PUBLICATIONS OF THE DEPARTMENT OF ROMANCE LANGUAGES
UNIVERSITY OF NORTH CAROLINA

General Editor: ALDO SCAGLIONE

NORTH CAROLINA STUDIES IN THE ROMANCE LANGUAGES AND LITERATURES

ESSAYS; TEXTS, TEXTUAL STUDIES AND TRANSLATIONS; SYMPOSIA

Founder: URBAN TIGNER HOLMES

Editor: JUAN BAUTISTA AVALLE-ARCE
Associate Editor: FREDERICK W. VOGLER

Other publications of the Department: *Estudios de Hispanófila, Hispanófila, Romance Notes, Studia Raeto-Romanica*

Distributed by:

INTERNATIONAL SCHOLARLY BOOK SERVICE, INC.
P. O. BOX 4347
Portland, Oregon   97208
U. S. A.

NORTH CAROLINA STUDIES IN THE
ROMANCE LANGUAGES AND LITERATURES

Essay 1

MOLIÈRE:

TRADITIONS IN CRITICISM, 1900-1970

MOLIÈRE:

TRADITIONS IN CRITICISM,
1900-1970

BY

LAURENCE ROMERO

WITH A PREFACE BY
JACQUES GUICHARNAUD

CHAPEL HILL

NORTH CAROLINA STUDIES IN THE ROMANCE
LANGUAGES AND LITERATURES
U.N.C. DEPARTMENT OF ROMANCE LANGUAGES
1974

Library of Congress Cataloging in Publication Data

Romero, Laurence.
   Molière: traditions in criticism, 1900-1970.

   (North Carolina Studies in the
Romance Languages and Literatures, 1)
   Bibliography: p. 168.
   1. Molière, Jean Baptiste Poquelin, 1622-1673—
Criticism and interpretation—History.
I. Title. II. Series.
PQ1860.R65   842'.4   74-536
ISBN 0-88438-001-7

I.S.B.N. 0-88438-001-7

IMPRESO EN ESPAÑA

PRINTED IN SPAIN

DEPÓSITO LEGAL: V. 1.439 - 1974.

ARTES GRÁFICAS SOLER, S. A. - JÁVEA, 28 - VALENCIA (8) - 1974.

CONTENTS

for C. and Chaps

AVANT-PROPOS

Au moment où ce livre est mis sous presse, que se prépare-t-il en cette année 1973 pour commémorer le losange noir qui, comme arraché à l'habit de quelque Arlequin endeuillé, marque dans le fameux Registre de Lagrange le 17 février 1673, date de la mort de Molière? Bon nombre de cérémonies officielles et d'hommages émus, où l'un des mots les plus galvaudés du monde sera employé à tort et à travers: le mot "génie"... Consolons-nous en nous disant que, pour une fois, il signifiera quand même quelque chose. Mais nous savons aussi —et cela est plus important— que conférences et colloques vont proliférer, ainsi que collections d'essais et numéros spéciaux de revues. En outre on nous promet de célébrer ce tricentenaire par d'originales et bouleversantes mises en scène. Avec le renouvellement récent des études historiques consacrées au XVIIème siècle, avec l'apport, discutable peut-être mais certainement fort considérable, des sciences humaines en crise de méthode, avec enfin les orientations modernes de la conscience théâtrale, il semble probable qu'au terme de cette année nous nous trouvions devant la tâche d'assembler un nouveau puzzle, au découpage et aux coloris inédits, où se précisera l'image, ou plutôt le modèle possible, d'un Molière dont nous n'entrevoyons encore que peu de chose. Il faut nous attendre à des cris et à des grincements de dents. Mais voilà qui est bon — car ce sera le double signe d'une vitalité critique et créatrice, en des temps par ailleurs assez pauvres, et de l'indiscutable permanence d'une œuvre.

On ne saurait s'autoriser pour autant à considérer comme négligeable et dépassée la totalité des portraits précédents. De décennie en décennie, d'école en école, des éclairages différents ont été projetés sur le visage de l'homme comme sur celui de l'œuvre. A vrai dire, aucun événement intellectuel du XVIIème siècle français n'a été aussi intensément et diversement exploré, à l'exception peut-être de l'événement Pascal. Trop aisément nous jugeons dépourvue d'intérêt pour nous telle ou telle entreprise et sommes sévères pour ce que nous estimons maintenant fausses

pistes ou rayons perdus. Mais il n'est pas dit que l'avenir proche
ne découvrira pas que certaines de ces pistes, si on les pro-
longe, peuvent conduire quelque part, et que ces rayons, si on les
règle, peuvent heurter et illuminer un objet pertinent. Quoi qu'il
en advienne, l'histoire de la critique et l'histoire de l'histoire elle-
même sont bien évidemment des disciplines valables et révélatri-
ces. Tel ou tel discours savant qui est venu, au cours des trois
derniers siècles, cheminer un moment le long des dialogues moliéresques, en les réfléchissant à sa manière, nous apprend ce qu'a
été Molière pour telle ou telle époque, pour telle ou telle race
de spécialistes. Plus profondément, cela ne nous apprend-il pas
ce que telle ou telle époque, telle ou telle race de spécialistes a
été pour Molière? Car ce n'est pas seulement d'un auteur qu'il
s'agit dans ce genre d'exercice, mais de nous, des curieuses variations dans le temps de notre compréhension des créations majeures.

   "Molière pour telle époque", "Molière pour telle discipline",
il faudrait sans doute lier chaque expression par des traits d'union,
et oublier les considérations essentialistes sur un "vrai Molière".
Car enfin, s'il y a de "faux Molière" inventés par la pure ignorance
ou créés par de légendaires méprises, il n'y a pas d'autres "vrais
Molière" (comme il n'y a pas d'autres "vrais Racine") que ceux
qui naissent de la rencontre entre l'observation de faits certains
(biographiques, mais surtout textuels) et les disciplines interpré-
tatives toujours changeantes. Quels que soient nos goûts, nous
ne saurions affirmer objectivement que le "Molière peintre et
critique de son temps" soit plus vrai ou plus faux que le "Molière
pur acteur et dramaturge", par exemple. En fin de compte, le
"vrai Molière", c'est celui que nous créons au nom de nos préfé-
rences, selon nos idéologies, nos définitions de l'homme, du phéno-
mène littéraire, de l'essence du théâtre — selon en fait ce qui
nous semble être la direction de pensée et de recherche la plus
valable et la plus enrichissante *hic et nunc*.

   Le bavardage qui précède, si on l'accepte, peut s'appliquer
bien sûr à n'importe quel artiste du passé. S'il s'impose particulièrement dans le cas de Molière, c'est à cause de la limpidité
immédiate de l'œuvre. Un jeune Français de douze ans peut
parfois "sentir" Baudelaire ou Rimbaud (Racine l'ennuie), mais
sans difficulté il "comprend" Molière. Il trouvera embarrassante
et bête une mise en scène trop farcesque, mais à aucun moment
il ne sera dérouté par les personnages, la conduite de l'action, la
langue même. Il y a certes les pièces dans lesquelles trois siècles
de critique se sont plu à multiplier les ombres: *Tartuffe, Le Misanthrope*, et surtout *Dom Juan;* mais, à tout prendre, des comédies
comme ces dernières ne comportent pas plus de psychologie des
profondeurs, d'obscurités poétiques ni de difficile philosophie
explicite que *L'Avare* ou *Le Bourgeois gentilhomme*. Molière a

pu choquer, mais il ne déroute pas; ses personnages et leur langage n'offrent pas d'autres surprises que celle de la surenchère: loin d'exploser comme dans la comédie absurdiste, loin d'être modelés par des hasards contradictoires comme dans le théâtre baroque, loin enfin de se métamorphoser dialectiquement comme dans le drame cornélien, ils se contentent d'être obstinément eux-mêmes, c'est à dire qu'ils vont jusqu'au bout d'une définition d'eux-mêmes donnée d'avance, et s'ils la dépassent, c'est dans le sens d'une extrapolation dont la logique n'est en rien démentie par le délire de la poésie théâtrale. Or n'est-il pas remarquable que ces déterminismes clairs, ces actions sans mystère, aient donné lieu à tant d'interprétations?

C'est sans doute que cette clarté, comme celle d'un ciel bleu, ne s'ouvre sur rien d'autre que sur elle-même. Pour obtenir cette lumière, Molière a fait feu de tout bois — sans nous dire, puisque tous ses papiers sont perdus, de quels bois il s'agissait: du coup, l'histoire littéraire, dans sa recherche des sources, a beau jeu. En outre, chaque comédie, chaque scène se suffit à elle-même: rares y sont les moments exclusivement culturels, nuls les symboles polyvalents... Et pourtant, cette œuvre qui ne pose jamais de questions conduit aux questions. Par le fait même qu'elle ne prend pas pour matière ses propres présuppositions, elle nous oblige à chercher ces dernières. Et ces dernières, encore une fois, nous les tirons de nous-mêmes tout autant que des textes et des faits, en oscillant entre un goût pour le secret d'un homme qui s'est rarement et si peu livré et le plaisir que nous procure la candeur d'une œuvre qui se dit sans ambiguïté.

On sait l'ampleur de la bibliographie qui offre une galerie des "vrais Molière" à travers les âges: Molière des moralistes, Molière des historiens, Molière des philosophes, Molière des psychologues, Molière des gens de théâtre — autant de Molière possibles qui, par un effet de boomerang, nous apprennent bien des choses sur les orientations de nombreuses disciplines et sur l'évolution des intérêts et des idées en général. Répétons-le: à cet égard, la bibliographie moliéresque est particulièrement éclairante à cause de la limpidité a priori de l'œuvre en question. Il était donc bon, à la veille du déluge de révisions et d'applications de nouvelles méthodes qui marquera en toute probabilité l'année 1973, d'opérer une mise au point de l'acquis, de mettre de l'ordre dans un corpus considérable, de nous offrir un guide raisonné de ce musée critique au moment où se bâtit fébrilement l'aile des modernes. C'est ce que Laurence Romero a fait — et, nous semble-t-il, avec bonheur.

JACQUES GUICHARNAUD

INTRODUCTION

The bibliography of critical works on Molière is vast. Recent compilations list over 2,500 items, and every year the volume of books and articles increases substantially. These studies range over a wide spectrum of methods and interpretations, from the rigorously historical to the purely polemical, from savory impressionism to lean formalism. The breadth of the subject of this book, Molière in the changing perspectives of twentieth century criticism, demands a few qualifying remarks. The term criticism here is to be understood in its broadest sense, as René Wellek defined it: "the judgments of individuals and authors, judicial criticism, practical criticism, evidence of taste." Since criticism is inherently "evidence of taste" for successive generations, it cannot be a single, continuous postulation. It is clear that since the Romantic period, critics have increasingly believed that literature can, in different periods, have different meaning and import and therefore be understood and appreciated according to varying standards. In this view, the essence of the work of art can change with time and become the focus of successive sets of values. The term "traditions" is taken in the meaning T. S. Eliot ascribed to it, "a way of feeling and acting which characterizes a group through-out generations." But there is also the etymological sense (from the Latin *traditio*) of a giving-up, a surrender, a condition liable to change. *Traditions in Criticism* means, therefore, continuity and change in various forms of critical appreciation of Molière and his works.

There are other more practical considerations. The critical studies surveyed in this book are from French, British and American sources, with only few exceptions. The starting point is

Lanson's famous piece from 1901, but the long opening chapter deals with more than 200 years of commentary from Molière's time to 1900. It aims at outlining some of the themes and preoccupations which persisted through time and which gave direction to some aspects of exegesis in the modern period. Subsequent chapters are organized into broad areas of inquiry which are but convenient categories for ordering the multifarious raw material. Chapter Two concerns biography and deals with the legend which grew up around Molière, Gustave Michaut's combative effort to check it, and the influence of biography on textual exegesis. Chapter Three considers various aspects of academic criticism: literary history, questions of philosophy and morality, and the emergence of the "new approach" around 1950. Chapter Four is a brief consideration of the writings of professional men of the theatre on Molière's work. Even if this particular part of Molière studies is modest in volume, it is both original and important, for it influenced the "new approach" and the impressive generation of critics following it. The last chapter deals exclusively with the most recent criticism, 1960 - 1970. It treats not only "books" but "boards" as well, some noteworthy stage performances of Molière during the last decade.

Since Molière criticism is an on-going, uninterrupted investigation, a few observations on the present and some projections for the future seemed most appropriate for the Conclusions.

No study of this kind could possibly account for every item in the inexhaustible bibliography on Molière. At almost every stage a selection had to be made with the hope that it would be representative, while other pieces of related interest are mentioned in the footnotes. Although there is much in this book which is necessarily expository and historical in nature, a number of modest judgments are occasionally made in order to bring into clearer relief some of the most original and innovative contributions. Often, however, judgments are highly subjective and the reader will want to take heed. While this work is not willfully partisan or intended to promote any single critic or method, it may express an occasional bias, especially when dealing with the most recent writings. But the dominant idea — and ideal — behind this book is to survey *some* of the trends and methods that have characterized the attempts in our century to seize Molière and make him ours. Only the reader himself can determine the ultimate worth of each contribution in this long process of valuation.

A word now on what this book is not. Although it aspires to be more than a mere catalogue of names and titles, it cannot deal effectively with the social background of the myriad attitudes expressed toward Molière's works in the twentieth century. Without doubt it would be fascinating to delve at length into the social and political matrix surrounding Faguet's conservatism, Michaut's positivism, Vilar's "silence" in his *Dom Juan* production, the "realism" of other recent stagings of *Tartuffe* and *Dom Juan;* but that is another book, for someone else to write. This one deals more in the relationships of critic to critic, studies on Molière to other studies on Molière. In that sense it may be hopelessly academic. But every book is a risk and this one will be modestly successful if it serves as an introduction and useful guide to modern Molière studies.

Acknowledgements

Several obliging and proficient librarians were helpful during the preliminary stage of research, especially in the libraries at Yale and Harvard, and in Paris, at the Centre dramatique Léon Chancerel and at the Archives of La Comédie Française. A grant from the American Philosophical Society, plus a travel allowance from Tufts University, made possible a brief but indispensable and pleasant research visit to the French capital.

Many friends and colleagues also helped. Among them, the author is particularly indebted to Professor Jacques Guicharnaud for advice and encouragement, and to Philip Bertocci for invaluable help in editing the manuscript. The author alone is responsible, however, for whatever errors or misjudgments might be found in this book.

L. R.

Wolcott, Vermont
Fall, 1972

CHAPTER I

ROOTS OF THE TRADITIONS

Molière's Contemporaries

All things considered, Molière weathered his contemporaries
well. True, the polemics were long, fierce, and often dangerous,
and the burden of work exhausting. Molière's life at Louis' court
was anything but a long *fête galante*. And yet an unmistakable
element of his genius was fortitude, or, less poetically, sheer
physical stamina. Molière persisted, survived, and triumphed in
large measure due to his unusual capacity for work, writing,
acting, directing his troupe, and assisting in the preparations of
the sumptuous royal *divertissements*. He also had a sharp instinct
for self-preservation: the prefaces and dedications offered to the
right royal personage, the *placets* sent to the King even in time
of battle, the circumstance plays of the early 1660's. Intelligence,
talent, energy, Molière had in abundance. And he had a friend.
His crucial relationship with Louis XIV seems to lend credence
to the popular expression, "It's not what you know but who [sic]
you know." It was one of those rare relationships, apparently
sustained by mutual admiration and simple pragmatism, for both
profited. Molière's advantages were obvious and he shrewdly
missed no opportunity to gain from them. For his part, the young
King was quite willing to project and test his growing powers at
the court through his manipulations of the series of polemics which
raged around his *troupe royale* during the first decade of his
rule. Erich Auerbach suggests that this turbulent period represents
a first synthesis of varied groups at court into a "homogeneous

culture." [1] Clearly, the King's success at controlling power within his court was based on this kind of ordering of disparate elements which were potential sources of competition and conflic. [2]

One important friend and countless enemies. So numerous and powerful were Molière's antagonists that, in retrospect, his intimacy with Louis XIV appears to have been a decisive factor in his ultimate survival. Who were these people? All kinds: from the envious actors of the competitive Hôtel de Bourgogne to the invidious *dévots;* from the tawdry Donneau de Visé to the eloquent Bossuet. These are the people who made up the growing and sophisticated *public:* merchants, would-be poets and dramatists, clerics, noblemen. Their arguments, petty quarrels, and pedantry constitute, for better or for worse, what is called "criticism" of the day and it was almost always personal and highly subjective. This accounts in part for the inordinate number of cliques and coteries and for their considerable influence in literary affairs. No author was invulnerable to their attacks. A quarrelsome coterie forced Corneille to suffer a fierce pamphlet war over *Le Cid,* and the machinations of a similar group against *Phèdre* might have hastened Racine's premature retirement from the theatre. Although Malherbe, and especially Boileau, attempted to codify the formal criteria of criticism, the actual rules were written according to the exigences of the moment in that never-never land between the *parterre* and the *ruelle.*

One of the first references to Molière is in Tallemant des Réaux, that indefatigable chronicler of *Historiettes:* "Un garçon nommé Molière quitta les bancs de la Sorbonne pour la suivre [la Béjart]; il en fut fort amoureux... et enfin s'en mit à l'épouser. Il a fait des pièces où il y a de l'esprit. Ce n'est pas un merveilleux acteur, si ce n'est pour le ridicule. Il n'y a que sa troupe qui joue ses pièces; elles sont comiques." [3] These cursory remarks

---

[1] Erich Auerbach, "La Cour et la Ville," in *Scenes from the Drama of European Literature* (New York: Meridian Books, 1959), pp. 133-179.

[2] See the interesting article by R. B. Landolt, "Molière and Louis XIV," in *History Today,* vol. 16 (1966), pp. 756-764.

[3] Tallement des Réaux, *Historiettes,* ed. Antoine Adam, (La Pléiade, 1961), vol. II, p. 778.

are noteworthy for they contain in germ two points which will later become sources for dispute in fixing Molière's biography: that Poquelin was a bad actor in the serious genre, and that he studied at the Sorbonne. Finally, the error in alluding to Madeleine Béjart as Molière's wife suggests that even at this early date there was some confusion about Molière's marital affairs.

La Fontaine seems to be the first man of letters to approve strongly of Molière's genius. The poet compared Molière favorably to Terence and to Plautus, and further suggested that Molière's art had at once revised and revived the comic form. In fact, this new concept of high comedy had signaled the death knell of low farce as exemplified by Jodelet. [4] This assessment of 1661 reflects a trend of favorable opinion for Molière. In August of 1660, Louis XIV had not only accorded a gratification of three thousand *livres* to Molière's troupe, but had provided the company with the Palais Royal theatre. In his official report requested by Colbert, *Mémoire des gens de lettres vivants en 1662*, Chapelain characterizes Molière as a naturally gifted comic poet, inventive (even when he borrows), and concludes: "Sa morale est bonne, et il n'a qu'à se garder de la scurrilité." [5]

On 26 December 1662, *L'Ecole des femmes* literally exploded on the stage of the Palais Royal theatre and *la cour et la ville* were never to be the same again. In the violent reaction to the play, one report reflects succinctly the confused opinion of the moment. It comes from the pen of one of the most blatant social-climbers of seventeenth century France, Jean Donneau de Visé, and it is considered one of the first extended critical observations on Molière's work. "Cette pièce a produit des effets tout nouveaux: tout le monde l'a trouvée méchante et tout le monde y a couru ... C'est le sujet le plus mal conduit qui fût jamais ... cette pièce est un monstre qui a de belles parties, ... jamais on ne vit tant de si bonnes choses et de méchantes choses ensemble ... Jamais comédie ne fut si bien représentée ni avec tant d'art; chaque acteur sait combien il y doit faire de pas, et toutes les œillades

---

[4] Jean de la Fontaine, *Œuvres,* ed. H. Régnier (Hachette, 1892), vol. 9, pp. 348-349.

[5] Quoted in Pierre Mélèse, *Le Théâtre et le Public sous Louis XIV, 1659-1715* (Droz, 1934), p. 129.

sont comptées." [6] Finally, the perfidious critic appends a phrase which later became the source for scandalous repetition: "Mais si vous voulez savoir pourquoi, presque dans toutes ses pièces il raille tant les cocus, et dépeint si naturellement les jaloux, c'est qu'il est du nombre de ces derniers." [7] Paradoxically, the total effect of these vicious attacks was merely to confirm Molière's growing presence in the theatre of the time.

The polemic surrounding *L'Ecole des femmes* continued apace. Molière wrote a pointed preface to *La Critique de l'Ecole des femmes* in August 1663, dedicating the play to none other than the Queen Mother, a model of seriousness and devotion. But scurrilous pamphlets continued to circulate. Donneau de Visé's *Zélinde ou la véritable critique de l'Ecole des femmes* is pure calumny, and Boursault's *Le Portrait du peintre* is of the same low order. [8] From the rival troupe of players at the Hôtel de Bourgogne, Montfleury contributes to the muck with his anodine *L'Impromptu de l'Hôtel de Condé*. This not being sufficient, he resorts to the vilest slander which Racine relates, and dismisses: "Montfleury a fait une requête contre Molière, et l'a dénoncé au Roi. Il l'accuse d'avoir épousé la fille et d'avoir autrefois couché avec la mère. Mais Montfleury n'est point écouté à la cour." [9] From Molière, there is one eloquent statement in Scene 5 of *L'Impromptu de Versailles* where he pleads for "courtoisie" in those private matters "qui ne font rire ni les spectateurs, ni celui dont on parle." [10] By early 1664, the "guerre comique" had run its course and Molière emerged even more firmly established as the court's "grand comédien".

---

[6] Molière, *Œuvres complètes*, ed. Despois-Mesnard (Hachette, "Les Grands Ecrivains de la France," 1900), vol. 10, p. 464. Hereafter this standard edition will be referred to simply as GEF. See also Mélèse, *Un Homme de lettres au temps du grand roi, Donneau de Visé, Fondateur du Mercure Galant* (Droz, 1936).

[7] GEF, op. cit., vol. 10, p. 468. See also, G. Mongrédien, "Donneau de Visé dans *la guerre comique* contre Molière," in *Revue générale Belge*, vol. 106 (1970), pp. 57-68.

[8] Boursault, *Le Portrait du Peintre ou la véritable critique de l'Ecole des femmes*, in *Collection Moliéresque*, ed. Paul Lacroix (Geneva: J. Gay et Fils, 1868).

[9] Jean Racine, *Œuvres complètes*, ed. R. Picard (La Pléiade, 1960), vol. II, p. 459.

[10] GEF, vol. 3, pp. 429-430.

But there was no peace. In the spring of 1664, *Tartuffe* caused a scandal which haunted the author to his grave. The spirit and quality of most of the debate on this play is exemplified by Pierre Roullé's pamphlet, *Le Roi glorieux au monde*, a dull, heavy-handed and fanatical tract addressed to the King. The author refers to Molière as "un homme, ou plutôt un démon vêtu de chair et habillé en homme, et le plus signalé impie libertin qui fût jamais en tous les siècles passés."[11] No one appears to have taken this seriously.

One of the best critical essays of the period was published in 1667 after a revised version of *Tartuffe* (entitled *L'Imposteur*) had been played once in the Palais Royal. Donneau de Visé was present at this single performance and is undoubtedly the author of the interesting and sympathetic *Lettre sur la comédie de l'Imposteur*. One wonders why Donneau de Visé suddenly shifted his position on Molière. The answer is not clear although one explanation seems plausible: in August 1665, Molière's troupe played *La Mère coquette* whose author was none other than Jean Donneau de Visé! Molière not only played Donneau de Visé's work, but sustained his troupe's performances against Quinault-the-younger's *La Mère coquette,* playing simultaneously at the rival Hôtel de Bourgogne. The aspiring young playwright had apparently come full circle into the camp of Molière's friends and from that time on Donneau de Visé appears to have been an ally. In fact it seems likely that as a gesture of gratitude, Donneau de Visé also wrote the *Lettre sur le Misanthrope* (1666) and *Observations d'une comédie du Sieur Molière intitulée Le Festin de Pierre* (1665). For a long time these texts were virtually ignored by critics, with only a few exceptions. Recently, however, at least two critics have made a strong case for accepting these essays not only as having been written by Donneau de Visé, but perhaps in collaboration with Molière himself. As Professor W. G. Moore suggested, several pertinent aspects of Molière criticism would have to be reconsidered if we accept that these pamphlets were either written or inspired by the master. Let us consider some of these points.

---

[11] Pierre Roullé, *Le Roi glorieux au monde*, in *Collection Moliéresque*, op. cit., pp. 34-35. See also GEF, vol. 10, pp. 316-317.

The *Lettre sur la comédie de l'Imposteur* relates in some detail
the August 1667 performance of *L'Imposteur,* and then reflects
on the essence of religion and the comic in the play. The first part
is particularly interesting for historical purposes because it sheds
light on what the earlier version of *Tartuffe* might have been
and provides a good idea of Molière's own conception for playing
the hypocrite. For example, there is this precise comment on
Orgon's famous line: "C'est un homme ... qui ... ah! un homme ...
un homme enfin" (I, 5). Based on Molière's performance, Donneau
de Visé interprets Panulphe as being "extrêmement un homme,
c'est-à-dire un fourbe, un méchant, un traitre et un animal très-
pervers, dans le langage de l'ancienne comédie." [12] If this is accepted, it could render specious all the speculation on how Molière
intended his hypocrite to be played. There are a number of other
similar examples.

The second part of the *Lettre* is short but dense. It proposes
interesting schematic definitions of "la religion" and "le ridicule",
at least within the specific context of this play. Since there is
essentially nothing from Molière on his attitude toward such
concepts, this discussion is of the highest interest. Consider this
poetic, Cartesian definition of religion: "Il est certain que la
religion n'est que la perfection de la raison, du moins pour la morale, qu'elle la purifie, qu'elle l'élève et qu'elle dissipe seulement les ténèbres que le péché d'origine a répandues dans le lieu
de sa demeure, enfin que la religion n'est qu'une raison plus
parfaite: ce serait être dans le plus déplorable aveuglement des
païens que de douter de cette vérité." [13] This could suggest that
Molière was neither an atheist nor even indifferent to religion,
and while this posture may not have completely satisfied Bossuet,
it would at least invalidate the excessive charges of Roullé and
the fanatics.

The second point concerns "le ridicule" and provides a basis
for defining Molière's *esprit comique.* The author of the *Lettre*
suggests that the soul takes a certain pleasure in the recognition
of truth and virtue, and inversely, that ignorance and error are
the source of "le ridicule ... c'est-à-dire ce qui manque de rai-

---

[12] GEF, vol. 4, pp. 536-537.
[13] *Ibid.,* p. 555.

son ... Le ridicule est donc la forme extérieure et sensible que la providence de la nature a attachée à tout ce qui est déraissonable ... la convenance est la raison essentielle ... la disconvenance est l'essence du ridicule ... nous estimons ridicule ce qui manque extrêmement de raison." [14] Professor W. G. Moore has already suggested that this could be the point of departure for a redefinition of the comic in Molière (see below). Few other critics have been willing to accept this text as valid and discussion of it is usually shrouded in caution and skepticism.

About another matter there has been little doubt: that Boileau remained a close friend and defender of Molière, especially between 1663 and the playwright's death ten years later. And yet the last lines of "Chant III" of the L'Art poétique are anything but enthusiastic:

Si moins ami du peuple en ses doctes peintures,
Il n'eût point fait souvent grimacer ses figures,
Quitté, pour le bouffon l'agréable et le fin,
Et sans honte à Térence allié Tabarin.
Dans ce sac ridicule où Scapin s'enveloppe
Je ne reconnais plus l'auteur du Misanthrope. [15]

This is an elitist view of comedy, with little appreciation for what are integral parts of Molière's comic vision, farce and broad humor. Boileau was rebuffed for this harsh appraisal of his recently lost friend. It appears that part of L'Art poétique had been read even before Molière's death (although apparently not "Chant III") to the famous group of friends at Auteuil. In February 1677, Boileau wrote his Epître à M. Racine to console the playwright on the failure of his Phèdre. Here Boileau wrote perhaps the best lines on Molière:

Mais sitôt, d'un trait de ses fatales mains,
La Parque l'eût rayé du nombre des Humains,
On reconnut le prix de sa Muse éclipsée.
L'aimable Comédie avec lui terassée
En vain d'un coup si rude espéra revenir,

---

[14] Ibid., pp. 559-560.
[15] Boileau-Despréaux, Œuvres complètes, ed. F. Escal (La Pléiade, 1966), p. 178.

Et sur ses brodequins ne put plus se tenir.
Tel fut chez nous le sort du Théâtre Comique. [16]

The other references to Molière in Boileau's works are of little interest. Even the famous *Satire II à M. de Molière* is rather anodine. Of a total of 100 lines, only 15 bear directly on Molière. Those verses applaud the comic poet's facility for writing verse, a compliment of dubious value. The remainder is a detailed exposition of the plight of the fledgling young poet, Nicolas Despréaux.

Brossette, the tireless apologist and commentator of Boileau, attempted to justify the latter's attitude toward Molière in *L'Art poétique.* He argued that this poem represented Boileau's only effort at codifying his precepts on comedy and was therefore the reason for being so exacting, even with Molière. Antoine Adam has reminded us, however, that Boileau was involved in several of the literary *cabals* of the time and that he took them very seriously. By the early 1670's, for example, Boileau had gained entry into the "cénacle" of the pious First President of the Parlement, M. Lamoignon. It is interesting that the membership list in this coterie reads like an index of Molière's enemies: the Jesuit Rapin, Bourdaloue, Cotin, and even Bossuet occasionally sent "communications" on various subjects. Boileau himself by this time had evolved toward a more serious position, going from his fitful youth and the *Satires* to the more staid *Epîtres* and finally to the *Art poétique, Traité du sublime,* etc. It appears that while Boileau remained a personal friend of Molière, he could not esthetically appreciate or condone certain elements of the dramatist's genius which his own tastes hardly allowed him to understand. Boileau's writings on Molière remain ambiguous and the relationship between the two men might stand reviewing.

One of the most precious documents on Molière after his death is the rather summary preface to the 1682 edition of the *Œuvres de Monsieur de Molière,* by Charles Varlet, *dit* de LaGrange, and Vivot. Both were close to Molière and the former is, of course, the same LaGrange who kept the invaluable *Registre* on the activities of Molière's troupe between 1659 and 1685. Although

---

[16] *Ibid.,* pp. 127-128.

the writers had first-hand information on the poet, they carefully imparted only the *vérité officielle*. There is no mention of the alleged translation into French of Lucretius' *De Natura rerum* (supposedly rendered around 1650), the veritable handbook of Gassendi and his disciples. No mention either of a possible association between the mathematician-philosopher and the comic playwright. LaGrange and Vivot also mistakenly assert that the Prince de Conti had remained to the end an admirer and bene-factor of Molière while in fact, after 1657 he had become a religious fanatic and had written ponderously disapproving tracts against *L'Ecole des femmes*, *Tartuffe* and *Dom Juan*. One phrase in the LaGrange-Vivot preface *a fait fortune*, mostly by dint of its vagueness. "Il observait les manières et les moeurs de tout le monde; il trouvait moyen ensuite d'en faire des applications admirables dans les comédies, où l'on peut dire qu'il a joué tout le monde, puisqu'il s'y est joué le premier en plusieurs endroits sur des affaires de sa famille et qui regardaient ce qui se passait dans son domestique. C'est ce que ses plus particuliers amis ont re-marqué bien des fois." [17] Unfortunately, the generality is sustained by only one concrete example: Molière playing on his lingering cough in *L'Avare* (II, 5). We shall see how this remark will be used to justify a very special reading of Molière's plays and, in fact, sustain an entire tradition. But does it not seem unlikely that this general assertion is to be taken literally? Were La-Grange and Vivot suggesting that Molière had exposed his most private and intimate domestic matters in his plays, that he was Arnolphe and Alceste, that his wife was "bête"? If this were the case, then the LaGrange-Vivot preface would be a very candid document indeed. But there is considerable debate on how this document should be read and some of the arguments will be discussed later. Suffice it to say for the moment that in spite of its ambiguities and limitations, the *Préface* stood as the most important source on Molière's life until 1705.

La Fameuse Comédienne ou l'histoire de la Guérin, author unknown, enjoyed a *succès de scandale* after Molière's death. The novel recounts the principal "escapades" of Armande Béjart who, four years after her first husband's death, remarried a

---

[17] GEF, vol. 1, pp. XV-XVI.

mediocre actor, Isaac-François Guérin d'Estriché. One of the most engaging episodes is the so-called conversation between Molière and his friend Chapelle in which the former speaks freely of his marital woes. The story presents Molière-Arnolphe who prepared his wife from childhood for a faithful marriage only to discover later certain "méchantes inclinations" impossible to curb. Thus he is destined to suffer his marriage with a woman he desperately loves but who continues to be unfaithful, sometimes even in spite of herself. [18] This anecdote has had the greatest success, and echoes of it resound in biography and in textual criticism as well. It is a brilliant set-pièce, at times moving, especially when Molière candidly confides his attitudes toward love to his friend. So high is the quality of the prose that there was speculation that Racine or even La Fontaine might have written it.

In spite of its special appeal, editions of La Fameuse comédienne were few and it does not appear to have circulated widely. The famous Molière-Chapelle tête-à-tête gained prominence mostly by the authority lent to it by subsequent writers who quoted freely from it. Pierre Bayle was perhaps the most important author who lent respectability to La Fameuse comédienne. In his article "Poquelin," in the Dictionnaire historique et critique, Bayle used this text as a primary source for biography. The article in question is curious: the main part is but an innocuous résumé of the LaGrange-Vivot preface to the 1682 edition. The pearls are contained in the notes, those treasure niches first carved by Bayle in the Dictionnaire and later perfected by Diderot as a diverting tactic in the Encyclopédie. It is mostly in note "C" that Bayle appended the well-known passage from La Fameuse comédienne as documentary evidence to explain Molière's almost obsessive preoccupation with the cuckold husband in his plays. [19] With Bayle's authority behind it, this anecdote and its implications began a long life in Molière "research."

Bayle had already published a short but perceptive note in his Nouvelles de la République des Lettres (1684) which objectively

----

[18] La Fameuse Comédienne ou l'Histoire de la Guérin, auparavant femme et veuve de Molière, in Collection Moliéresque, op. cit., pp. 19-20.
[19] Pierre Bayle, Dictionnaire historique et critique (Desoer, 1820), vol. 12, pp. 256-260.

questioned the already established cliché that Molière's comedies had reformed the morals of the time. (All of Molière's partisans believed this, although the *dévots* and churchmen were of another mind.) "Quantité de personnes disent fort sérieusement à Paris que Molière a plus corrigé de défauts à la Ville, lui seul, que tous les prédicateurs ensemble et je crois qu'on ne se trompe pas, pourvu qu'on ne parle que de certaines qualités qui ne font pas tant un crime qu'un faux goût, ou qu'un sot entêtement... [mais] pour la galanterie criminelle, l'envie, la fourberie, l'avarice, la vanité et choses semblables, je ne crois pas que ce comique leur ait fait beaucoup de mal." [20] Nonetheless, the tradition of "Molière moraliste" continued. Partisans of this theory delighted in quoting from Boileau's *Satire X* which asserted that as early as *Les Précieuses ridicules,* and thereafter with even greater zeal, Molière developed into a conscious moralist and social reformer. This opinion is not rare even in our day, although Antoine Adam and Paul Bénichou radically refocused the question, as we shall see.

Among the many attacks on Molière, one of the sharpest came from Bossuet's acrid pen. His *Maximes et Réflexions sur la comédie* (1694) were written as a rebuttal to Father Caffaro's *Lettre d'un théologien illustre,* which proposed that the Church be more tolerant toward the theatre. But Bossuet had always been vehemently opposed to the theatre, considering it one of the prime sources of sensual pleasure, harboring "crimes publics et cachés... la concupiscence répandue dans tous les sens." For the prime example of this kind of theatre, Bossuet fell on Molière: "Il a fait voir à notre siècle le fruit qu'on peut espérer de la morale du théâtre, qui n'attaque que le ridicule du monde en lui laissant cependant toute sa corruption. La postérité saura peut-être la fin de ce poète comédien, qui, en jouant son *Malade imaginaire* ou son *Médecin par force,* reçut la dernière atteinte de la maladie dont il mourut peu d'heures après, et passa des plaisanteries du théâtre, parmi lesquelles il rendit presque le dernier soupir, au tribunal de celui qui dit: 'Malheur à vous qui riez, car vous pleurerez.'" [21] This severe attitude moved even Lanson to admit that,

[20] Pierre Bayle, *Nouvelles de la République des lettres* (Amsterdam: Chez David Mortier Libraire, 1715), pp. 200-201.
[21] Bossuet, "Maximes et Réflexions sur la comédie," in Ch. Urbain et E. Levesque, *L'Eglise et le théâtre* (Grasset, 1930), p. 185.

in this instance, Bossuet "fut plus pharisien que disciple de Jésus."

The general case Bossuet championed against the alleged immorality of the theatre was part of a long polemic, the so-called *Querelle du théâtre* which continued through most of the eighteenth century. This preoccupation with morality in art is, *mutatis mutandis*, part of the Classical belief in "la nécessité d'instruire." "Plaire" is important, but the work of art must also instruct. In his defense of *Tartuffe*, Molière had written that "Le devoir de la Comédie [est] de corriger les hommes en les divertissant . . ." [22] Thus it was not unusual for Molière's comedies to be judged by these norms. Nor was the subjectivity unusual for the time. As we have already noted, literature, and especially the theatre, were highly personal experiences in seventeenth century Parisian society, and much in Molière's comedies was interpreted as "sujets d'actualité." Moreover, with countless authors, critics, and pedants envious of Molière's success, it was practically impossible during the playwright's lifetime to attempt an objective evaluation of his work. Even the three interesting essays by Donneau de Visé were probably written as circumstance pieces. Finally, Molière's numerous enemies profited from the discretion which characterized the poet's private life to spread their venomous calumnies. The literature of scandal and the reactions to it produced the basic source material for the legend which flourished after Molière's death.

The Age of Enlightenment

Situated as it is in 1705, Grimarest's *Vie de Monsieur de Molière* offers a synthesis of seventeenth century attitudes on Molière, as well as a projection of some of the preoccupations of the eighteenth century. This life study has not always enjoyed the highest esteem. Indeed, its credit suffered from the very beginning when Boileau (whom Grimarest had not consulted) passed prescriptively on it shortly after its publication: "Pour ce qui est de la *Vie de Molière*, franchement ce n'est pas un ouvrage qui mérite qu'on en parle. Il est fait par un homme qui ne savait rien de la vie de Molière et qui se trompe dans tout ne sachant

---

[22] GEF, vol. 4, p. 385.

pas même les faits que tout le monde sait."[23] More recently, but with similar disdain, Gustave Michaut amused himself at sorting out and listing twenty-five errors in Grimarest's *Vie;* he also refers lightly to "le biographe marron de Molière." Georges Mongrédien has adopted a contrary attitude and his recent edition of Grimarest's work is a scrupulous assessment of this first and important full-length biography. He argues that Grimarest's errors are often factual oversights, for it is clear that the biographer was not very meticulous. On important matters, however, he is either well-informed or at least reflects the prevailing opinion of his time. To his credit, Grimarest is usually cautious about material of questionable veracity and, from the beginning, he recognized one of the problems of using source materials: "Il y a peu de personnes de son temps, qui pour se faire honneur d'avoir figuré avec lui [Molière], n'inventent des aventures qu'ils prétendent avoir eues ensemble."[24] Grimarest uses LeBoulanger and Boursault with circumspection, and chastizes Bayle for his sometimes careless use of documents. Unfortunately, the biographer is not adverse to inventing his own anecdotes whenever needed, although his *histories* are always well-intentioned. Thus, to counter the popular conversation between Molière and Chapelle at Auteuil from *La Fameuse Comédienne,* Grimarest imagines an exchange between Molière and the physician Jacques Rohault. Here Molière is made to appear more rational, less effusive, and more discreet, particularly concerning his relationship with Armande. About the latter's parentage, Grimarest accepts the notion, held by practically all his contemporaries, that she was "la fille de la Béjart" and he even writes that Madeleine was jealous and opposed to the marriage between Armande and Molière.[25]

In spite of Boileau's negative attitude, Grimarest's *Vie* did enjoy some success in the beginning of the eighteenth century and it served as an important source for biographies written during the entire period. In fact, Mongrédien has shown how all subsequent biographies during the eighteenth century (Bruzen de la Martinière,

[23] Boileau, *Lettres à Brossette* (Belles Lettres, 1942), p. 95.
[24] Grimarest, *Vie de Monsieur de Molière,* ed. G. Mongrédien (M. Brient, 1955), p. 7.
[25] *Ibid.,* pp. 81-83; for Grimarest's comments on Armande's parentage, Molière's marriage and Madeleine's reaction, cf., pp. 57-58.

La Serre and Voltaire's, among others) were but reworkings of Grimarest. [26] To a degree, this situation can be explained by a gradual
shift of interest at the time, from the anecdotal side of Molière's
life to a more critical interest in the comedies. By 1705, memories
of Molière the man had dimmed and readers were less concerned
with minute details of the actor-playwright's personal life. Grimarest's biography (and whatever could be borrowed from it for
other life studies) satisfied remaining curiosities as attention was
gradually refocused on the works.

Voltaire's *Vie de Molière* (1738) reflects this new seriousness.
It proposes to avoid "des détails inutiles et des contes populaires
aussi faux qu'insipides . . . on ne dira de sa propre personne que
ce qu'on a cru vrai et digne l'être rapporté; et on ne hasardera
sur ses ouvrages rien qui soit contraire aux sentiments du public
éclairé." [27] The last phrase indicates Voltaire's attitude and in
fact there is considerable propaganda in his commentaries on
Molière. The following is but one example. Grimarest had treated
the touchy details of Molière's funeral with characteristic brevity,
assuming as it were that ". . . tout le monde sait." La Serre, a later
biographer and contemporary of Voltaire, had added simply that
the King ". . . engagea l'Archevêque de Paris à ne lui pas refuser
la sépulture dans un lieu saint." [28] Commenting on the same event,
Voltaire makes two points: that the Archbishop in question was
of doubtful moral character, and that, ironically, Molière was a
'philosophe', a man of unquestionable integrity. "Le malheur
qu'il avait eu de ne pouvoir mourir avec les secours de la religion,
et la prévention contre la comédie, déterminèrent Harlay de Chan-
valon, Archevêque de Paris, si connu par ses intrigues galantes,
à refuser la sépulture à Molière . . . La populace, qui ne connaissait
dans Molière que le comédien, . . . ignorait qu'il avait été un
excellent auteur, un philosophe." [29]

---

[26] Georges Mongrédien, "Les Biographes de Molière au 18e siècle," in
La Revue d'Histoire littéraire de la France, vol. 56 (1956), pp. 342-354.

[27] Voltaire, *Œuvres complètes* (Garnier Frères, 1879), vol. 23, p. 88.

[28] Molière, *Œuvres,* ed. La Serre (Amsterdam et Leipzig: Chez Arkstée
et Merkus, 1750), vol. 1, p. LXVIII.

[29] Voltaire, *Œuvres, op. cit.,* vol. 23, p. 96. See also R. Lowenstein,
Voltaire as an Historian of Seventeenth Century French Drama (Baltimore:
The Johns Hopkins Press, 1935), pp. 105-106, and also chapters I and IV.

In *Le Siècle de Louis XIV*, Voltaire reiterates this point in emphatic terms. "Molière avait d'ailleurs une sorte de mérite que ni Corneille, ni Racine, ni Boileau, ni La Fontaine, n'avaient pas: il était philosophe, et il l'était dans la théorie et dans la pratique." [30] This remains the basic theme throughout the "Notices" Voltaire wrote on each play for a 1750 edition of complete works. The short commentaries contain basic historical information (often incorrect), plus some very Voltairian insights into the meaning of the plays and their implication for the times. Critics have insisted on how much Voltaire follows his predecessor La Serre's *Vie* and commentaires, but this charge holds only for certain facts and notions that were common currency at the time. Throughout the rest, there is much freshness and originality.

This recurring theme of "Molière philosophe" is one of the most interesting ideas in Voltaire's commentaries on Molière. From Voltaire's pen, the designation *philosophe* represents the highest expression of approbation. The term connotes all those qualities the writer himself held dear: brilliance, generosity, tolerance, moral integrity. Thus Voltaire writes that Molière "...fut le premier qui fit sentir le vrai et par conséquent, le beau." [31] In the Voltairian creed, any esthetic sentiment is inextricably linked to a moral and social commitment. Thus he interprets Molière's successfully amusing attack upon the doctors as having served a socially useful purpose, for by impugning their bad faith, Molière took the first important step in moving the medical profession toward a more responsible position in society. In this view, the playwright's efforts are part of the long evolution toward civilization. As a result of such pressures, "L'esprit de raison s'est introduit dans toutes les sciences et la politesse dans toutes les conditions." [32]

It is hardly surprising that Voltaire should prefer *Tartuffe* to all of Molière's comedies. This play represents a meeting of minds, for fanaticism was Voltaire's *bête noire*. He had not the slightest doubt that the play was directed against "les faux zélés ... l'espèce

---

[30] Voltaire, *op. cit.*, *vol.* 15, p. 105.
[31] *Ibid.*, vol. 23, p. 104.
[32] *Ibid.*, p. 109.

34   MOLIÈRE: TRADITIONS IN CRITICISM

d'homme la plus dangereuse." No doubt too that the play was
"l'éloge de la vertu et la satire de la seule hypocrisie... il [Mo-
lière] a diffamé l'hypocrisie et non la vertu." [33]

In a personal way there is a kinship of souls between Voltaire
and Molière. The "maître de Ferney" sees in the classical playwright a prime example of the persecuted genius, the artist-
pariah, which is the rôle Voltaire himself assumed, often without
choice during much of his life. On Molière's difficulties with *Tartuffe*, Voltaire concludes: "Voilà comment ce grand homme fut
traité de son vivant: l'approbation du public éclairé lui donnait
une gloire qui le vengeait assez; mais qu'il est humiliant pour une
nation, et triste pour les hommes de génie, que le petit nombre
leur rende justice, tandis que le grand nombre les néglige ou les
persécute." [34] One can be reasonably certain that Voltaire counted
himself among the persecuted "hommes de génie."

Too much has already been written about Voltaire's negative
criticism of Molière's stagecraft. True, eighteenth century audiences, particularly between 1730 and 1750, demanded more an-
imation on stage than did the public of Louis' court. Voltaire's
reservations about Molière's facility with intrigues, continuity in
scenes, resolutions, etc., are typical of the times and no more
interesting than the commentaries of countless less talented critics.
But Voltaire's attitude is somewhat different for it views Molière's
shortcomings in technique as ultimately secondary, even going
so far as to admit that most of them are "négligences que la comédie tolère." [35] In this perspective, Voltaire's "critique de fautes"
is subordinate in importance to his other substantial commentaries
on Molière's theatre. The Classical comic poet had played his
part in that brilliant moment in French history which brought
France closer to the ideal enlightened and tolerant state. He stood
out by virtue of his sharp insights into the human personality, his
defense of justice against the false gods and, not least of all,
his great talent in entertaining the "public éclairé." Raymond
Naves sums it up well: "Molière est, de tous les écrivains du
17ème siècle, celui que Voltaire a le plus aimé, pour sa personne

[33] *Ibid.*, p. 117.
[34] *Ibid.*, p. 119.
[35] *Ibid.*, vol. 14, pp. 105-106.

autant que pour son œuvre, et s'il a désiré chez lui plus d'habileté et de perfection technique, il n'a jamais pu désirer plus de cœur et d'intelligence." [36]

Jean-Jacques Rousseau's remarks on Molière are of a different order, and much has already been written on the subject. The basic argument in the *Lettre à M. d'Alembert sur les spectacles* (1758) is simply, "qu'Alceste dans la pièce est un homme droit, sincère, estimable, un véritable homme de bien; que l'Auteur lui donne un personnage ridicule." [37] Thus Molière is blamable for having mocked true virtue in Alceste and for having allowed the dubious integrity of Philinte to triumph. The lack of measure and perspective can be explained in part by Rousseau's intimate association with Alceste, which makes his writings on this character but a thinly veiled apology for himself. In 1790, Fabre d'Englantine actually wrote a *mise en œuvre* of Jean-Jacques' ideas in a new play entitled *La Philinte de Molière*. Originally proposed as a sequel to *Le Misanthrope*, it gradually turned into a refutation of the original, an awkward reworking with a complete shift of focus. Alceste, played by the popular actor Molé, was kindly, generous, virtuous, while the real villain, Philinte, was made into an outright fraudulent, dishonest hypocrite. In the prologue, the author stands firmly behind his authority, Rousseau, to whom he acknowledges, ". . . je dois mon ouvrage et sa conception." [38]

There has always been a strain of purism and pedantry directed against certain aspects of Molière's comedies. La Bruyère had written, "Il a manqué à Molière d'éviter le jargon et le barbarisme et d'écrire purement . . ." and had warned against "un ridicule bas et grossier" in moliéresque comedy. [39] Fénelon and Vauvenargues made similar comments. Marmontel was one of the first to defend Molière against the purists, particularly in the playwright's use of sub-culture language: ". . . le jargon du monde de la cour a

---

[36] Raymond Naves, *Le Goût de Voltaire* (Garnier, 1938), p. 351.

[37] J.-J. Rousseau, *Lettre à d'Alembert sur les spectacles* (Geneva: Droz, 1949), p. 49.

[38] P. F. N. Fabre-d'Eglantine, *Le Philinte de Molière ou la Suite du Misanthrope* (Amsterdam: Chez Gabriel Dufour, 1792), p. 11.

[39] La Bruyère, *Œuvres*, ed. G. Servois (Hachette, 1865), vol. 1, pp. 128-129.

sa place dans le comique. Molière en a donné l'exemple." [40]
Unfortunately, Diderot is not very original in discussing Molière
and often repeats the old chestnuts on the poet's "langage bas."
Preoccupied with his own experimentations in the *drame bourgeois*, Diderot obviously had little inclination for probing Molière.
One interesting remark comes from a good, one-page essay in *De la
poésie dramatique*, entitled "Du drame burlesque." "Cependant
une farce excellente n'est pas l'ouvrage d'un homme ordinaire.
Elle suppose une gaîté originale; les caractères en sont comme
les grotesques de Callot, où les principaux traits de la figure
humaine sont conservés. Il n'est pas donné à tout le monde d'estro-
pier ainsi. Si l'on croit qu'il y a beaucoup plus d'hommes capables
de faire *Pourceaugnac* que *Le Misanthrope*, on se trompe." [41]
This recalls Diderot's innate sense and appreciation for the comic
in all its forms, even farce. This open attitude toward farce is
especially unusual during the eighteenth century. (Voltaire had
been very cautious about *Monsieur de Pourceaugnac*.) Regrettably
there is too little in this vein. After a detailed study of Diderot's
reading of Molière, a recent scholar aptly concluded: "Diderot
semble connaître de Molière à peu près ce que tout le monde
en connaît. La culture moliéresque de Diderot est celle de
l'honnête homme de son temps, sans curiosité particulière ni
originalité marquée." [42]

The *Histoire du théâtre italien* (2 volumes, 1727-1731), by the
famous Italian actor Louis Riccoboni, is noteworthy both as an
introduction of Italian theatre into France and for its remarks
on Molière. In an attempt at presenting his native theatrical
traditions as an important source for French theatre, Riccoboni
undertook the first quasi-systematic and partially objective study
of Molière's sources. His excesses aside (all of *Tartuffe* comes
from an obscure Italian play), this well-intentioned work remained
for many years the main source for subsequent source studies

---

[40] Marmontel, *Œuvres complètes* (Chez Verdière, 1818), vol. 14, p. 197.
See also Claire Zanetta, "Marmontel et Molière," in *De l'Encyclopédie à la
Contre-Révolution: J.-F. Marmontel* (Clermond-Ferrand: G. de Bussac, 1971),
pp. 105-116.
[41] Diderot, *Œuvres Esthétiques* (Garnier, 1959), p. 202.
[42] Adrienne D. Hytier, "Diderot et Molière," in *Diderot Studies*, vol. 8
(1966), p. 79.

(Moland, Toldo, etc.). In his *Observations sur la comédie et sur le génie de Molière* (1736), Riccoboni attempts to exonerate Molière from the charges of plagiarism: "Molière nous enseigne... comment il faut se servir d'une fable étrangère et de quelle manière on peut la rendre propre aux moeurs et à la langue de son pays. Il faut voir qu'il ne suffit pas de traduire un bon original... Une fable qui serait bonne dans son premier état peut devenir parfaite dans l'imitation." [43] In his advanced age Riccoboni was seized with religious fervor and in his *De la Réformation du théâtre* (1749), he proposed cuts and changes for purifying the comedies.

Jean-François d'Estandoux Cailhava is generally considered the first "moliériste." By dint of his many studies on Molière and his obsessive preoccupation with every detail of the poet's life, he could have had charter membership in the cult which flourished toward the end of the nineteenth century. For our purposes, two elements of Cailhava's criticism are worth noting. He was one of the first to admit that in Molière's biography the actual known facts were too meager to be used as a basis for interpretation of the comedies. He concludes by exhorting the reader, "LISEZ LA PIECE DE MOLIERE." His own commentaries, although somewhat dogmatic and lacking in depth and originality, are nonetheless based on a close reading of the texts. Cailhava also established that imitation is one of the foundations of Molière's art and that this did not detract from its validity. To substantiate this point, the critic distinguishes between "un imitateur, un copiste, un plagiaire." [44] Behind these discussions of imitation in Molière is a central preoccupation of the eighteenth century, the matter of *imitatio naturæ* and *ut pictura pœsis*. For this period, the beauty of art and poetry is determined by an intellectual comparison between the model and the imitation. The importance of this idea for interpreting Molière is that it necessitated a close, although often dogmatic, reading of the texts which nonetheless

---

[43] Quoted by Xavier de Courville, *Un Apôtre de l'Art du Théâtre au XVIIIe siècle, Luigi Riccoboni, dit Lélio* (Librairie Théâtrale, 1958), vol. 3, p. 186.

[44] J. F. d'Estandoux de Cailhava, *De l'Art de la comédie* (de l'Imprimerie de Ph.-D. Pierres, 1786), vol. 2, pp. 2-3.

represented some progress over the quality of criticism in Molière's time.

The century ends in a flurry of praise for Molière. In his *Eloge de Molière* (1769), Chamfort reflects the spirit of his time by insisting on the utility of the comedies, their positive propaganda value: "Le théâtre et la société ont une liaison intime et nécessaire... les poètes comiques [par] des maximes utiles, répandues dans leurs ouvrages, ont corrigé peut-être quelque particulier." [45] Due to Molière's particular contribution, "... la comédie [devint] un jour l'école des moeurs, le tableau le plus fidèle de la nature humaine et la meilleure histoire morale de la société." [46] Chamfort opines that Molière's work is more pertinent than Corneille's or Racine's, for the comic poet had demonstrated by his example how great an asset to the nation artistic genius could be and had taught the body politic the uses it could make of such talent. Finally, it is interesting that Chamfort was the first to note that Molière never dared discuss finances in his comedies and he suggests that the poet was on orders from Colbert. A curious idea which, if proven, could compromise Molière's integrity. Thus far, however, there is absolutely no proof for such a contention. The question of Molière's relationship with the King and the nobles continues to fascinate readers of Molière.

We saw how Voltaire, Chamfort, and others defined Molière's genius according to a value scale forged by the *philosophes*. Palissot's notes on the comic poet are an amusing counterthrust. The aging critic had fought long and hard against the *philosophes* and their esprit but with only limited success. In his *Mémoires*, he makes one last foray against the arch-enemy. Palissot holds that Molière's genius flourished in the particularly ideal setting of Louis XIV's splendrous court, with a benevolent prince affording the luxury and protection necessary for creative endeavors. And all of this available in an ambience of pervasive good taste, at a court which served as a meeting place for all of admiring Europe. What a contrast with the tawdriness and greyness of Palissot's own time, a condition caused by the *philosophes:* "... l'esprit

---

[45] Chamfort, *Maximes et Pensées, Anecdotes et Caractères* (Larousse, 1928), p. 181.
[46] *Ibid.,* pp. 195-196.

de gaîté est alors généralement répandu par suite de la consi-
dération et de la prosperité dont jouissait la nation; cet esprit de
gaîté que la manie philosophique a depuis desséché dans sa fleur,
lorsque las pour ainsi dire, d'être français, quelques raisonneurs
mélancoliques ont voulu nous livrer aux délires des idées an-
glaises." [47] Naturally, Palissot sees but a desert in comic theatre
since Molière: "Toutes les innovations que l'on s'est permises
depuis ce grand homme, sous prétexte de réformer ou d'ennoblir
le genre, n'ont tourné qu'à la ruine de la vraie comédie." [48] This
is typical of the way Molière was used in polemics and propaganda
throughout the century.

In retrospect the eighteenth century actually contributed little
to original Molière exegesis. Between the exploitation for propaganda, the dogmatism of the critical method and the concern
for grammar and sources, there was relatively little inquiry into
the actual comic substance of the comedies. Although there was
some enthusiasm for Molière, it was often naïve and superficial.
The first important new discoveries were left to the following
century.

The Nineteenth Century

Sainte-Beuve referred to a renewed and particularly vigorous
interest in Molière after 1794 sustained by "les transports d'un
public ramené au rire de la scène, et par l'esprit philosophique
régnant alors et vivement satisfait." [49] This impetus continued
almost unabated during most of the nineteenth century, which was
an extremely rich period in points of view on Molière and in
scientific research. The two notable phenomena which characterize
the enormous body of critical literature from this period are the
subjective, Romantic image of the comic poet and the gradual
founding of the "critique scientifique" based on the discovery
of numerous civil documents concerning Molière, the Poquelins,
the Béjarts, and the "Illustre Théâtre."

---

[47] Palissot, *Mémoires pour servir à l'Histoire de notre littérature* (de
l'Imprimerie de Monsieur, 1788), vol. 3, p. 304.

[48] *Ibid.,* p. 306.

[49] Sainte-Beuve, *Les Grands Ecrivains français,* ed. M. Allem (Garnier,
1927), "XVIIe Siècle, Les Poètes dramatiques," p. 190.

For the Romantics, the complexities of Molière's existence as director-playwright-actor-husband at Louis XIV's court were so overwhelming that they quite naturally overflowed into his works to the point where the comedies were dramatizations of Molière's domestic and professional experiences. This approach was not a discovery of the nineteenth century, however. We have seen how the allusions of *La Fameuse comédienne*, Donneau de Visé's insinuations, and other libelous tracts of the seventeenth century had already laid a groundwork for such an approach. The nineteenth century shifted the focus and instead sketched a very sympathetic portrait of Molière which was nonetheless often subjective. To a point however, this view has been over-emphasized. Musset's remark on *Le Misanthrope*, for example, was probably as much a boutade as a serious reflection, and it is not typical: "Quelle mâle gaîté, si triste et si profonde / Que, lorsqu'on vient d'en rire, on devrait en pleurer!" [50] Chateaubriand was more cautious and saw the potentially serious side of the plays in the perspective of the comic. [51] Mme. de Staël refers to Molière as the model in French comedy with whom to compare German writers and she does so in favor of Molière. *Dom Juan* is a good example of how the "esprit français" is capable of a fine mixture of the metaphysical and the comic while remaining essentially light: "Un prodige qui fait frissonner sert de mobile aux situations les plus comiques et les plus grand effets de l'imagination se mêlent aux nuances les plus piquantes de la plaisanterie." [52] Molière represents the French comic spirit par excellence, more subtle and *fin* than the basically serious German *Geist*.

The republicans also had a special approach to Molière. Victor Hugo preferred the charm and spontaneity of the young Molière (particularly his use of the salty "langue de Louis XIII") to the preciosity of the Sun King's court literature. [53] Stendhal thought Moliére equal to Shakespeare and, predictably, he detected an

---

[50] Alfred de Musset, *Œuvres complètes* (Louis Conard, 1923), vol. 2, p. 235.

[51] Chateaubriand, *Œuvres complètes* (Garnier frères, n. d.), vol. 6, p. 394.

[52] Mme de Stael, *De l'Allemagne* (Garnier frères, 1894), p. 341.

[53] Paul Stapfer, *Les Artistes juges et parties, Causeries parisiennes* (Sandoz et Fischbacher, 1872), p. 55.

anti-royal strain in *Le Misanthrope:* "Alceste est un homme how-beleur [sic] que se révolte contre le gouvernement monarchique . . . Louis XIV aurait pu exiler Alceste qui faisait voir le ridicule et l'odieux de la monarchie." [54] The young Beyle had already taken pleasure in recalling Chamfort's suggestion that the absence of financiers in Molière's comedies could probably be explained by clandestine orders from Colbert. No evidence is advanced to support the theory.

The most striking elaboration of the republican spirit is in Michelet who contended that Molière was a victim of royal injustice and despotism. The "historien terrible" considered Molière's position at Louis' court unique. In Michelet's chronology, Molière's ascendency in Louis' entourage corresponds directly to the growing preëminence of the Sun King's court as the center of power and elegance for all of Europe. (But Michelet categorically refused to refer to this period as "le grand siècle.") "L'apparition du *Tartuffe* et la conquête de Flandre marquent l'apogée littéraire et politique du siècle de Louis XIV." [55] But the insidious enemy, "les tartuffes," worked relentlessly against the play and managed to have it squelched. Michelet reads the next two great plays as thinly veiled revenge statements against this injustice.

Dom Juan, for example, is an overt attack on the essential group at the court, the marquis, who represented the royal group which harbored most of the intriguers, the scoundrels, and "faux dévots." Michelet sees Dom Juan, lying, stealing, heartless rogue, as a serious parody of the marquis. And yet the court, gullible and unsuspecting, ". . . admira Dom Juan, le trouva parfait gentilhomme." [56] *Le Misanthrope* is even more audacious. Michelet characterized it as "une pièce infiniment hardie (plus que *Tartuffe* peut-être et plus que *Dom Juan*)." [57] After all, as the

---

[54] Stendhal, *Molière, Shakespeare, La Comédie et le Rire,* ed. H. Martineau (Le Divan, 1930), p. 156. See also A. Thibaudet, "Stendhal et Molière," *NRF,* 1924 (2), pp. 592-604.

[55] J. Michelet, *Du Prêtre, de la Femme, de la Famille,* 3rd edition (Comptoir des Imprimeurs-Unis, 1845), p. 114, note 1.

[56] J. Michelet, *Louis XIV et la Révocation de l'Edit de Nantes,* 3rd edition (Chamerot, 1863), pp. 69-70.

[57] *Ibid.,* p. 83.

historian saw it, the play represented a direct affront to the
King. For Michelet, Alceste's violent moral indignation is really
directed not against Célimène but against the entire court and
".... qu'est'ce que la cour sinon le monde du roi, arrangé par lui
et pour lui?"[58] Unfortunately, all these efforts came to naught.
Michelet reads *Amphitryon* as the last desperate attempt to reach
the King. Accordingly the play was written at that delicate moment
when Louis had consented to showing *Tartuffe*, but only verbally,
and Lamoignon and the Archbishop were still holding out against
it. In this view, Alcmène's supplications to Jupiter are but a
transposition of Molière's pleading with Louis XIV for official
release of his play. "Molière essayait tout, priait les nouveaux
dieux, espérait dans Alcmène. S'il se pouvait qu'aux heures où
Jupiter voit trouble, elle tirât de lui l'émancipation du *Tartuffe!* ...
Voilà le secret de Sosie, le salaire espéré de la farce, des coups
de bâtons."[59] Sosie-Molière is helpless and he finally capitulates:
"Allons, cédons au sort dans notre affliction." This, Michelet
affirms, is the final indignity for Molière: "Le pis, c'est que Sosie
avoue que le dur argument de Mercure, le bâton, lui touche l'âme
et qu'il commence à l'admirer. Misère, misère profonde, contre
la force de l'injustice de ne pas garder le mépris."[60] The Sosie-
Molière situation is a micro-example of how Michelet viewed the
comic playwright's situation: sad, abused and so beaten by
enormous injustices that he is finally broken into meek and
mindless acceptance, without strength for protest or even indignation. This "Molière malheureux," with its political implications,
is different from the established romantic view, although it remains
within the same tradition.

Sainte-Beuve's sketch of Molière in the third volume of *Port-
Royal* is often cited as the outstanding example of the romantic
conception of Molière: "Il a au cœur la tristesse ... il était triste;
il l'était plus que Pascal, qu'on se figure si mélancolique..."[61]

---

[58] *Ibid.*
[59] *Ibid.*, p. 112.
[60] *Ibid.*, p. 114. For a diametrically opposed view of Louis' court and
Molière's role in it, see D. Nisard, *Histoire de la littérature française* (F. Didot,
1886), vol. 2, pp. 126 ff.
[61] Sainte-Beuve, *Port-Royal*, 6th edition (Hachette, 1901), vol. 3,
pp. 274-276.

And yet to limit Sainte-Beuve's view of Molière to this notion is to oversimplify. For thirty years the critic read and reflected on Molière, always with sympathy and generosity. Even the well-known "Aimer Molière" passages from an article of 1863 exude an admiration for Molière, for his honesty, and artistic and moral integrity, which goes far beyond the simplistic "triste Molière" scheme. There is an attempt in the critic's commentaries to describe an ambience, an attitude one feels after having known Molière. Consider this Voltairian observation: "Aimer Molière c'est être guéri à jamais, je ne dis pas de la basse et infâme hypocrisie, mais du fanatisme de l'intolérance et de la dureté en ce genre, de ce qui fait anathématiser et maudire... c'est être également à l'abri et à mille lieus de cet autre fanatisme politique, froid, sec et cruel, qui ne rit pas, qui sent son sectaire, qui, sous prétexte de puritanisme, trouve moyen de pétrir et de combiner tous les fiels, et d'unir dans une doctrine amère les haines, les rancunes et les jacobinismes de tous les temps." [62] Professor Otis Fellows' conclusion on Sainte-Beuve's criticism of Molière seems quite judicious. While admitting to "romantic" elements in the critic's writings, Professor Fellows is of the opinion that Sainte-Beuve's sharp critical insights and his broad, eclectic approach had brought him to a fuller understanding of the comic poet than any other nineteenth century critic. "In heeding the personal, the humanitarian, the creative and the purely dramatic aspects of Molière, [Sainte-Beuve] arrived at a definitive conception which places Molière among the few great geniuses the world has known. This conception is embodied in Sainte-Beuve's definition of a true classic." [63] This is a better measure of the critic's view of Molière. Simply to label Sainte-Beuve's Molière a "romantic Hamlet" is to deny the great critic that special broad view that he himself brought to bear on the comic playwright's work, and indeed to all of criticism.

If this period is referred to as the time of "moliéromanie," it is largely due to the volumes of serious scholarship which stand as a monument to the times. It is significant, for example, that between

---

[62] Sainte-Beuve, *Les Grands Ecrivains français, op. cit.*, p. 360.
[63] Otis Fellows, *French Opinion of Molière* (Providence: Brown University Press, 1937), p. 113.

1812 and 1824 four major editions of Molière's *Œuvres* were published and widely circulated. It was during this time that Louis Beffara, a Paris police commissioner, published his *Dissertation sur J.-B. Poquelin-Molière* (1821), a compendium of civil documents culled from Paris archives. These documents included Molière's baptismal and marriage certificates, among other interesting items. Beffara's thin volume was the beginning of the first great period of Molière research which reached a frenetic peak during the 1880's. The *Dissertation* established the first scientific trend in Molière scholarship which coexisted with the more impressionistic commentaries. Beffara was one of the first scholars to suggest that, accord:ng to the marriage certificate, Armande Béjart may not have been Madeleine's daughter but her youngest sister. But the discovery of civil documents and their implications did little at first to change the existing attitudes toward on Molière's life, except of course to correct a few factual errors of names and dates. Jules Taschereau's *Vie de Molière* (1824) is a case in point. The biographer considered himself a disciple of Beffara and was proud to present the first full-length scientific biography, based on the latest research, and designed to replace Grimarest. And yet Taschereau sought to substantiate many elements of the legend and cites questionab'e sources with only occasional reference to possible "invraisemblances." He repeats the old canards of Molière's amorous escapades in the provinces, the Molière-Chapelle conversation from *La Fameuse Comédienne*, and the "en-cas-de-nuit" tale. Here, Louis XIV is reported to have personally invited Molière to sup with him in order to spite noblemen who objected to "bourgeois-comédien" Poquelin's constant presence in the King's entourage. [64] In spite of the emerging scientific method, Taschereau had not been as critical as he intended and his book did little to check the growing legend. That task was left for another, more rigorous volume.

Anaïs Bazin was a little-known historian and lawyer, author of an *Histoire de Louis XIII*. In two long articles in *La Revue des Deux Mondes,* he launched what is considered the first attempt at *tabula rasa* in Molière biography. Michaut called Bazin's revised

---

[64] J. Taschereau, *Histoire de la Vie et des ouvrages de Molière,* 3rd edition (J. Hetzel, 1844), p. 79.

and augmented *Notes historiques sur la vie de Molière* (1851) the first scientific text on the subject which could serve as a starting point for future research. The *Notes* are gritty, often dry, and sometimes ponderous. The author is arrogantly conscious of the debunking value of his study and the opening line is a good indication of his attitude: "On peut tenir aujourd'hui pour constant que Molière naquit à Paris, non pas en 1620 ou 1621, mais le 15 janvier 1622; non pas sous les piliers des Halles, mais dans la rue Saint-Honoré, où demeurait son père; qu'il était fils de Jean Poquelin, tapissier, et de Marie Cressé (non pas Boutet) sa femme." [65] The rest is a point-for-point refutation of many hypotheses (including some from Grimarest), during which the author hammers away with documented evidence. But even Bazin occasionally balked before the facts. He stubbornly contends that Armande is Madeleine's daughter, the marriage certificate notwithstanding. By curious reasoning, he does conclude, however, that the Comte de Modène was Armande's father and not Molière.

For all its value, Bazin's method was very confining. Aside from a few new documents, he depended almost entirely on the LaGrange-Vivot *Préface* of 1682, believing it to be the only valid document Molière could have wanted to leave to posterity. But for all his care and circumspection, Bazin was not very sensitive to the shortcomings of the LaGrange preface and hardly mentions the "official" quality of that document. Nor was the historian adverse to an occasional speculative extrapolation. Michaut calls attention to Bazin's reading of Sosie's complaint early in Act I of *Amphitryon*. Like Michelet, Bazin interprets "Sosie, à quelle servitude / Tes jours sont-ils assujettis?" as a "bouderie" on Molière's part for having been left in the lurch by the King in the dispute over *Tartuffe*. [66] But these are details and the fact remains that Bazin's *Notes historiques* gave biography research new direction, and, in general, new seriousness to research on Molière.

After Bazin, from 1850 on, there was an abundance of Molière scholarship. The Beffara-Bazin tradition is maintained by

---

[65] A. Bazin, *Notes historiques sur la vie de Molière* (Techner Libraire, 1851), pp. 9-10.

[66] *Ibid.,* p. 151.

Eudore Soulié in his excellent *Recherches sur Molière et sur sa famille* (1863). This modest volume brought to light some sixty-odd new documents of considerable interest and importance. They included the "accord entre les comédiens de l'Illustre Théâtre," the "Contrat de mariage entre Molière et Armande-Gresinde-Clair-Elisabeth Béjart," and the "Inventaire fait après la mort de Molière." The new documentation is preceded by an essay in which Soulié sketches a biography of Molière in light of Beffara, Bazin and his own research. For the most part, it is a careful and lucid text, a good example of the best kind of scholarship of the time. If there is one element in Soulié's method that dates his work, it is his partial acceptance of Taine's "milieu-race" theory of literary history which was in vogue at the time. Briefly stated, this notion emphasizes the importance of the social class and milieu of the artist to a full understanding of his work. For Molière research, this theory exerted both a positive and a potentially negative influence. On the one hand it served as an impetus to search even further into archives and notarial record deposits for documents relating to Molière and his entourage; on the other hand, it tended to foster, unwittingly, the ceaseless but not always productive attempts at justifying each play with biographical or historical facts.

The unlikely admixture of two opposing attitudes in Molière research, the Romantic and the scientific, gave a curious character to scholarship in the closing years of the nineteenth century. No single publication is more representative of this predicament than *Le Moliériste*. From the start, there was no question as to the function of this journal: to gather and publish the latest findings which would foster the "culte de Molière." Under the able guidance of Georges Monval, it served that function from 1879 to 1889, and was the rallying point of some of the most unabashed cultists. Monval's editorial in the first number of 1 April 1879 establishes the character of the journal and the collaborators: ". . . dévots de Molière dont l'admiration va jusqu'au culte et pour lesquels la découverte d'une signature, l'indice seul d'un autographe du Maître prend les proportions d'un événement public. C'est l'organe de cette petite église littéraire que nous voulons fonder, quelque chose comme 'les Annales de propagation de la foi' dans notre religion spéciale."[67] The journal was the forum not only for the "grands prêtres et adorateurs du Dieu," but also for "chercheurs obscurs, moliérisants, moliérophiles, moliéromanes mêmes (c'est toute une armée qui n'avait pas son 'Moniteur officiel')."[68] True to its policy, Le Moliériste represented all of these "chercheurs" during its ten years, along with some substantial and respectable scholars. But articles like "Anecdote sur Baron," "La Mâchoire de Molière," "Le Fauteuil de Molière," and "Pourceaugnac en Chine," give a good idea of the anecdotal quality of this unique journal.

Aside from the limited value of some of these volumes for scholarship today, the phenomenon of Le Moliériste is pertinent for the moment it represents in the evolution of Molière studies. The decade of its publication represents the apogee of detailed research on Molière spawned by the important works of Beffara, Bazin and Soulié. The mad rush to discover a signature or the "mâchoire" of Molière is the outgrowth of "moliéromanie." But there was another more positive aspect of Le Moliériste. An open forum, it also became the locus of another current of scholarship whose source was the Sorbonne, and which was gradually in the process of re-establishing equilibrium, sanity, and a measure of objectivity in Molière studies. Gustave Larroumet was one of the first to take issue with the excessive aspects of some of the active cultists. In one of the volumes of Le Moliériste, he engaged a cultist, Auguste Baluffe, in a sharp polemic over Molière's relations with the Béjart family and displayed a sharp edge of condescension for Baluffe's erratic method and untenable propositions. Brunetière accused the moliéristes of inanities, fabrications and gross errors in their publications. His amusingly sharp definition of a moliériste is worth quoting: "Un moliériste est un érudit qui s'inquiète beaucoup plus de savoir en quelle année Molière donna des représentations à Angoulême ou à Montauban que de comprendre Tartuffe ou Le Misanthrope, et qui se soucie beaucoup moins de relire Dom Juan ou l'Avare, que de courir d'étude en étude de notaire pour y chercher au bas d'un contrat de

---

[67] Le Moliériste, ed. George Monval (Libraire Tresses, 1880), vol. 1, p. 3.
[68] Ibid., p. 4.

vente ou d'un acte de mariage la signature de Molière." [69] The tide
was turning and this negative reaction to the excesses of "moliérisme" is indicative of the new direction taken in the closing
decades of the nineteenth century.

Several publications after 1870 are indicative of the trend
toward renewing the priority of serious scholarship. In part, this
attitude is but a reaffirmation of the skeptical, scientific methods
established around mid-century. An example of the very sound
scholarship at this time is Eugène Despois' *Le Théâtre français sous Louis XIV* (1874), which was the background work
for the "Grands Ecrivains" edition of Molière's complete works.
This latter edition of Molière's work is the outstanding publication
of the time in terms of erudition. It belongs to the prestigious
Hachette series of "Grands Ecrivains de la France," and the
fourteen volumes on Molière were more than twenty-five years
in preparation. Soulié began the work in 1873 but he died only
three years later, after having published the first three volumes.
Then Eugène Despois directed the project for a few years
before Paul Mesnard began work. From the volume on *Tartuffe*,
through the last volumes of bibliography and iconography, Mesnard was editor. By any measure it is an outstanding edition
and is highly respected even today, although it is somewhat
out of date. Each play is prefaced by a long "notice" which
situates the work historically and brings to bear all incidental
material which might elucidate the text. Generally, the commentaries are terse and contain only the most pertinent information. This is followed by important texts or documents of the
time (Molière's prefaces or "placets," De Visé's critical texts, etc.).
Mesnard also included Voltaire's "Sommaires" from the 1735
edition which are still quite pertinent. Within the text, the ample
footnotes include variant forms, sources, references to the mass
of libelous literature of the time, and selected bits of criticism
from earlier periods. (The Taschereau edition of 1824 had done
this more systematically.)

The outstanding contribution from Paul Mesnard is Volume 10,
Notice Biographique sur Molière (1889). Mesnard culled with the

[69] F. Brunetière, "Trois Moliéristes," in *La Revue des Deux Mondes*,
vol. 66 (1884), p. 703.

greatest care from the mass of documentation and anecdotes which previous generations had amassed. The result is an erudite but never ponderous text which is still useful today, although naturally a few of the passages are dated. The biographer hedges on Molière's relationship with Gassendi but finally accepts that Molière was probably the philosopher's student; he refers to the alleged translation of Lucretius as a sort of absent "pièce justificative." Although Mesnard refuses to deal with the incest calumny, he is very cautious about deciding on Armande's parentage, and here, where information is scanty and confused, he simply relies on his intuition and his good faith in Molière: "Mieux vaut ne s'appuyer que sur l'estime dont notre poète a toujours été entouré." [70] Mesnard was one of the first to maintain that Molière had really broken with his bourgeois family and embraced the bohemian life out of a serious dedication to poetry and not to the vocation of theatre. Finally, Mesnard does accept a limited degree of subjectivism in Molière's plays, particularly with regard to Armande: "Il n'y a guère à se tromper sur son dessein de lui faire entendre par la bouche d'Alceste la menace d'une rupture sans espérance de retour . . ." [71] But Mesnard's position was shared by many other serious "universitaires."

Gustave Larroumet's La Comédie de Molière (1903) also belongs to this tradition. While it is a serious and careful study, Larroumet's Molière is nonetheless "triste, d'une tristesse silencieuse . . . il recherchait la solitude . . . et le silence . . . l'amertume croît dans son âme et finit par déborder." [72] By somewhat specious argumentation, Larroumet also links Molière's melancholy to the broader symptoms of acute hypochondria, so acute and so persistent that the critic believes it to be a mild form of psychosis, a kind of madness! To sustain his case Larroumet can only refer to Elomire hypocondre, a libelous text from 1670, in which Elomire-Molière consults the charlatans of the Pont-Neuf in one of his stages of delusion. Finally, Larroumet muses on the perverse delights doctors might take in the bizarre paradox of "la savoureuse vengeance qui consisterait à faire passer pour légèrement

---

[70] GEF, vol. 10, op. cit., p. 263.
[71] Ibid., p. 337.
[72] G. Larroumet, La Comédie de Molière (Hachette, 1903), pp. 341-349.

fou l'homme qui s'est moqué de la médecine elle même." [73] A curious hypothesis without a shred of proof to sustain it.

The last important figure of this generation was Brunetière who placed Molière in the long-honored gallic tradition of "libre esprit." In fact Molière is, according to Brunetière, the only important link in the seventeenth century between Rabelais and Montaigne on the one hand and Voltaire and Diderot on the other. In forceful prose, Brunetière argues that since conditions at Louis' court were essentially immoral, there was no profit for anyone pretending religious fervor, nothing to gain from acting the "faux dévot." The true object of Molière's sharpest attacks was not the false zealots at all; on the contrary, "les ennemis ou les adversaires de Molière [furent] les vrais dévots, non pas les faux... ceux dont l'imagination et le crédit menaçaient ou pouvaient menacer la liberté de son art... c'est au profit de la nature qu'il a voulu détruire la religion de l'effort et de la contrainte morale." [74] Molière is really anti-religion, a dangerous atheist who attempted to destroy established dogma. This was not an uncommon position on Molière taken by the ultracatholic critics of this period. Nonetheless, Brunetière's reading of Molière does represent a shift in focus away from anecdotal, cultist preoccupations. It was perhaps the same general spirit which moved Emile Augier to suggest straightforwardly that Tartuffe, Arnolphe and Alceste were simply "personnages comiques." [75] At about the same time, Coquelin l'Aîné dared to play Alceste in a comic vein and his brother did likewise in the rôles of Harpagon and Tartuffe. [76] The winds were shifting.

---

[73] *Ibid.*, p. 349.

[74] F. Brunetière, *Etudes critiques,* 4th series (Hachette, 1898), p. 202 and p. 209.

[75] Emile Augier, "Tartuffe, Arnolphe, Alceste, personnages comiques," in *Le Moliériste, op. cit.*, vol. 7, p. 99. See also Hillemacher's response in same volume, pp. 131 ff.

[76] M. Descotes, *Les Grands rôles du théâtre de Molière* (P. U. F., 1964), pp. 112-114.

Chapter II

PROBLEMS IN MOLIÈRE BIOGRAPHY, 1900 - 1959

It has been said that Molière's life as we know it begs for legend. This remark suggests the paucity of details available on the dramatist's life, in spite of many marginal documents. To judge from their writings, it is clear that many literary biographers have sought to reveal the character of Molière's genius by ordering and explaining the sparse collection of facts on the playwright's life. In the case of many biographers, these attempts led to the gradual building of a legend, for the contrast between available data and the biographer's needs forced many writers into the realm of almost pure imagination.

Often the writers of fictionalized biographies utilized in a most uncritical way documents of dubious value from the seventeenth century and then sought to confirm their fictions with slanted readings from the comedies. In other cases, the inadequate data on Molière — much more inadequate than for Corneille, Descartes, Racine — moved biographers to attempt to deduce the man from his works. The root of the problem is that Molière left not a single letter, and aside from the plays themselves, his writings include only a few prefaces and poems which offer very little about the man.

The incontestable, and rudimentary facts are easy to summarize. Jean-Baptiste Poquelin, called Molière after 1644, was born in Paris on 15 January 1622, the son of a middle-class cloth merchant with an appointment to Louis XIV's household staff; at twenty-one he became enamored with the theatre and forsook the security of the family profession to throw himself into the disreputable vocation of the boards; failing in his first attempt at establishing his troupe, he left Paris and for thirteen years he wandered through the provinces; during this time he began writing material for his troupe, *L'Illustre-Théâtre;* in 1658 he returned to Paris, and for the following fifteen years Molière wrote and performed in about twenty-eight plays in Paris, Versailles, Chantilly, Saint-Germain en Laye, in other "residences," and in private; in 1662 he married Armande Béjart who bore him three children, of whom only one daughter survived; he died on 17 February 1673. This is the framework on which various kinds of biographies will attempt to reconstruct Molière.

The objectives of this chapter are to adumbrate some of the general problems of establishing Molière's biography and to identify some of the persistent elements of the moliéresque legend as well as the attempts at checking it. Finally, biographically oriented methods of explication will be discussed in order to show how they influenced textual exegesis.

The Legend

In the previous chapter, we saw how a number of undocumented and unverifiable elements of the poet's life gradually became accepted by critics and biographers. This tradition tacitly accepted the validity of some of the most questionable documents relating to Molière and it viewed the comedies as mirror reflections of the poet's personal life. Often referred to as the subjectivist method, it continued into our century and had one of its earliest partisans in Abel LeFranc. In a series of lectures at the Collège de France in 1904-1905, LeFranc stated unequivocally that for him subjectivism was "la règle générale," and that he regretted that "On a sensiblement exagéré le caractère impersonnel, objectif et classique de la littérature française du 17ème siècle." [1] LeFranc utilized rather freely many of the suspect texts on Molière from the seventeenth century, including *Elomire hypocondre* and *La Fameuse comédienne.* Moreover, he accepted uncritically almost all of Grimarest's *Vie de M. de Molière* and thereby re-established

---

[1] Abel LeFranc, "La Vie et les ouvrages de Molière," in *Revue des cours et conférences,* vol IV/2 (1906), p. 194.

credit for this work which had fallen into relative obscurity, especially during the nineteenth century. On yet another point of contention, LeFranc argued that Molière clearly acknowledged that he himself, his family, and his "domestique" would be the primary subject for his works. LeFranc was referring to the ambiguous passage in the LaGrange-Vivot preface and maintained that this document justified the subjectivist method in biography writing and in textual exegesis.

On the relationship between Molière and Gassendi, LeFranc was also categoric. For the critic, Gassendi was without doubt "le maître de Molière, celui qui a exercé probablement l'action la plus profonde sur le développement de sa pensée . . . L'influence de Gassendi sur Molière ne saurait donc être contestée." [2] In this view, many of the plays reflect Gassendi's influence. *Les Femmes savantes*, for example, favors the Gassendist temperament concerned with "la guenille — mon corps" and is opposed to "le spiritualisme cartésien." LeFranc also delighted in the mystery and confusion surrounding Armande, "Mademoiselle Molière," and her identity. The mere ambiguity of it all seemed to make it even more attractive. "Le grand secret [la naissance d'Armande] domine toute la biographie et même en partie l'étude de l'œuvre de l'auteur du *Misanthrope*." [3] There is little doubt that LeFranc's attitude toward Armande, his uncritical use of documents, and his vivid imagination helped to relaunch the subjectivist tradition in the early years of the twentieth century in France.

But LeFranc's method was not the only one being used at this time. In fact several commentators objected mildly to the exaggerations of the subjectivist method and proposed more moderation. Eugène Rigal's *Molière* (1908) was one of the earliest biographies in the first decade of the century to adopt the objective method of Bazin and Soulié. But while Rigal seems to reject many of LeFranc's contentions, he neither refutes them completely nor excludes possible influences from the dramatist's "vie sentimentale" in the comedies. [4] Georges Lafenestre's *Molière* (1909) is even

---

[2] *Ibid.,* pp. 506-508.
[3] *Ibid.,* p. 309. Quoted by Michaut and others.
[4] Eugene Rigal, *Molière,* 2 vols. (Hachette, 1908); cf. particularly "L'Homme dans l'œuvre," vol. 1, pp. 1-29.

less successful. The author delineates sharply between Molière's life and works by isolating a succinct chronology of the subject's life, and then discussing the works. Unfortunately, the method is artificial and Lafenestre seems almost too determined not to fall into anecdote. For example, he discusses Molière's marriage without ever raising the question of Armande's parentage and with only the most cursory reference to the controversies that had raged around it. [5] Nonetheless, Rigal and Lafenestre displayed a measure of caution in their works which distinguishes them from the more imaginative subjectivists.

Within the next two decades, three important and reliable biographies appeared in English: Brander Matthew's *Molière, His Life and His Works* (1916), Arthur Tilley's *Molière* (1921), and John Palmer's *Molière* (1930). All of them have the distinction of being sensible, especially about many of the major points of the moliéresque legend. On the Armande question, John Palmer observed judiciously: "The discovery of Beffara . . . far from terminating the controversy, only added to its complexity. Its astounding convolutions during the next hundred years are only explicable on the assumption that there is an unconscious human bias in favor of scandalous readings. The tradition must at all costs be saved; therefore the documents are false."[6] But this enlightened view was a minority opinion, and it hardly existed at all in France. Nonetheless, the winds were shifting, and by 1920, the subjectivist tradition was headed into a violent storm. It was time for the first important reassessment and it came in 1922.

In spite of the sharp controversy surrounding the man, Gustave Michaut remains an unquestionable authority in Molière studies in the first half of the century. His works on Molière include the well-know *La Jeunesse de Molière* (1922), *Les Débuts de Molière à Paris* (1923) and *Les Luttes de Molière* (1925). On the question of Molière biography, two other articles are pertinent: "La Biogra-

---

[5] Georges Lafenestre, *Molière* (Hachette, 1909), pp. 44-45.
[6] John Palmer, *Molière* (New York: Brewer and Warren, 1930), p. 227; quoted by W. G. Moore from the British edition in *French Studies*, vol. 1 (1947), p. 293.

phie de Molière" (1932), and "Molière dans son œuvre" (1937), plus a curious edition of documents, *Molière raconté par ceux qui l'ont vu* (1932). The first three volumes follow Molière's career through *Le Misanthrope*. A fourth and final volume, *Le Triomphe de Molière,* never appeared although notes from it were used in Michaut's edition of Molière's complete works. These works represent a systematic attack on all aspects of the moliéresque legend and its effects on textual interpretation. Even incomplete, Michaut's three volumes constitute an impressive synthesis of all the important problems in Molière criticism and biography up to 1925. Specifically, Michaut saw biography as the particular area in Molière studies which had been led astray by a certain Romantic prestige, and which had fallen prey to fiction or hypotheses instead of respecting "l'austérité de la méthode et de l'esprit critiques." By 1920, the problem had become acute for this "genre" had progressed virtually unchecked. According to Michaut, these arbiters "... admettent que Molière s'est mis tout entier dans son œuvre, que sa vie a passé dans ses comédies, qu'il s'y est peint et raconté et qu'on peut dire de son théâtre ce que Michelet dit de lui-même et de son histoire: qu'il y a identité du livre et de l'auteur." [7] He objects to the oversimplification in relating psychological or exterior factors of the poet's biography directly to the plays with the result that "... le lecteur finit par ne plus bien savoir si c'est la tragédie supposée de son existence qui nous conduit à l'interprétation tragique de ses comédies ou si c'est l'interprétation tragique de ses comédies qui nous entraîne à supposer la tragédie dans son existence." [8]

A good example of Michaut's method on an important aspect of Molière's youth is his discussion of the comic poet's education and possible contact with Gassendi. That Molière had been Gassendi's student and that his philosophy had influenced the plays directly had been more or less accepted as fact. In addition to Abel LeFranc, Michaut cites several other well-known commentators who subscribed to this thesis. Michaut's own method is

---

[7] Gustave Michaut, "Molière dans son œuvre," in *Pascal, Molière, Musset* (Editions Alsatia, 1942), p. 139.

[8] Gustave Michaut, *La Jeunesse de Molière* (Hachette, 1922), p. 14; quoted by Moore and others.

rigorously historical. First, he insists on establishing the final date of Molière's studies at the Collège de Clermont. Then in ten pages of close argumentation, Michaut shows how it is unlikely that Molière was still doing his "humanités et philosophie" in 1641, the year Gassendi arrived in the French capital. [9] Michaut's main argument rests on a detailed consideration of the chronology of Molière's activities between 1636-1641, based on all the available documents. Primarily, Michaut tries to discredit Grimarest who was one of the main sources on the question. On the matter of Gassendi's influence on the comedies, Michaut cannot be sure. He seems to think that Molière occupied a position between "Bernier gassendiste" and "Boileau cartésien," without specifying exactly how much at odds Molière might have been with either of these philosophies. He does maintain that either of these attitudes could have allowed the playwright to be part of the wave of anti-aristotelianism which prevailed at the time.

In *Les Débuts de Molière à Paris*, Michaut devotes an entire chapter to "Le Mariage de Molière." The critic could not avoid this particular issue for it was the single most controversial point in Molière's biography and constituted the "épine dorsale" of the subjectivist method; LeFranc's remark cited above suggests this clearly. This school holds that Armande was the illegitimate daughter of Madeleine Béjart, probably fathered by the baron de Modène, but perhaps even by Molière himself. The sources for this view are disparate. Boileau and Grimarest seem to have believed, along with many of their contemporaries, that Armande was Madeleine's daughter, without thinking that Molière's marriage was incestuous. Bayle, alas, gave the incest theory a considerable boost by inscribing it in his *Dictionnaire*. The original sources for the calumny at the court were Montfleury, Le Boulanger de Chalussay in his *Elomire hypocondre* (1670), the anonymous *La Fameuse Comédienne* (1688?), and Guichard in his *Factum* of 1676. The absence of any reference to Armande's parentage in LaGrange's *Registre* also led to speculation that Molière's friend and fellow board-player was simply avoiding a sticky issue. Michaut categorically refuses to consider the libelous pamphlets

---

[9] *Ibid.*, pp. 67-77.

circulated against Moliére by his enemies. Being so warped and vicious, these texts could not possibly be considered dependable, particularly on this issue. Instead, he addresses himself to the more substantial and valid documents. He argues for accepting the marriage contract between Armande and Molière and the actual marriage certificate of 20 February 1662 as accurate and dependable; both documents clearly identify Armande as the youngest daughter of Marie Hervé Béjart, Madeleine's mother. Michaut makes the same case for accepting as valid Marie Hervé's death certificate which indicates that she was 47 or 48 at the time of Armande's birth (and not 52), which is not too advanced an age for childbearing. Logically, Michaut contends that La Grange kept the *Registre* for his own purposes, like a press agent's diary, and did not need to make annotations of facts and details already obvious to him, such as the names of Armande's parents. Since Boileau's remark on Armande comes to us only through Brossette, it could be an error, as many of Brossette's remarks have proven to be. Necessarily, Michaut is often reduced to refuting hypothesis with hypothesis, but his reasoning is sound, his use of the documents careful, and his conclusions invariably appear closer to the truth than the speculations of the subjectivists. He concludes that existing evidence indicates that Armande was Madeleine's youngest sister and that the contrary case has been sustained by the "force d'une opinion préconçue."

In his essay of 1937, Michaut returned to another important source in the subjectivist credo, the LaGrange-Vivot *Préface* of 1682. Here is the crucial passage: "... l'on peut dire qu'il a joué tout le monde, puisqu'il s'y est joué [dans ses comédies] le premier en plusieurs endroits, sur des affaires de sa famille et qui regardaient ce qui se passait dans son domestique." [10] Michaut's tack here is to suggest that the mind finds what it seeks, and that this phrase has been taken too literally by innately subjectivist critics. He returns to the *Dictionnaire de l'Académie* of 1694 and shows that the terms "famille" and "domestique" had a broader, more generic meaning in the seventeenth century and should not be understood too literally. Moreover, he points out how LaGrange

---

[10] GEF, vol. 1, pp. xv-xvi; quoted by Michaut in *Pascal, Molière, Musset, op. cit.,* p. 148.

and Vivot carefully state "dans ses comédies," and not "dans *toutes* ses comédies;" "plusieurs endroits," and not *partout;* "bien de fois," and not *toujours.* Michaut interprets the preface to mean that Molière used in his plays only those details of everyday life which can become grist for any anecdote or any piece of imaginative literature. The substance of daily, domestic existence does not, however, extend to the intimacy of Molière's relationship with his wife, father, possible mistresses, etc. [11] To support his case, Michaut recalls that the authors of the *Préface* refer only to Molière's well-known cough as the single instance of the playwright's use of personal material in his plays. Indeed, it had already been noted that Molière had a special knack for profiting from the physical features of all of his players, even from the unflattering ones: René du Parc's obesity is depicted as such in *Le Dépit amoureux;* Jodelet's thin line is supposed to be the result of his fatigue from the wars in *Les Précieuses ridicules;* La Flèche limps in *L'Avare,* as did in reality Louis Béjart who created the role in 1668. Michaut insists that these cases are the only documented examples of Molière's use of material from his "domestique," and that those are the instances LaGrange and Vivot must have alluded to. Anything else is pure conjecture and goes counter to the sense of discretion Molière exhibited in *L'Impromptu de Versailles.*

After this systematic attack on many salient points of the moliéresque legend, one wonders what Michaut might have considered valid and judicious biography for Molière? The answer may be in his *Molière raconté par ceux qui l'ont vu* (1932). The idea of the volume is to collect and present pertinent documents of a "témoignage" nature from the contemporaries of the subject. Since the total documentation on Molière from the seventeenth century would represent a considerable corpus, Michaut limited his collection to those items which touched directly on Molière the man, director of his troupe, actor and playwright. The "choix de textes" extends from Molière's baptismal certificate of 1622, to Perrault's sketch in his *Hommes illustres . . .* of 1696. As much as possible the editor lets the documents speak for themselves,

---

[11] For a full discussion of this point, see Michaut, *Pascal, Molière, Musset, op. cit.,* pp. 147-151.

for his slim volume contains only a meager "avertissement" and introduction, and no conclusion. The notes are few and mostly limited to historical information. Lest one were to miss the point, however, an occasional note does orient the reader in this hodge-podge, and Michaut's few interventions clearly reaffirm his attitude on Molière biography. The short note appended to the LaGrange-Vivot *Préface* restates Michaut's firm conviction that "En matière de biographie moliéresque, c'est le document capital, malgré les quelques erreurs qu'on y a relevées." [12] Chapter headings and subtitles also qualify and limit the value of the document according to Michaut. In this volume, Somaize is "l'injureux copiste," Donneau de Visé is a "plagiaire," LaGrange and Vivot's *Préface* is "officielle," and Le Boulanger de Chalussay earns the title of "biographe haineux." Inevitably, there are also some glaring omissions. There are no extracts from *La Fameuse comédienne* or from Grimarest's *Vie*. It seems clear that the documents included in this volume, with reservations and qualifications, are those Michaut considers essential to Molière's biography. In an area so depleted of reliable information, so confused and distorted, these documents taken as a whole provide a good adumbration of what the dramatist's life might have been. And, although individual pieces are not always objective and trust-worthy, the totality of the collection, edited and arranged, does impart a feeling of sobriety and reliability, at least as a proto-biography. For Michaut's acute "esprit scientifique," this slender volume appears to represent an attempt at reaching Ranke's ideal of presenting history "wie es eigentlich gewesen ist."

To assess Michaut's contribution in this specific area of Molière studies is not an easy task. The very negative nature of his undertaking, his unlimited skepticism, his sometimes overly rigorous methodology, his sharp, polemical style, all of these characteristics have made an objective evaluation of his work difficult. And from the publication of his first volume in 1922, the reaction was chilly if not hostile, especially in France. There were scornful innuendoes concerning the great research efforts Michaut had poured into proving "ce que la vie de Molière n'était pas."

[12] Gustave Michaut, *Molière raconté par ceux qui l'ont vu* (Stock, 1932), p. 225.

English and American scholars, literally and figuratively more distant on the question, were generally more receptive to Michaut's attempts at exposing the untenable legendary aspects of Molière's life. Somewhat simplified, the two most oft-repeated French attacks on Michaut were that "il n'apporte rien de nouveau," and "sa critique est trop systématiquement négative et sèche." But both of these criteria are irrelevant. It is plain that Michaut's task was not to seek out new documents but to bring order, reason, and a measure of sanity to the use and understanding of existing documentation. Unavoidably, his method was negative and the works of many scholar-colleagues would be questioned. It is curious that many critics who raised a hue and cry about Michaut's approach either did little to justify their alarm, or unashamedly admitted that they could not bear the loss of the vividness which much of the legend had brought to Molière biography. And yet, *grosso modo*, Michaut's volumes have survived and many scholars today consider them standard. The best measure of the value of Michaut's works is the implicit tribute by W. G. Moore when he divided the last hundred years of Molière studies into the pre- and post-Michaut periods.

Some historians were content to accept, actively or tacitly, the results of Michaut's investigations. Daniel Mornet, for example, seems to reflect Michaut's attitude, at least in the rapid biographical sketch of his *Molière* (1943). His outline adds nothing new but prides itself in being "prudent et clair," two qualities which recall Michaut's method. For other historians, however, the task has not been so easy. While Michaut's scrupulously scientific method was difficult to dismiss, many academics wanted nonetheless to preserve certain elements of the legend, especially to fill in the "points obscurs" of the poet's life. Georges Mongrédien's *Vie privée de Molière* (1950) occasionally suggests this. This biography returns to the documents and yet the author's position is ambivalent. He defends the rigor of the scientific method and yet he usually manages to accept as valid all the documents on Molière, usually for lack of something better. Moreover, he admits belonging to the subjectivist school. In keeping with this position, Mongrédien sees a measure of "actualité" in all of the comedies and Molière "apparaît comme un 'revuiste' de génie." [13] On other questions, however, he is more circumspect. He tends to believe that Armande is Madeleine's daughter but, finding the evidence too inconclusive, he concludes, "il est impossible de nous prononcer." [14] While he strongly repudiates the suggestion that Molière's marriage was incestuous, he is convinced that Molière's marriage was a sad one. "Molière est, avec Napoléon et Victor Hugo, un des exemples traditionnels de maris trompés parmi les grands hommes." [15] Mongrédien's work is an example of sound, serious scholarship, although it hedges occasionally on certain aspects of the legend.

Antoine Adam's biographical section on Molière in his *Histoire de la littérature française au XVIIe siècle* (volume 3, 1954) is also noteworthy. Although a scant half-dozen pages in length, it nonetheless sketches a conception of Molière the man which gives an interesting shade to the historian's interpretations of the works. For example, he insists on bourgeois Poquelin's modest, unromantic, even unattractive physiognomy: "Molière n'était pas beau,... il faut même parler de laideur... il était bas sur jambes... le cou très court, la tête trop forte et enfoncée dans les épaules lui donnaient une silhouette sans prestige..." [16] The portrait here is essentially one of a sturdy bourgeois, prepared to be stubborn, and Adam thinks many of the early plays are polemical. *L'Ecole des femmes* is a provocative satirical attack against a conception of religious morality; *Tartuffe* is the next bitter installment and it represents a bold thrust against the powerful "Colbert-cabale dévote" clique; Trissotin is a personal slur against L'abbé Cotin, etc. Unfortunately, Molière was not the tough pugilist all of his life. Adam recalls that toward the end of 1665 the dramatist fell ill and his condition deteriorated to the point that by the spring of 1667 rumors circulated that he was *in extremis*. From this time on, his work takes on a different tone. Adam thinks Alceste reflects the general pessimism into which Molière had fallen. Beyond *Le Misanthrope*, his increasing

---

[13] Georges Mongrédien, *La Vie privée de Molière* (Hachette, 1950), pp. 12-13.
[14] *Ibid.*, p. 100.
[15] *Ibid.*, p. 102.
[16] Antoine Adam, *Histoire de la littérature française au XVIIe siècle* (Del Duca, 1952), vol. III, p. 224.

debility is also reflected in the other plays. "Pour comprendre Harpagon et Argan, mais aussi Monsieur Jourdain et Chrysale, il faut les imaginer joués par ce Molière que ronge la maladie et que sa volonté seule soutient." [17] This odd mixture of biography "dans les œuvres" is not the subjectivist method of systematically seeking detailed "clefs," but it does not go as far as some recent critics in disassociating biography from the comedies. In fact, Adam's position suggests a certain disabused sympathy with the Romantic tradition, while bringing considerable historical precision to the entire question.

Historical rigor was apparently not a primary concern of Henri Poulaille who occupies a unique place in moliéresque criticism. He believes that Molière was really Pierre Corneille in clever disguise. To be sure, Jean-Baptiste Poquelin really lived between 1622 and 1673, but only as a front for the more frivolous side of the otherwise serious Corneille, who never deigned publish anything like idle farce under his own name. In 1951 Poulaille published his first bold volume, *Pierre Corneille: Tartuffe ou la comédie de l'hypocrite.* He admitted here that his thesis was not original, for Pierre Loüys and a certain Mme Elizabeth Fraser had already presented a similar case which he intended to reaffirm. He argues that only the forceful, important scenes of *Tartuffe* were written by the master Corneille, while the burlesque fillings were scribbled by the "comédien Sganarelle." [18] The sequel to this study, *Corneille sous le masque de Molière* (1957), offers another good example of Poulaille's method, especially the chapter "Essai de biographie véridique de Molière." In this part, he maximizes the contradictions and inconsistencies of the poet's life and thus produces a sense of total confusion and inconclusiveness in the service of his own conjectures. He insists that Corneille is beyond doubt the true master, while Molière is but an idle rhymester. All of the memorable scenes in the great plays are from Corneille's pen, while the rest comes from the mediocre "gêneur": "Nous ne pouvons pas ne point dire nos regrets de constater le bousillage des chefs-d'œuvre qu'eut en main Molière

---

[17] *Ibid.*, p. 225.
[18] P. Corneille, *Tartuffe ou la comédie de l'hypocrite,* édition de H. Poulaille (Amiot-Dumont, 1951); for the reconstituted text, cf. pp. 130-210.

et qu'il abîma par une sotte vanité qui lui donnait la démangeaison d'écrire." [19] *Honni soit qui mal y pense.* But this view is an aberration and should not occupy us longer. [20]

"The Man in his Works" Tradition

When Ramon Fernandez published his *Vie de Molière* in 1929, Michaut predictably objected to the technique of finding Molière everywhere in the plays, even in such minor works as *Les Fâcheux.* Although Michaut correctly detected "une méthode psychologique inspirée ou teintée de freudisme ou de pirandellisme," he did not seem to have fully appreciated this rather special work.

The example of Fernandez' interpretation of *Les Fâcheux* is a good starting point. The author sketches a Molière harassed by the enormous demands made upon him as director-actor-playwright to his troupe, the backbone of his company. Thus in *Les Fâcheux*, we are struck by the protagonist's nervousness and his impatience with the many pests who distract him from his work. "Le temps est infiniment précieux à Molière," [21] writes Fernandez. The playwright's nervous temperament affects his work, for "chez Molière la conception poétique et le tempérament de l'homme sont inséparables." [22] These notions are part of a larger view Fernandez has of a "Molière sensuel." According to the *NRF* critic, Molière's marriage to Armande confirms this notion because

---

[19] H. Poulaille, *Corneille sous le masque de Molière* (Grasset, 1957), p. 241.

[20] F. R. Freudmann has written a good synthesis of Poulaille's efforts which will probably suffice for most readers: "Is there 'Un Cas Molière'?" in *Modern Language Quarterly*, vol. 19 (1958), pp. 53-59. For complete references to the original article which prompted the Corneille-Molière debate (P. Loüys' piece in *Le Temps*), see P. Saintonge and R. W. Christ, *Fifty Years of Molière Studies 1892-1941* (Baltimore: Johns Hopkins Press, 1942), pp. 53-54; see entries 398-415 and especially item 403 which gives detailed references to the early stages of the debate. On a related question, Molière and the "Masque de fer," see items 420-426 (p. 55), and especially Anatole Loquin's contributions, items 423-426. Loquin claims that Molière's alleged death and burial were but a ruse, that instead the playwright was taken to the Bastille where he remained in solitary confinement behind an iron mask until his actual death in 1704.

[21] Ramon Fernandez, *Vie de Molière* (Gallimard, 1929), 12th edition, p. 112.

[22] *Ibid.*, p. 180.

it fulfilled the sensualist's need for someone new, young, and innocent. For such a man it follows that this kind of marriage, inevitably tenous and tempestuous, would provoke deep-seated feelings of fear and suspicion and Fernandez believes that Molière was tortured by jealousy. This view suggests the Romantic tradition thinly veneered with a new "psychologisme," and many critics, behind Michaut, decried the utter futility of such a biography. [23] And yet it is clear that Fernandez was attempting an ambitious redefinition of biography. As a premise for formulating certain lines of interpretation, he suggests ignoring the mass of unsure documentation and working with a few assumptions in an effort to "rejoindre l'homme à travers l'œuvre . . . comprendre comment la ligne d'une vie coïncide avec la courbe d'un métier." [24]

For Fernandez, Molière's life could only be deduced from the plays, for only the plays recorded fully Molière's attempt at realizing himself. There and there alone, ". . . on aperçoit que les nuances particulières de son génie et jusqu'au genre particulier où il excelle, sont relatives au problème personnel qu'il a dû résoudre pour trouver son équilibre et s'affirmer de sa naissance à sa mort." [25] To recapture and give meaning to the existential adventure which the comedies recount, Fernandez proposes to "suivre la méthode bergsonnienne, accumuler les lignes qui convergent vers un centre idéal," from which certain forces radiate and reflect both the poet's genius and his deepest convictions. The biographer insists on the conditions under which the plays were written and the circumstances which in turn shaped the works. Thus the pressures under which the actor-director-playwright worked, coupled with the latent obsession with Armande, produced in him the restlessness and anxieties echoed in the recurring preoccupation with the "fâcheux" theme. In Molière's case, this nervous temperament is not a negative attribute. On the contrary, it

---

[23] This *Vie de Molière* prompted considerable discussion and much dissension. Prominent among the dissenters was Fernandez' formidable colleague at the NRF Albert Thibaudet, who commented "amicalement" in the *Revue de Paris*, 1930, fascicule 2, pp. 372 ff. See also Fernández' *apologia pro domo*, "Poésie et Biographie," in NRF, vol. 33 (1929), pp. 824-828.

[24] *Vie de Molière, op. cit.*, p. 9.

[25] "Poésie et Biographie," *op. cit.*, p. 826.

represents an essential "élan vital," characteristic of Molière's personality and an intrinsic impetus to his genius.

Having established his premise, Fernandez' comments on a possible reason behind *Les Précieuses ridicules* are both original and coherent within his system of analysis. He argues that since Molière is *l'homme instinct,* driven by sentiment and demanding perfect transparency between the heart and the intellect, he is instinctively the enemy of those who shelter their emotions, even to the point of distorting language. Here is Fernandez in a long passage which exemplifies the perspicacity and logic of his thinking:

> La préciosité est justement une défense contre l'instinct, un frein compliqué destiné à en retarder la satisfaction, et le retard, sous toutes ses formes, était essentiellement antipatique à Molière. Elle exprime une permission, une vacance qu'on se donne, une marge de liberté vis-à-vis de l'animal humain. Le précieux a le temps, ou se donne le temps, ou oblige les autres à prendre leur temps, et surtout son temps. Quand l'instinct est fort, surabondant, il peut s'octroyer le luxe de se freiner soi-même, de pro-longer ou de faire renaître son désir, comme il apparaît dans la préciosité shakespérienne. Mais il arrive, chez les femmes surtout, que l'instinct freiné s'atrophie, que la vacance devienne un vide. Les idées et le langage précieux, qui sont une seule et même chose, ne sont plus qu'une traduction ingénieuse des nécessités de la vie qui permet de trahir celles-ci. Molière devant les Précieuses, c'est l'instinct urgent, c'est la précipitation devant la froideur qui retarde, devant l'ingéniosité qui suspend. [26]

This passage illustrates Fernandez' attempt to go beyond traditional use of documents and biography. It also shows how a subtle, intelligent mixture of *vie et œuvre* can be penetrating and enlightening.

In terms of a possible moliéresque philosophy, Fernandez thought that the comic mode almost invariably implied an attitude

---

[26] *Vie de Molière, op. cit.,* pp. 71-72. There is a slightly modified version of this passage in Fernandez' "Molière" in *Tableau de la littérature française* (Gallimard, 1939), vol. 2, pp. 74-75. This essay is a fine *mise au point* and a vigorous reaffirmation of the substance of his biography of ten years earlier.

toward life and the world. "L'interprétation comique du monde implique une vision qui à son tour implique une philosophie... L'idéal comique... aboutit presque automatiquement à souligner le désaccord de la raison et de la vie, et l'illusion dérisoire de la volonté."[27] But this conception of a moliéresque philosophy is essentially poetic, for it represents Molière's attempt at finding and imposing himself in the existential adventure which was his art. The critic believes that at first Molière "avait souhaité de corriger le monde," in the belief that "la raison peut changer le monde."[28] Gradually, Molière realizes the futility of his early dream. *Le Misanthrope* is the outstanding work for it unfolds in microcosm the entire destiny of Molière's life in his art. Fernandez sees Alceste as a giant clinging valorously to his rigid conception of truth, heavily armed with "la raison." The hero's goal is to "démontrer qu'on est capable de résister au comique, de la vaincre, et que la vertu est plus forte que la société."[29] But Alceste and Molière were wrong. Society, harnessed in convention, proved stronger and the only solution was Alceste's "désert." The protagonist's misadventure represents "la faillité d'une volonté," and in human terms this failure is total: "Qu'est-ce que le rêve de Dom Quichotte, qu'est-ce que le défi d'Alceste, sinon l'irruption dérisoire de l'absolu dans le relatif? On voit peut-être maintenant pourquoi les excès d'humeur d'Alceste témoignent du génie de Molière: il n'est pas de petites mesures pour un esprit absolu qui a refusé une fois pour toutes de s'adapter au monde."[30] After *Le Misanthrope*, Molière resigns himself to the cruel fate of farce; and abandons all responsibility for changing the world and all pretentions of "sérieux." *Le Bourgeois gentilhomme* is a clear

---

[27] *Tableau de la littérature française*, op. cit., vol. II, p. 73.
[28] *Vie de Molière, op. cit.*, p. 204.
[29] *Ibid.*, p. 185.
[30] Ramon Fernandez, "A propos d'Alceste", in *NRF*, vol. 48 (1937), p. 278. Much of François Mauriac's essay "Molière le tragique" (*Trois Grands hommes devant Dieu*, 1947) either follows or contradicts Fernandez. Mauriac believes that Molière's bitterness is in part a reaction against his own pitiable self (p. 15). The essay compares Molière to Pascal and finds the comic poet by far the more tragic because he refuses to engage himself in Pascal's "pari": "Ce n'est pas qu'il nie le surnaturel; mais il refuse d'en être occupé et trouve comique l'homme qui a souci de son âme..." (p. 7). At the source of Molière's anguish is the fact that he is "un homme qui aime sans être aimé" (p. 15).

abjuration, because it forcefully depicts "le triomphe de la société." Jourdain is like a child before the world in that he makes no objections, threatens no system. On the contrary, he wants nothing more than to join in. Jourdain is a completely defeated Alceste.

Fernandez' attempt at defining a philosophical attitude is both penetrating and generous. It expresses the poet's instinctive drive for life at its fullest, against vacuity and sham. The critic had the talent to go beyond the documents and history and seek out in intelligent speculation a certain poetic ambiance which reflects both Molière's talent and convictions. There was room in Molière biography, particularly after Michaut, for this kind of coherent, intuitive inquiry. In a short and sympathetic review of the *Vie de Molière*, a colleague of the author's at the *NRF* wrote very aptly that "les vraies biographies sont des interrogations." This is precisely the quality that makes Fernandez' work a valuable contribution to Molière biography. [31]

Other "l'homme dans l'œuvre" biographies have been less ambitious. In most of these works, propositions on Molière's affective essence remain an end in themselves without leading to further philosophical or psychological inquiry. Mme Béatrix Dussane's *Un Comédien nommé Molière* (1936) is a good example of this kind of biography. It is less a fictionalized biography than a *vie théâtralisée*, for Molière's life unfolds in a series of dramatic sketches. Thus, even the signing of the first pact, the contract for the *Illustre Théâtre* in 1643 takes on a secret significance. Mme Dussane imagine the signing "en bonne compagnie," after which a toast is offered. "Madelaine et Jean-Baptiste choquaient leurs verres avec une secrète solennité: ce contract, c'était un peu leurs épousailles." [32]

This biographer's treatment of Armande's parentage is rather elusive, contrary to what one might have expected. She leaves the question open, but her exposition is nonetheless "romanesque." Dussane supposes that Molière first saw Armande in Madeleine's

---

[31] The book is available in English in a paperback edition: *Molière: The Man Seen Through His Plays* (New York: Hill and Wang, 1960), translated by W. Follett.

[32] B. Dussane, *Un Comédien nommé Molière* (Plon, 1936), p. 55.

mother's arms and naturally thought the child belonged to
Mme Béjart. After the marriage in 1662, there were echoes and
innuendoes concerning the young bride which Molière did not
understand. Then a letter came to Molière from his friend Cosnac
relating Montfleury's accusation of incest made before the King.
Brimming with rage, Molière confronted Madeleine. She defends
herself by insisting (but rather halfheartedly) that Armande is
her sister and by reminding Molière of the circumstances in which
he had first seen Armande. Finally, she produces civil documents
to sustain her story. Yet this entire episode is presented in such
a way as to remain at best inconclusive. Through it all Madeleine
is nervous and upset, the way the guilty usually are when confronted, and she does not seem to be convinced by her own
arguments. The reader is left with certain suspicions and the
matter rests there. Dussane presents this entire scene as a very
dramatic theatrical tableau. [33] While much of this is invented,
the author's enthusiasm for Molière and her love for the theatre
combine to make this a very readable volume.

Pierre Brisson also establishes his biography, *Molière - Sa
vie dans ses œuvres* (1942), outside of the scientific tradition.
While utilizing all available material, the author fills in whenever
necessary in his attempt at "une reconstitution humaine." [34] For
him, Molière is a simple man, an artist gifted only for the theatre
and mediocre in everything else. For such a man, his own heart and
soul, his affects and sentiments, become the prime source for
his art. "Dans une âme comme le sienne, le partage quotidien
a de puissants effets. La confrontation permanente de l'illusion
et du réel l'éloigne des chimères." [35] In this case, the biographer's
task is simple, for Molière was given so completely to the theatre
that his decision for his art was a veritable ". . . prise de possession
absolue, l'identification totale d'une vie et d'une fonction." [36] Thus
the plays serve as the prime source for defining the stages of the
dramatist's life and Brisson proceeds to deduce the man from
his works.

---

[33] *Ibid.*, pp. 163-165.
[34] Pierre Brisson, *Molière, Sa Vie dans ses œuvres* (NRF, 1942), 19th
edition, p. 7.
[35] *Ibid.*, pp. 313-314.
[36] *Ibid.*, p. 313.

It follows that Brisson is naturally attracted to those comedies which best mirror what he believes to be the playwright's own affectivity. As a result, the biographer is impatient with *Amphitryon* and *Dom Garcie*. Concerning the latter play, Brisson contends that Molière attempted to write it during an interim, a calm moment, and at a time when he had gained a measure of success. He was after all moving to a larger, more elegant theatre (the Palais Royal theatre, January 1661), was closer now to the court, and he was very ambitious. It was also a propitious moment for improving his image before Armande. For these reasons he let himself be tempted into moving toward a more serious and noble genre, tragedy. According to Brisson, the result, in *Dom Garcie*, was catastrophic: ". . . . c'est la disparition de Molière. Disparition totale, absolue, impressionnante. On cherche une trace quelconque, si légère soit-elle . . . l'ombre d'une ombre: rien. Vous penchez sur un gouffre, un néant." [37] For the same reasons *Dom Juan* also fails, for it too does not portray Molière's private situation. It is "un accident." The protagonist is but a vague *précieux* lover. "Ce n'est pas un personnage, à peine un rôle; c'est une rumeur . . ." and the don's romantic ideal recalls "un badinage, une stratégie de Grand Cyrus." [38] The entire enterprise has neither shape nor direction. Don Juan is not a dangerous atheist, immoral corruptor of women. He is so extreme that he simply cancels himself out and in the end, he is as inanimate as the "Commandeur." These two examples demonstrate how a preoccupation with biography, with systematically seeking "Molière dans son œuvre," can lead to a certain myopia when it comes to dealing esthetically with certain texts.

The subjective prism through which Brisson filters the comedies gives his biography another curious effect. In it, all of Molière's contemporaries are polarized into well-defined camps of good friends and archenemies (the latter group is easily the larger). For Brisson, Molière's relationship with his contemporaries has a direct bearing on his works. Corneille is depicted as a "vieil et infatigable rimeur," either plotting against Molière or simply being a "fâcheux." On the other hand, for political expediency,

---

[37] *Ibid.*, p. 64.
[38] *Ibid.*, p. 136.

Louis XIV is firmly aligned with Molière after the battle of *L'Ecole des femmes* and this relationship had a salutary influence on the playwright: "La faveur du roi ne l'avait pas seulement ébloui; elle avait apporté une délivrance. Cette protection royale, pesante mais libératrice, s'identifiait avec la liberté." [39] Racine and la Du Parc deserve one another for having abused Molière's confidence, tricked and deserted him. This particular affair upset Molière and the predictions of sure success for Racine's upcoming *Andromaque* angered him: "Que va-t-il (Racine) extraire d'Euripide? Cette gréco-manie horripile Molière." [40] According to Brisson, the only antidote against a severe case of "gréco-manie" is a good solid dose of the gay Latin poets. Having turned to Plautus, Molière's recovery was remarkable, for he wrote *Amphitryon* and *L'Avare* in the same year. The pedants Cotin and Ménage also pay heavily for having crossed Molière and for their crimes against spontaneity and comedy. Rather perversely, Brisson thinks that Molière's last good moments were the ones surrounding the triumph of *Les Femmes savantes,* which destroyed his enemies Cotin (Trissotin) and Ménage (Vadius). "La pièce est jouée onze fois jusqu'à Pâques, devant des salles pleines. Le sinistre Cotin, complètement anéanti, se cache sous les meubles, ose à peine retourner parmi ses confrères, renonce à écrire. Ménage se répand partout en jurant qu'il n'est pas Vadius. Victoire totale. Molière vient de vivre ses derniers beaux jours." [41]

In this biography, Molière's life is one long struggle. Brisson finds *Tartuffe* "l'œuvre la plus intime" because the battle of the play's survival from 1664 to 1669 illustrates the tremendous fighting spirit and sheer staying power he associates with Molière. But another play is even greater: "*Le Misanthrope* est son aveu public, sa confession batailleuse et désenchantée, la seule pièce sans référence et sans emprunts qu'il tira tout entière de lui-même." [42] Naturally this great play is directly related to Armande: "Sans elle, Alceste n'existerait pas." [43] Thus *Le Misanthrope* is considered the best play because it is the most personal, the most

---

[39] *Ibid.,* p. 60.
[40] *Ibid.,* p. 192.
[41] *Ibid.,* p. 248.
[42] *Ibid.,* p. 150.
[43] *Ibid.,* p. 154.

autobiographical. In fact, it is all the more admirable because, in his best fighting spirit, Molière displayed both the courage to write it and the audacity to show it publicly. Once more, the quality of the work depends on the degree to which it exposes the playwright's intimate life.

Antoine Adam called Brisson's work "la plus intelligente et la plus chaleureuse des études critiques." This kind of praise is not too surprising, for Brisson's work represents, for many critics, the acceptable medium between Fernandez and Mme Dussane: a certain amount of speculation wrapped in a colorful, discreet narrative which usually avoids "romanesque" excesses and over-effusiveness. Without slavish adherence to anecdotes or adding to them, Brisson's *Molière* nevertheless preserves much of the spirit of the moliéresque legend. It remains a model for those who begrudge Michaut.

One of the striking pieces of more recent subjectivist criticism is René Jasinski's *Molière et Le Misanthrope* (1951). Much more than merely an interpretation of one play, this book constitutes a sort of erudite "biographie sentimentale" of the playwright. Jasinski's position on subjectivism is clear: "Une création dans l'abstrait, échappant à l'actualité vivante, purement intellectuelle et livresque, paraît invraisemblable en tout temps." Later he adds that "*Le Misanthrope* constituerait un des chefs-d'œuvre de la littérature personnelle." [44] Like Abel LeFranc, Jasinki regrets that objective textual criticism has tended to reduce the biographical richness implicit in much of French classical literature. One senses that Jasinski might have intended his book on *Le Misanthrope* as a model for a renewed effort at more subjective criticism for the entire body of seventeenth century French literature.

Apart from the debatable approach, the book is exemplary in many respects. The section "sources livresques," for example, is a concise and excellent synthesis of the literary background to Molière's play. Paradoxically, however, Jasinski's heart is elsewhere and he considers the literary background secondary to Molière's

---

[44] René Jasinski, *Molière et le Misanthrope* (A. Colin, 1951), p. 111 and p. 120. His *Histoire de la littérature française* (1947) had already outlined this position: see vol. 1, p. 424 and pp. 430 ff.

"propres aventures dans *Le Misanthrope . . .*" which really constitute "la source essentielle." But these "aventures" were complex
and Jasinski eschews oversimplification. He observes, for example,
that Molière is both Alceste and Philinte: "Alceste incarnait son
désespoir et peut-être en le poussant un peu à bout, en le discré-
ditant aussi par le ridicule, contribuait-il à l'en délivrer, tandis que
Philinte, expression de sa raison assouplie et trempée par l'expé-
rience, lui montrait une voie rude encore mais possible, apaisée,
finalement rassurante." [45]

In spite of its finesse, Professor Jasinski's work tends to be
overly systematic on certain points. Convinced that *Le Misanthrope*
reflects a specific life experience for Molière, the critic is then
led to defining the other characters in the play as intimate
friends or acquaintances of the poet. For all the obvious reasons,
Célimène is Armande, Eliante is la De Brie, and Arsinoé is la
Du Parc; "le grand flandrin de vicomte" refers to Guiche,
Acaste resembles Lauzun, etc. [46] Jasinski's erudition and his
imagination enable him to unlock all the doors. True, he admits
that while inspired by reality, "Molière . . . parachève et . . . trans-
figure." But the evidence he submits accentuates the realism in the
comedy and minimizes whatever is imaginative. And regardless of
its many fine pages, Jasinski's study has become dated, for around
1950 perspectives were changing and biography-oriented exegesis
was losing ground. In retrospect, Jasinski's work represents one
of the last important contributions to subjectivist criticism from
an eminent academic critic.

Alfred Simon's conception of Molière's life and works in his
spirited and original *Molière par lui-même* (1957) is that of the
artist struggling for his freedom and integrity at an oppressive,
autocratic court where the rule was submission and silence ("avilis-
sement des nobles . . . asservissement des artistes"). In this perspective, Simon sees Molière at a moment of crisis in 1666. The
question is whether the playwright should engage in open political opposition or simply remain faithful to his art. According
to Simon, *Le Misanthrope*, which is both "un sommet et un

---

[45] *Molière et le Misanthrope, op. cit.,* p. 120.
[46] *Ibid.,* pp. 115-118.

cul-de-sac," provides the painful but noble response. By his
forthright honesty, Alceste "met en cause la caste des gens en
place, un certain régime dont la brigue, la concussion, la dénon-
ciation même sont les ferments actifs. Il n'épargne pas le pouvoir
établi..." [47] But even Alceste reaches a point beyond which he
cannot go without grave risks and he chooses instead the silence
and exile of his "désert." "La rupture d'Alceste avec son siècle
et les hommes, sa retraite en ce désert... sont pour Molière le
signal de se retirer en un autre désert." [48] But this "démission
de Molière" represents at least "la victoire de la comédie," for
after *Le Misanthrope*, Molière throws himself into the purely
esthetic adventure of theatre for theatre. Simon interprets *Les
Fourberies de Scapin* as the apotheosis of Molière's withdrawal
into pure theatre and as a prophetic final statement. Scapin
operates like a demiurge, charged with giving Providence a
helping hand. He represents "l'intelligence déliée de toute entrave,
de tout préjugé, de tout scrupule." [49] This power is at once Scapin's
great liberty and Molière's final liberation through his art. Simon
concludes that with Scapin, Molière "... a créé une équivoque
entre le théâtre et la vie, entre le spectacle et la rue. Il peut
bondir de la coulisse sur la scène, puis dans la salle, puis dans
la ville, sans partir de son élément, car tout devient théâtre sous
ses pas... Mais il n'y a pas de réconciliation possible. Aussi
traître que Tartuffe, aussi démoniaque que Dom Juan, aussi
solitaire qu'Alceste, il sauvegarde le pouvoir de rire et de faire
rire, parce qu'il s'est dépossédé de toute humanité et qu'ainsi,
ne compromettant que lui, il permet à Molière de jouer le jeu
jusqu'au bout." [50] At the end, Scapin's theatrical death, his retreat
into a sort of voluntary retrenchment, represents Molière's own
retreat into "un autre désert." Ergo, the title Simon affixes to
this section of his book, "La Scapinade providentielle."

Simon's monograph is highly speculative, even tenuous in some
of the implications of Molière's alleged political consciousness.
But his arguments are engaging, his grasp of Molière and his

---

[47] Alfred Simon, *Molière par lui-même* (Le Seuil, 1957), p. 128.
[48] *Ibid.*, p. 129.
[49] *Ibid.*, p. 143.
[50] *Ibid.*, pp. 144-145.

times is solid, and his republicanism is very much in the temper
of the times.

The "Métier" Approach

The increasing general interest in Molière as a professional
man of the theatre influenced biography writing. Since practically
all the normal sources for biography were lacking (correspondence,
personal papers, etc.), the notion of a "vie professionnelle" gradually developed as the only valid and appropriate life-study
for Molière. The idea was to confine the poet's existence to his
activities in the theatre. To a degree this represented a non-
or anti-biographical concept since it denied traditional moliéresque
biography many of its criteria. In the main, this approach refused
to validate hypotheses on the poet's domesticity, his "vie intime,"
his philosophy or morality. The beginning of this new concept of
Molière is related to a gradual evolution toward a larger *theatrical*
view of the man and his works.

Gustave Lanson's famous piece, "Molière et la farce" (1901), is
not concerned with questions of biography as such. On the contrary,
it deals with elementary forms of moliéresque comedy and relates
them to the Italian farce tradition. Nonetheless, several points in
Lanson's argument bear indirectly on biography, especially as
a source for textual exegesis. After remarking how Molière played
in the Italian style, Lanson posits this pertinent question: "S'en-
suit-il que Molière auteur ait eu les mêmes maîtres que Molière
acteur? que son œuvre écrite ait les mêmes origines que son
jeu?"[51] The historian's unequivocal answer is "yes," that there
is a direct relationship between "un certain jeu" and "un certain
style" when the playwright is an actor writing his own material.
Further, Lanson refers to "la permanence" of each character
type in force and in many Molière roles. This trait is defined
as an inalterable part of the essence of the characters, who "ne
peuvent dire 'oui' après avoir dit 'non,' un 'non' qui était dans
la nécessité de leur essence."[52] Hence Lanson suggests that many

---

[51] Gustave Lanson, *Essais de méthode, de critique et d'histoire littéraire,*
ed. Henri Peyre (Hachette, 1965), p. 199.
[52] *Ibid.,* p. 207.

roles in Molière, inherently fixed, take life only by interacting in
a purely dramatic or theatrical universe without reference to
exterior reality. But in Lanson's article this is only implied, not
developed, and no one followed up on the idea, until Bray.

Jacques Audiberti's *Molière dramaturge* (1954) is a love story,
told by an *homme de théâtre* who shared Molière's passion for
the theatre. But the story evolves in fits and starts because Audiberti eschews systematic presentation. Excerpts and brief commentaries are sprinkled throughout but they usually concern the lesser
plays. The rationale behind this method is to recall the "Molière
insolite" in brief passages from the more naïve plays. For the
idea is to rescue Molière from the pedants who have too long
held sway over the playwright's *fortune,* those "qui ont fait de
lui, dans son œuvre et dans sa vie, une idole sévère, une statue
fermée." [53] Thus, in the impressionistic chapter "Lignes géné-
rales et analogies," Audiberti relates the young Molière to Charlie
Chaplin who shared a common human fate. "La farce devient
une morale, la tarte à la crème une philosophie. Les pantins sont
salués comme des champions monumentaux d'une humanité non
plus antiquaire et théorique, mais qui, sur-le-champ, chacun
peut toucher du doigt ... Jean-Baptiste ou Charles-Spencer apparaît, en personne, comme le suprême commun dénominateur des
martyrs de son répertoire à l'insoluble cocasserie." [54] Audiberti
is fully aware of his eclectic and iconoclastic approach and of
the freedom he occasionally takes with Molière. And the author
feels that this is the spirit Molière best imparts to our time.
"Grâce à lui notre nation ... fait entendre, sans système, sans
dogmatisme, non pas même au nom du bon sens mais au nom
d'un spectacle gai, la protestation contre tout au monde qui nous
absoudra." [55]

This amusing aversion for established Molière criticism, for
"l'histoire historienne" and the "plumitifs" who live by it, sometimes goes too far. Audiberti is convinced that Armande is
Madeleine's child, that Molière more or less adopted her early
and attended to her growing up. His justification for this view

[53] Jacques Audiberti, *Molière dramaturge* (L'Arche, 1954), p. 94.
[54] *Ibid.,* pp. 65-66.
[55] *Ibid.,* p. 132.

is not very sound: the Armande who is the child of Marie Hervé Béjart is merely the product of specious reasoning on the part of meddling historians, beginning with Beffara. "Un historien s'en mêla. Il s'appelait Louis Beffara (Beffa, niche, bourde)." Of course, it is all wrong and we have merely been duped by "la pudibonde et rétroactive ardeur que Beffara consacre à ... désinfecter ... l'union de Molière et de la petite Béjart." Audiberti implies that the substance of the Arnolphe-Agnes misadventure corresponds to the Molière-Armande situation and that the relationship was ". . . en quelque sorte un cas masculin de grossesse extra-utérine prolongée de dix-sept ans." [56]

These eccentricities aside, Audiberti's book is a refreshing approach to Molière as player and playwright, a life which evolved essentially in and for the theatre. This *vie* does not even attempt to answer all the questions a biography normally raises. Its uniqueness lies in its resolve to ignore many worn and unsolvable enigmas and to offer instead many insights and unconventional perspectives into Molière's "vie théâtrale." In that sense, it constitutes a kind of anti-biography.

As we have seen, the problems of Molière biography have revolved around two basic approaches: one which interprets Molière in light of a variety of historical legends about the man, and another which seeks to uncover the man in his works. Michaut did much to discredit many assumptions in the moliéresque legend and to point out that biographically-oriented methods of textual interpretation were very tenous.

Professor W. G. Moore's thin volume, *Molière: A New Criticism* (1949), turns resolutely in that direction and takes a very disabused attitude about the verifiable aspects of Molière's life. But it is René Bray's *Molière Homme de théâtre* (1954) which breaks completely with tradition and pointedly rejects biography as a valid criterion for textual analysis.

The entire first section of Professor Bray's study concerns the problems of "l'œuvre et la vie." The author does not hesitate to write: "La vie privée a peu à faire avec la création poétique ...

---

[56] *Ibid.*, p. 28.

Molière homme privé n'intéresse guère le critique." [57] An example of Bray's attitude and method is his treatment of the relationship between Trissotin and L'Abbé Cotin. It appears as fact that Molière sketched Trissotin of *Les Femmes savantes* as a caricature of the Abbé and Bray does not deny this. He confirms it as historically plausible and then proceeds to show how unimportant it is in an esthetic consideration of the role of Trissotin:

> Il n'y a pas de doute, Molière a voulu que le spectateur pensât à Cotin en particulier, à un être déterminé et à ce seul être. Et pourtant Trissotin n'est pas Cotin: les différences sont nombreuses de l'un à l'autre et leur importance n'est pas mince . . . . Molière a isolé dans le personnage historique quelques traits sur lesquels il a construit le personnage comique . . . . Cotin c'est un être de chair qui s'inscrit lourdement dans l'histoire; Trissotin est un fantôme léger qui habite notre imagination. Cela ne veut pas dire qu'en définitive cette légèrete ne pèse pas plus que cette masse. [58]

This view implies that the only valid relationship to consider in critical interpretation is the relationship between the fictive characters in the world they inhabit, the imaginative, dramatic universe of the play itself. All other allusions to real world people and events are untenable.

Molière Homme de théâtre is primarily important for the position it assumed in textual criticism *per se*. And yet this attempt at discrediting faulty methods in Molière biography and biographically-oriented exegesis is not merely a side issue for Bray. It represented the first substantial and sustained effort by a French academic to disqualify biography as a valid tool in assessing the comedies. In a later chapter, we will return to Bray's book for a more detailed appreciation of its formalistic approach.

---

[57] René Bray, *Molière homme de théâtre* (Mercure de France, 1954), pp. 17-18.
[58] *Ibid.*, p. 190.

CHAPTER III

ACADEMIC CRITICISM

This chapter will attempt to deal with the large corpus of criticism from the university, with the exception of writings on biography. The chapter is organized under three dissimilar rubrics, each dealing either with a methodology or a particular problem in exegesis. The first part concerns problems in literary history; the second, debate on questions surrounding Molière's *morale;* the third, the "new criticism" which revitalized Molière studies around 1950.

Literary History

Albert Thibaudet characterized the first two decades of this century as the period of "les grandes synthèses universitaires" in moliéresque criticism. Some of the first syntheses were source studies. Between 1906 and 1910, at least three thick volumes analyzed Molière's alleged debt to the Spanish and Italians. E. Martineche's *Molière et le théâtre espagnol* (1906) suggested that the primary sources for the comedies could be traced back to Spanish literature. "Il [Molière] n'a rencontré nulle part de plus précieuses ressources qu'au delà des Pyrénées." [1] G. Huzár, a student and admirer of Brunetière, went much further. In his *Molière et l'Espagne* (1907), he asserted forcefully that all of Molière's inspiration and his borrowings came from Spain. Moreover, he argued that the French dramatist was not very original in his reworkings of comic material drawn from Spanish literature and

---

[1] E. Martinenche, *Molière et le théâtre espagnol* (Hachette, 1906), p. 273.

that Molière's place in European letters has been exaggerated. Huzár considered the great Spanish authors superior to Molière in their inventive genius, their gift for humor and in their sharp sense of satire. But Molière was French and he profited from "l'universalité de l'esprit français." "Si l'œuvre de Molière eut une destinée plus glorieuse que celle des Espagnols, il le doit presque autant à sa qualité de français qu'à son propre génie." [2]

Pietro Toldo's *L'Œuvre de Molière et sa fortune en Italie* (1910) reviews many eighteenth century Italian ideas on Molière, particularly on the question of sources in Italian literature. Also there are some excellent analyses of Molière's influence on Italian comedy in the eighteenth century, especially on Goldoni.

Gustave Attinger's book traces the "spirit" of the *commedia dell'arte* in French theatre. [3] The author holds that the French seventeenth century destroyed the essence of the Italian *commedia* in which fixed character types were integrated into an improvised spectacle, consisting mostly of sequential *lazzi*. In France, according to Attinger, this kind of spectacle was replaced by a more highly structured comic form, usually played by well-known actors, following a completed text. Molière's theatre reflects both traditions, but mostly the latter. Attinger distinguishes between the great plays up to *Le Misanthrope* in which one main character usually dominates. Molière's remaining work returns in part to the *commedia* tradition, in which Harpagon, Jourdain, Argan and Scapin are integrated into a spectacle where they are often the victims. The author also gives an excellent account of the technique of pantomime as practiced by Scaramouche (Tiberio Fiorelli). The argument of this book reaffirmed the importance in moliéresque comedy of gesture, mime and other techniques

---

[2] G. Huzár, *Molière et l'Espagne* (Champion, 1907), pp. 296-297. The question of Molière's originality and his use of sources which plagued the eighteenth century reaches a ridiculous extreme in Georges Maurevert's *Le livre des plagiats* (Fayard, 1922). For this critic, French literature is but one long series of clever plagiarisms, and Molière is "Prince et roi des plagiaires."

[3] Gustave Attinger, *L'Esprit de la Commedia dell'Arte dans le théâtre français* (Neuchâtel: La Baconière, 1950). See also I. A. Schwartz, *The Commedia dell'arte and its Influences on French Comedy* (1933), and K. M. Lea, *Italian Popular Comedy* (1934).

related to the Italian tradition of comedy, a view shared by many critics after 1950.

One of the most readable books from the time is Maurice Pellisson's *Les Comédies-ballets de Molière*. Like Sainte-Beuve, Pellisson intended to dismiss the idea that the "comédie-ballet" was a negligible part of Molière's total work, that they had been hastily scrambled together at royal command, and, worst of all, that they absorbed time and energy Molière would have spent more profitably on his greater works. Quoting from *L'Impromptu de Versailles* and *La Critique de l'Ecole des femmes*, the author recalls that Molière himself did not consider the genre inferior and that in the "Avertissement" to *Les Fâcheux*, Molière had provided a good outline of the form of the "comédie-ballet." Pellisson sees Molière's innovation in the genre as welding the heretofore disjointed elements of dances, songs, and *récits* into a structured dramatic unit. Molière himself was not unaware of his originality, as evidenced by the "Avertissement" alluded to above: "Pour ne point rompre le fil de la pièce par ces manières d'intermèdes, on s'avisa de les coudre au sujet du mieux que l'on put, et de ne faire qu'une seule chose du Ballet et de la Comédie... Quoi qu'il en soit, c'est un mélange qui est nouveau pour nos théâtres."[4] Pellisson also asserts that Molière adapted his prose especially for the genre and that the resulting supple language represented a minor innovation in Molière's style.[5]

Raoul Allier's important study, *La Cabale des dévots*[6] (1902), and A. Rébilliau's subsequent articles on the same subject in *La Revue des Deux mondes* (1902-1909), represented important new research into the secret religious organizations. Allier includes a chapter on *Tartuffe* in which he refutes Brunetière by suggesting that Molière was not attacking religion, nor the Jesuits, nor even the Jansenists as such, but the whole "cabale" which plotted against the extravagances of the young Louis XIV. In a later article on *Tartuffe*, Allier sums up his views: "Molière n'a pas

---

[4] M. Pellisson, *Les Comédies-ballets de Molière* (Hachette, 1914), p. 60.
[5] *Ibid.*, pp. 174-184. Henri Ghéon suggested that all Molière's prose works "sont conçus comme des ballets dans un sens à la fois plastique et dynamique..." See his *L'Art du théâtre* (Montréal: Ed. Serge, 1948), pp. 90-91.
[6] R. Allier, *La Cabale des dévots* (A. Colin, 1902), p. 399.

dit que son personnage avait un original, mais des originaux. Lui-même nous indique que la comédie n'était pas une pièce à clefs. Elle dresse devant nous un vice que Molière a cru distinguer dans tout un groupe d'hommes et dont il dénonce le danger. De ce vice il a cru voir l'incarnation dans la cabale des dévots, dans ce que nous savons aujourd'hui avoir été la compagnie du Saint-Sacrement; mais ce serait sortir de la vérité historique que de faire de son œuvre un document de reportage." [7]

Allier's cautious generalizations did not suffice for other scholars. Antoine Adam observed that historians who had delved into the secrets of the "cabale" erroneously believed "qu'ils avaient du même coup découvert le sens secret de *Tartuffe*." Henri d'Almeras thought that *Tartuffe* attacked the extreme Jansenists, those of the Compagnie du Saint-Sacrement. [8] F. Baumel, in his *Taruffe et ses avatars* (1925), believed that the genesis of the play went back to the peregrination years when the playwright was hounded by the *dévots*. But although Molière met these fanatics and hypocrites everywhere, the most finished type who became the model in the play was the Lyon barber Crétinet, whose life Baumal sketches. [9]

Source hunting reaches extravagant proportions in P. Emard's *Tartuffe, sa vie, son milieu* (1932). For him, Tartuffe is without doubt copied on the life and escapades of Charpy de Sainte-Croix (the source is Tallemant), whom Molière met in Turin and later had as a neighbor in Paris. Emard is so convinced by his hypothesis that he proceeds to identify systematically almost every character in the play. [10] He also arrives at a different conclusion from Allier when he asserts that Charpy alone was attacked in *Tartuffe,* and that if the play seemed to allude to the "compagnie

---

[7] R. Allier, "Le Problème de Tartuffe," in *La Revue de Genève,* II (no. 7), 1921, pp. 3-26.

[8] Henri d'Almeras, *Le Tartuffe de Molière* (Amiens: Ed. Edgar Malpère, 1928), p. 44.

[9] F. Baumal, *Tartuffe et ses avatars; de Montufar à Dom Juan* (Nourry, 1925). Cf. also his *Molière et les dévots; la genèse de Tartuffe* (Bougault, 1919).

[10] Paul Emard, *Tartuffe, sa vie et son milieu* (Droz, 1932), pp. 205-209. Antoine Adam is rather kind about this work; cf. his *Histoire,* III, p. 300, n. 3.

du Saint-Sacrement," it was "hors des intentions de l'auteur." [11] Molière's enigmatic protagonist continues to fascinate and recent articles have added yet other possibilities to an already long list. [12]

Since 1900 there have been at least three outstanding "grandes synthèses universitaires" on Molière's work. They rank with any from the previous century and have provided an invaluable contribution to knowledge in Molière studies: G. Michaut's three volumes (1921-1925); H. Carington Lancaster's two volumes, "The Period of Molière" (1936), in his nine-volume *A History of French Dramatic Literature in the Seventeenth Century;* Antoine Adam's volume III, "L'Apogée du siècle, Boileau-Molière" (1953) in his *Histoire de la Littérature française au XVIIè siècle.*

We have already seen how Michaut's systematic review of documents and criticism debunked a great deal of the moliéresque legend. His *Les Luttes de Molière* (1925) is less concerned with questions of biography. It covers only six plays, from *Le Mariage forcé* to *Le Misanthrope.* [13] The *pièce de résistance* here is the new and substantial case for accepting the original version of *Tartuffe* (1664) as a complete play in three acts. Michaut is dubious about all of the sources which refer to the first version as incomplete, because all of them (except for LaGrange's notation in his *Registre*) are dated later than September 1665, sixteen months after the first performance. He also contends that LaGrange's entry was probably made toward the end of 1664 at the earliest, after Molière's first *placet* to the King. Thus LaGrange spoke of "the first three acts," knowing that Molière had subsequently added a fourth and fifth in hopes of getting the play reinstated. LaGrange is known to have made errors in his notebook and there are indications that he regularly made post-dated entries. [14]

---

[11] *Ibid.,* p. 197.

[12] D. Mornet, "Un prototype de Tartuffe" in *Mélanges Ed. Huguet* (Boivin, 1940), pp. 308-312; and R. Derche, "Encore un modèle possible de Tartuffe," in *Revue d'Histoire littéraire de la France,* vol. 51 (1951), pp. 129-153.

[13] This was the third and last volume to appear. The notes for the projected fourth volume, *Le Triomphe de Molière,* were used in his edition of Molière's *Œuvres complètes* (Imprimerie nationale, 1949), 11 vols.

[14] These have been discussed and the entire matter of the *Registre* and la Grange cogently exposed in B. E. and G. P. Young's admirable edition,

Moreover, Michaut claims that Molière never presented an incomplete play and had even allowed *La Princesse d'Elide* to be performed part in verse and part in prose in order to meet a deadline. And nowhere does Molière ever refer to *Tartuffe* as anything but a complete play. [15] As for the structure of the first version, the historian thought it probably included the essential parts of the first three acts of the final text. [16] These views were a sharp departure from prevailing opinion and did not convince everyone. In 1956 John Cairncross returned to the question and, using Michaut as a starting point, made an even more convincing case for a completed version in 1664. In his *New Light on Molière*, Cairncross goes further than Michaut on this question, and even reconstructs the first version which he dubbed the *Urtartuffe*. Unlike Michaut, he concludes that it was probably made up of Acts I, III and IV of the final version, eliminating Mariane and her potential misadventure. [17] The theory has apparently been accepted, for no scholar has offered a substantial refutation of it.

H. Carrington Lancaster's multi-volume *History of French Dramatic Literature in the Seventeenth Century* still remains a good reference for sources, techniques, and history of the stage. The third part in two volumes covers "The Period of Molière" and catalogues performances, playwrights and sources from 1652 to 1672. Although Lancaster's very detailed research left him open to charges of having missed the forest for the trees, he deserves credit for having understood Molière as a man of the theatre primarily, a view which was not firmly established at the time in academic criticism. On the nature of *Tartuffe,* for example, he concurs with his French predecessor: "M. Michaut is quite right in insisting that Molière's primary purpose was to write comedy, not to attack hypocrisy or, as Brunetière claimed, religion . . . Molière's earliest plays had shown that he was a dramatist rather

---

Le Registre de La Grange, 1659-1685 (Droz, 1947), 2 vols.; see particularly, vol. 2, pp. 94-99.

[15] G. Michaut, *Les Luttes de Molière* (Hachette, 1925), pp. 59-67.

[16] *Ibid.,* p. 79.

[17] J. Cairncross, *New Light on Molière* (Minard, 1965), pp. 28-53. This section was subsequently reproduced in his *Molière bourgeois et libertin* (Nizet, 1963), pp. 118-164. See also J. Guicharnaud's pertinent résumé of this question in his *Molière, Une Aventure théâtrale,* pp. 537-539.

than a reformer." [18] But Lancaster differs with Michaut on at least one point when he favors the conclusions of a professional man of the theatre to Michaut's academic position. [19] In fact, Lancaster takes a forceful stand for Molière "homme de théâtre" as opposed to the moralist or philosopher: "He sought to make his characters live and to make them comic. He rarely abandons his art to preach or to condemn." [20] In his best pages, Lancaster suggests an image of Molière which coincides with much of the new criticism of the postwar period.

Antoine Adam gives Molière "la part du lion" in his third volume of the *Histoire de la littérature française au XVIIè siècle*. M. Adam believes that the comedies should be seen in their historical context, especially in light of events and documents from the time. For example, he utilizes an anonymous and obscure pamphlet, *Le Livre abominable* (probably from around 1664), to refute the long-standing notion that *Tartuffe* was directed against La Compagnie du Saint-Sacrement. The pamphlet was apparently directed against Colbert and a small group of fanatics in the entourage close to him and the Queen Mother. Adam asserts that logically, Molière probably intended to attack this group, for it represented a danger to almost everyone at the court. The historian finds his argument confirmed in several remarks from *La Lettre sur l'Imposteur*, that important text which he uses to elucidate other questions as well. [21] Professor Adam was perhaps one of the first well-known academics in France to consider seriously the implications of *La Lettre sur l'Imposteur*, a text we will return to later.

This historical perspective is perfectly legitimate and in Professor Adam's deft analyses, a number of corrections and nuances are brought to past literary histories. And yet the perceptions are quite special. The firm commitment to interpret the plays

---

[18] H. C. Lancaster, *A History of French Dramatic Literature in the Seventeenth Century* (Baltimore: Johns Hopkins Press, 1936), Part III, pp. 623-624.

[19] *Ibid.*, pp. 657-658. Lancaster is referring here to the controversy between Jacques Arnavon and Michaut concerning Alceste.

[20] *Ibid.*, p. 855.

[21] A. Adam, *Histoire de la littérature française au XVIIè siècle* (Del Duca, 1966), vol. 3, pp. 307-312.

in the context of Molière's times tends to emphasize the satirical side of the comedies. Although Adam does not use the term, he seems to consider Molière a highly-talented *revuiste*, [22] consciously engaged in polemics and whose works are usually responses to outside stimuli. In turn, this impression influences Adam's conception of Molière the man. In this view, the little-known *Sganarelle* (1660) assumes particular significance. Artistically, the psychological make-up of the protagonist represents an important step toward the creation of a more human type, especially when compared to the marionette qualities of the earlier Mascarille. Subjectively, Sganarelle is a model, the first, of Molière's image of himself. "Il [Sganarelle] est pour Molière une sorte de double fraternel et méprisé, l'expression de ses inquiétudes et de sa jalousie, du conflit en lui, de la foi en son génie et du doute qu'il ne parvient pas à exorciser." [23] Adam follows this *Doppelgänger* through the circumstance plays surrounding *L'Ecole des femmes,* and finds him emerging again in the human qualities of Cléante. But by 1668, the character has changed considerably. Adam suggests that the key to understanding *L'Avare* is the simple fact that Molière chose to play Harpagon himself, at a time when the dramatist was physically debilitated and morally spent. [24] The same is true of Molière playing Jourdain and Pourceaugnac. The apotheosis of this evolution comes when Molière plays Argan and dies in the role. According to Adam, Argan is "nerveux, irritable, traqué... malade d'esprit, hypocondriaque... Il est frère d'Harpagon, et, malgré les apparences, frère de Monsieur Jourdain. Pauvre homme, jouet de ses nerfs, esclave de sa manie. Un Sganarelle vieilli et retombé, le dernier avatar du petit homme." [25]

---

[22] For an excellent study of this aspect of Molière's career, especially the productions of the "comédies-ballets," see Raymond Ismay, "Molière revuiste," in two parts in *Hommes et mondes,* fascicules 22 and 23, May and June 1948, pp. 68-79 and 241-255. Mongrédien also called Molière "un revuiste de génie" in his *La Vie privée de Molière,* p. 13. In his *Molière, Homme de Théâtre* (p. 31), Bray claims enigmatically that "Bénichou surtout a développé cette thèse" (Molière "revuiste"). This can only be an error.

[23] Adam, *Histoire,* p. 268.

[24] *Ibid.,* p. 374.

[25] *Ibid.,* p. 398. Adam insists that this play is a satire and shows how it broadened into a more philosophical attack against "l'aristotélisme des

It would be unjust to over-emphasize this aspect of Professor Adam's excellent history, although it is an integral part of his understanding of Molière. The playwright here is at once vulnerable to pain and admirably resilient; he is a warm human being, fully esconced in his time. "Molière ne devance pas son siècle, il l'exprime." [26] Professor Adam's writing follows in the humanistic tradition and his *Histoire,* so lucid and just, will be the standard work for a long time.

Philosophy and Morality

There is a tradition in moliéresque criticism concerned with establishing a relationship between the comedies and a philosophical and ethnical world-view. This preoccupation began even in the dramatist's own time, when his *morale* was considered suspect. Baillet believed that Molière was "un des plus dangereux esprits;" Rouillé exclaimed that he was "un démon vêtu de chair et habillé en homme;" Bossuet and Bourdaloue were hardly more generous. In the main, these attacks were personal in nature, superficial and unfounded, and often intended to discredit Molière and his prestige at the court.

During the eighteenth century, *Tartuffe* was the most popular work and it was thought to represent the author's progressive attitude. This play and Molière were often mentioned in the long "querelle de la comédie et de l'Eglise," but the discussions it engendered offered nothing new. Except in terms of its own propaganda, the eighteenth century did not attempt to relate Molière or his works to an established philosophical tradition.

The actual focusing on a specific philosophical and religious context really began in the nineteenth century. From the modest suppositions of Bazin and Soulié, to the dogmas of Michelet and Brunetière, Molière the would-be philosopher and libertine first took shape and form. This line of inquiry continued into our own times. In every play, even the vaguest allusions of a philosophical or religious nature were microscopically examined: the

---

Facultés," the official ideology of the Church and state. Peter Nurse also makes this point in his excellent edition of *Le Malade imaginaire* (Oxford: University Press, 1965).

[26] *Ibid.,* p. 286.

"maximes du mariage" in *l'Ecole des femmes,* the king in *Psyché* and Dom Juan as blasphemers, *Tartuffe* libertine and "faux dévot," suspect love in *Les Amants magnifiques* and in *Amphitryon,* the morality of *Le Misanthrope.* Thibaudet referred to this aspect of moliéresque criticism as "la phase religieuse," in which "le génie de Molière semble s'opposer au génie du christianisme." Mornet writes of the academic and pedagogic tradition which made of Molière ". . . un 'penseur' . . . un 'philosophe' à la fois profond et mystérieux dont il fallait sans cesse sonder les desseins hardis et cachés." Bénichou reminded us that "Agnès n'a été trouvée inquiétante qu'au XIXè siècle."

The earliest preoccupations centered around Molière's *morale.* Even as well-meaning a book as C.-J. Jeannel's *La Morale de Molière* (1867) concluded that the comedies were indeed suspicious. Although the author is careful not to question the poet's intentions, he detects nonetheless a certain "joyeuse et séduisante immoralité. . . [dans] . . . l'ensemble des tableaux." [27] Following Brunetière, the extreme conservative Catholic position was expressed by Louis Veuillot in his *Molière et Bourdaloue* (1877). By a juxtaposition of texts from Bourdaloue's eloquent prose and Molière's immoral bantering, he intended to expose the moral shabbiness of the comedies. [28] The book apparently attracted little attention. Emile Faguet is more urbane and judicious. He opined that Molière was not a moralist at all, but simply one who counseled ". . . ce qu'il faut être pour n'être pas ridicule;" this attitude makes the poet a "législateur des bienséances." [29] Faguet amuses himself by listing a number of aspects of seventeenth century French society which a true moralist would have attacked

---

[27] C.-J. Jeannel, *La Morale de Molière* (E. Thorin, 1867), p. 257.

[28] Louis Veuillot, *Molière et Bourdaloue* (Palme, 1877). Mme Dussane provides an interesting counter-argument when she states that Bourdaloue could have been misled by the "dévots" on questions concerning Molière and, as a result, over-reacted in his condemnation of *Tartuffe.* She suggests that the cleric and the dramatist had in fact shared a common aversion for hypocrisy and other vices. "Eternellement l'ortodoxie de Bourdaloue et le libre jugement de Molière diront les mêmes choses dans un langage différent et sans pouvoir se résoudre à un accord." (In *La Revue universelle,* v. 28, pp. 641-656; essentials of this article are reprinted in her edition of *Tartuffe,* 1932, pp. 239-251.)

[29] E. Faguet, *En lisant Molière* (Hachette, 1914), 3rd edition, p. 164.

("les hommes d'argent" for example), and on which Molière is conspicuously silent. Thus the poet is really amoral or at least a non-moralist. Faguet admits that "... pour moi c'est avoir mis une immoralité ou plutôt une démoralisation à la place de la morale." [30]

In his curious *Morale de Molière* (1945), Jacques Arnavon writes that Molière could not allow himself to express clear, didactic intentions for fear of losing contact with his public. Thus the lack of system in the comedies tends to obscure Molière's responses to specific questions. But without doubt, there is implied throughout Molière's works a basic righteousness which is expressed in a constant search for "bonheur." The dramatic tension in the comedies stems from the prejudices, lies, and jealousies which disorient this basic human thrust. The crux of Arnavon's argument rests on the special connotation the author attaches to this exclusive "morale": "Ce n'est pas dans la satisfaction des appétits, ou dans une passivité inerte qu'il [le bonheur] consiste mais dans une activité libre et désintéressé, dans l'union du dévouement et du travail." [31] Hence, Molière's philosophy includes sublimations of passions, self-sacrifice, discipline, hard work. [32]

---

[30] *Ibid.*, p. 137; see also conclusions, pp. 314-315. In fact, M. Harpin in *La Comtesse d'Escarbagnas* provides a brief but cutting picture of a "receveur de tailles," gross and self-centered. On this question, see Stoyan Tzoneff, *L'Homme d'argent dans le théâtre français jusqu'à la Révolution* (Gap: Imprimerie Louis Jean, 1934), pp. 54-59; and Emile Henriot's general article, "La Littérature et les finances," in *Courrier littéraire-XVIIè siècle* (Albin Michel, 1958), nouvelle édition, vol. 1, pp. 418-423. On Colbert and a possible caricature of him in Molière, see J. Marion, "Molière, a-t-il songé à Colbert en composant le personnage de Jourdain," in *Revue d'Histoire littéraire de la France*, vol. 45 (1938), pp. 145-180. The answer to the question of the title is "yes," but the argument remains tenuous.

[31] Jacques Arnavon, *Morale de Molière* (Editions Universelles, 1945), p. 224.

[32] *Ibid.*, and p. 229. Although Arnavon refuses to link Molière with any philosophical current, in his *Le Dom Juan de Molière* (1947), he does allude to the libertines of the time and suggests that the comic poet belongs to those "qui s'écartent des enseignements officiels," and finally, that Molière might be considered an agnostic (pp. 60-64). In his *Histoire de la littérature française*, Lanson suggests that Molière was a partisan of "la nature" in the tradition of Rabelais and Montaigne, without being an enemy of religion. The poet is really a moderate: "Molière ajoute la raison à la nature ... [qui] fixe à la nature, à l'instinct, leur mesure et leurs bornes." *Histoire* (Hachette, 1938), 18th edition, p. 527.

We have already seen how, at the beginning of the century, Abel LeFranc linked Molière with Gassendi's philosophy and how later Michaut attempted to discredit the idea. The question is complex however, and Michaut only proved it unlikely that Molière had actually been Gassendi's student in Paris in the early 1640's. This left open the more pertinent matter of determining to what extent "le gassendisme" influenced Molière's works. (Gassendi's philosophy is characterized by its scepticism, epicureanism, anti-aristotelianism). Recently, George Mongrédien recalled that Gassendi's influence appears to have been limited during his lifetime (he died in 1655), except for the indirect disemination of his ideas through his students Chapelle, and Bernier. But Mongrédien insists that this circle of friends was very active in the intellectual life of Paris, and that Molière was known to have frequented Chapelle. In any case, Mongrédien believes that Molière could easily have come in direct or indirect contact with Gassendi's ideas and cites a number of allusions in the comedies which are more-or-less Gassendist in spirit. [33]

Georges Poulet made an interesting effort at linking intellectually Molière with Gassendi. The critic detects in Molière's work "un univers des passions ... où l'on est dans une tension incessante, dans une agitation sans trêve, dans un recommencement perpétuel des mêmes désirs." [34] He then interprets this cyclical, ever-renewing temporality as a central axiom in Gassendi ("maître de Molière"). The phenomenon is linked with the essentially nominalistic fashion in which Molière develops his characters: "répétition constante des traits essentiels." Unfortunately Poulet's essay is very abstract, refers only obliquely to a few minor plays, and is founded in large part on a disputed text, *La Lettre sur la comédie de l'Imposteur*. The results are necessarily inconclusive, a fact which the author himself has admitted. [35]

---

[33] G. Mongrédien et al., *Pierre Gassendi, Sa Vie et son œuvre 1592-1615* (Albin Michel, 1955), pp. 128-134.

[34] G. Poulet, *Etudes sur le temps humain* (Plon, 1966), p. 85 ff. See also L. Goldmann, *Sciences humaines et philosophie* (Gonthier, 1966), p. 114.

[35] See M. Poulet's letter to René Wellek on the limits of his Molière essay, in S. Lawall, *The Critics of Consciousness* (Cambridge: Harvard University Press, 1968), p. 92. For an impressive demonstration of "gassen-

In his long piece, "Molière and la Mothe Le Vayer" (1933), A. L. Sells concentrates on the importance of La Mothe's *La Prose chagrine* (1661) for *Le Misanthrope* and *Les Femmes savantes*, and he detects a number of similar themes in the philosopher's texts and Molière's plays. Alceste and Philinte, for example, present the case for and against scepticism, and in so doing reflect the argumentative spirit which characterizes much of La Mothe's work. Alceste obviously lacks the philosophical detachment of the real sceptic however, and Sells suggests, ". . . not in Alceste should one look for Pyrrhonism but in Philinte and in Molière himself." [36] But Molière is neither a systematic philosopher, nor a moral doctrinaire. "His main interest was in practical morals and more especially, social morals. Instead of speaking of Molière's 'philosophy,' it would be more accurate to say Molière's 'ethics.'" [37]

On these questions, René Jasinski goes much further than Sells. The chapter "La Leçon du Misanthrope," in his *Molière et le Misanthrope* (1951), treats the philosophical import not only of this play, but for all of the poet's life and works. Jasinski wrote that although Molière was obviously familiar and sympathetic with Gassendi's epicureanism, ". . . il ne s'y rallie pas." [38] This system was too detached, contemplative, and hedonistic, while Molière's personality was too vibrant. By temperament, the comic playwright was naturally attracted to a more aggressive and engaging code. Christian scepticism, especially La Mothe's brand, offered just the measure of commitment Molière wanted. And, "d'étroites affinités de pensée relient Molière au vieux philosophe." [39] Jasinski acknowledged A. L. Sells' suggested affinities between *Le Misanthrope* and *La Prose chagrine* but is not satisfied with them. In a close analysis of the play and La Mothe's text, the French critic establishes an impressive number of similarities and he concludes: "Ainsi le thème général du *Misanthrope* s'accorde étroitement à celui de *La Prose chagrine*. Molière suit

diste" influences in one of the lighter plays, see G. A. Astre, "Magies d'*Amphitryon*," in *Cahiers Renault-Barrault*, no. 10 (1955), pp. 74 ff.

[36] A. L. Sells, "Molière and La Mothe Le Vayer," in *Modern Language Review*, vol. 28 (1933), p. 359.

[37] *Ibid.*, p. 444.

[38] René Jasinski, *Molière et le Misanthrope* (A. Colin, 1951), p. 258.

[39] *Ibid.*, p. 260.

ici La Mothe Le Vayer." [40] Further inquiry into the works of the philosopher and poet allows Jasinski to broaden these conclusions: "Ainsi s'affirme dans toute sa pensée, le lien entre la pensée de Molière et celle du vieux philosophe. On retrouve de part et d'autre la même thèse générale, complétée par des thèses secondaires analogues ... Molière se rallie de près aux idées de La Mothe Le Vayer ..." [41] The evolution of Jasinski's argument comes to this far-reaching conclusion: "On saisit maintenant l'originalité suprême du *Misanthrope*. Par une tentative sans précédent, Molière ne porte pas seulement à la scène une allégorie philosophique: sans rompre avec la vie, bien plus, en créant des types immortels, il illustre, en l'affermissant, un système, et pose, au sens le plus élevé du mot, les principes d'une 'philosophie'." [42] This attitude in Molière is not applicable for *Le Misanthrope* alone, but rather a morality which is "... celle de Molière dans sa plus haute expression." [43] This is in fact Molière's life philosophy. Finally, Jasinski interprets the implications of this *morale*. "Molière aboutit à une morale toute humaine, libertine certes, mais au sens le plus élevé du mot. Elle ne heurte pas ouvertement le dogme ni la foi. Mais elle s'en passe. Elle s'édifie en dehors d'eux. Elle trouve en elle-même ses moyens et ses fins." [44] Jasinski's attempt at relating Molière to a single "maître à penser" and at creating a systematic philosophical view of human nature represent the most ambitious recent arguments for a "philosophie de Molière" by a literary critic.

J. S. Spink's opinion represents somewhat of a synthesis of the major currents of opinion on this question. Spink links Molière to both Gassendi's epicureanism and La Mothe Le Vayer's scepticism. "Both the old intellectualism and the new intellectualism seem to be out of favor in Molière's eyes. Does that mean that the old (Aristotelian) naturalism and the new (Epicurean) naturalism were given a positive preference? That Molière's doubting unbelief caused him not to hold the balance between a

---

[40] *Ibid.*, p. 267.
[41] *Ibid.*, p. 271.
[42] *Ibid.*, p. 272.
[43] *Ibid.*
[44] *Ibid.*, p. 274.

naturalistic and an intellectual view of man's estate? That his
sympathies swayed him to the naturalistic view? That indeed is
the answer which best accounts for the facts." [45] Further, Spink
believes that Molière's attitude was related to "the rehabilitation
of Epicurus" which took on new force after the Fronde and
had its *aboutissement* in the elegant writings of Saint-Evremont.
This is not to say however, that Spink aligns Molière with Brunetière and LeFranc. One of the main points of his argument concerning the new epicureanism is that it was highly tinged with
cartesian rationalism which combines naturalism and pure scepticism. "The criterion which Molière seems to have had was a
conception of a coherent and coordinated life, governed by its
own inner principle, spontaneous and therefore natural, ordered
and therefore rational." [46]

The histories of both libertinage and religious sentiment in
the seventeenth century have differed considerably in treating
Molière. One of the first, F.-T. Perrin's *Les Libertins en France
au 17è siècle* (1899), places Molière without reservation in the
libertine camp. "Molière, lui, est libertin jusqu'aux moelles." [47]
After considering *Tartuffe* and *Dom Juan,* the historian can only
conclude that in fact Molière is an aggressive libertine, that he
attacked the clergy and religion, and that along with La Fontaine
he was "...la gloire du libertinage." [48]

A very different view is expressed by Jean Calvet. He is of
the opinion that in the case of many so-called free-thinkers there
was never a dramatic break with orthodoxy, but instead a more
subtle "séparation de la vie et de la religion." In this situation,
religion becomes "... un rite traditionnel, un décorum social, une
hygiène personnelle. Nous pouvons le pratiquer pour nous et

---

[45] J. S. Spink, *French Free Thought from Gassendi to Voltaire* (London: Athlone Press, 1960), p. 148.
[46] *Ibid.,* p. 149.
[47] F.-T. Perrins, *Les Libertins en France au XVIIè siècle* (Calmann Lévy, 1899), p. 342.
[48] *Ibid.,* p. 353. Although René Pintard does not discuss the comedies as such, he does hold that Molière seems to have belonged to the Gassendist, free-thinking group of "Chapelle et ses amis." In a rather inconclusive foot-note, Pintard sketches what might have been a refutation of Michaut's position concerning Molière and Gassendi. René Pintard, *Le Libertinage érudit dans la première moitié du 17è siècle* (Boivin, 1943), vol. 2, p. 624.

chez nous, à notre gré. Dans le monde il faut simplement être honnête homme; et si le chrétien peut se distinguer des autres par quelques nuances, ce sera par une tolérance plus accomodante et plus souriante." [49] This is Molière's stance, as it had been Montaigne's, and it is essentially the ethic of a "mondain" and not of a "libertin." Hence, where Faguet had labeled Molière "le législateur des bienséances," Calvet suggests a more nuanced "le législateur des convenances." This is the thesis of Msgr. Calvet's *Molière, est-il chrétien?* (1954), which claims that this separation was inherent in Molière's life. As a student of the Jesuits, he had been reared in the Church but had been cut off from his faith by the excommunication implicit in his vocation. Therefore, with regard to religion, Molière was really an outsider and he slowly evolved toard the ethic of a "mondain." According to Calvet, this attitude was widespread and in fact it became the established morality for the entire court beginning around 1668. "Alors commença cette période de gloire et de plaisir qui dura quinze ans environ; c'est le règne de la Montespan et de la doctrine mondaine de Molière." [50] The result was that the poet inevitably lost touch with the spirit of the reform doctrines of the 1660's and saw only the excesses. Thus he proposes "... des maximes de sagesse profane pour remplacer celles de l'Evangile." [51] In this view, Molière tends to overreact and his *Tartuffe* contains "... certains mots ... de colère, certains traits ... grossis par le parti-pris ou déformés pour la polémique." The play is a "... déposition sincère d'un mondain sur un problème qu'il connaît mal et d'un comédien sur un problème qui ne relève peut-être pas de la comédie." [52] Bossuet and Bourdaloue had also expressed similar views on *Tartuffe*.

But for Msgr. Calvet, Molière was not a libertine either. The "separation" in the poet's life operated between "sa vie personnelle qu'il veut libre, [et] la religion qu'il veut respecter et

---

[49] Msgr. Jean Calvet, *La Littérature religieuse de François de Sales à Fénelon* (J. de Gigord, éditeur, 1938), vol. 5, p. 548.

[50] *Ibid.*, p. 550.

[51] Jean Calvet, *Bossuet, L'Homme et l'œuvre* (Boivin, 1941), p. 154.

[52] J. Calvet, *Molière, est-il chrétien?* (Fernand Lanore, 1954), p. 60.

protéger." [53] In this view, *Dom Juan* clearly exposes the blasphemer to ridicule. Sganarelle, le Pauvre, Elvire and dom Louis, in subtle ways, all represent a triumph of morality and religion over the waywardness of the elegant don. Calvet's Molière occupies an ambivalent position between the faithful and the libertines: "Il a l'instinct religieux qui croit une religion nécessaire; il n'a pas le sens religieux qui comprend ce qu'est une religion." [54] Molière's conception seems to have been a sort of "déisme de bon ton," which lacked a profound feeling and respect for the potential greatness of true devotion: "Il est l'homme pour qui la sainteté n'a pas de sens." [55]

Henri Busson's excellent *La Religion des Classiques* (1948) treats Molière cautiously but vigorously. The author does not impute a specific religious creed to the poet, but he does place his "morale" within a broad ethical context in a state of flux at the time. "Si Molière avait une religion apparemment c'était celle de son temps.... La morale de Molière a évolué comme sa physique, avec celle de son temps." [56] Busson discusses Molière within the evolution of religious thought which led to a crisis of the sprit in France between 1660 and 1685. According to the author, this crisis was marked by the loss of credit for the final vestiges of peripatetic philosophy and scholasticism, a weakening of the prestige of stoicism, and the rising pre-eminence of intellectual libertinism. Molière, of course, is linked to this new attitude. Busson's main arguments are based on two unlikely plays, *Les Amants magnifiques* and *Psyché*, in which the poet's ideas ostensibly reflect the intellectual libertine position. For example, Busson contends that the rational free-thinkers of the time were obviously sceptical about the value of oracles and did much to discredit this outdated belief. Often however, their arguments were but thinly veiled attacks on the Church. He relates this line of action to the strategy of the false oracle in *Les Amants*

---

[53] *Ibid.*, p. 124. See also Msgr. Calvet's original and debatable interpretation of "la scène du pauvre," pp. 99-110.

[54] *Ibid.*, p. 96.

[55] *Ibid.*, p. 73.

[56] Henri Busson, *La Religion des classiques* (P. U. F., 1948), p. 229 and p. 234. See also the useful synthesis of points of view on this question, pp. 229-270.

magnifiques. The idea here is that the false oracle in the play is really "une imposture sacerdotale." "Mais précisément, c'est là une thèse soutenue par tous les libertins quand il s'agit des oracles anciens. Molière rejoint ici Vanini et il annonce Voltaire." [57] In this reading, Eriphile and Sostrate are akin to Dom Juan. [58] In the same spirit, *Psyché* represents a final break with stoicism at precisely the time of its sharp decline in France. In Molière's play, it comes in the form of a categorical refusal of "toute consolation," laic or religious, which Busson claims was a central tenet of "la philosophie du Portique." [59] The author also detects a kind of crisis in Molière's life around 1670 in which the doctrine of stoicism was found "insuffisante pour la vie." This was a major shift from a philosophy which had been inculcated in many characters in the comedies, including Alceste and Done Elvire. Busson concludes that Molière was abreast of philosophical currents of his day and that his plays reflected the growing influence of rationalism in religious questions. Like Jean Calvet, Busson thinks that "Molière n'est peut-être pas irreligieux; mais tenu hors de l'église par sa profession, il n'a vu la religion que de l'extérieur et elle ne l'intéresse que pour son comportement social." [60]

On questions of morality and philosophy, Antoine Adam reaffirms much that had already been established in literary history. He reviews Molière's association with the "libre-pensée" circles, as Mongrédien and others had done, insisting on the importance of Molière's close friendship with La Mothe Le Vayer and Bernier, and suggests that "Molière fut un chrétien moins que tiède." [61] It would be incorrect, however, to seek a system in the comedies, and *Tartuffe* represents not a critique of religion, but "une certaine manière de concevoir le christianisme." Quoting the well-known line from *La Lettre sur l'Imposteur,* "la religion n'est qu'une raison plus parfaite," Adam concludes: "Elle est la grande puissance

---

[57] *Ibid.,* p. 262.
[58] *Ibid.,* p. 265. On the subject of oracles and the like, see a curious article by E. Bouvier, "La Croyance au merveilleux à l'époque classique," in *Mélanges . . . offerts à Daniel Mornet* (Nizet, 1951), pp. 99-108.
[69] Busson, *op. cit.,* pp. 239-245.
[60] *Ibid.,* p. 271.
[61] A. Adam, *Histoire de la littérature française au XVIIè siècle* (Del Duca, 1962), vol. 3, p. 310.

d'ordre, d'harmonie, de solidarité que maintient la société civile.
La raison, ayant une valeur universelle, est présente chez les
hommes de tous les climats et de toutes les époques. Et par conséquent la religion, expression suprême de la raison, peut s'en-
seigner hors des Eglises, elle condamne l'esprit de secte et de
cabale, elle unit les hommes au lieu de les opposer les uns aux
autres." [62] This view implies that Molière is reaffirming the humanistic values of Erasmus and the Renaissance, of his contemporaries
Gassendi and La Mothe Le Vayer, values which will later become
those of Voltaire and the Enlightenment. [63]

The most radical departure on the question of philosophy and
morality is Paul Bénichou's *Morales du grand siècle* (1948). The
term "morales" has a special connotation here, for it represents
the aspirations and ideals of a certain humanism inherent in the
major authors and implied in the broad historical movements
of the period. The three "morales" Bénichou defines are, "une
morale heroïque, une morale chrétienne rigoureuse, une morale
mondaine," as represented in Corneille, Pascal and Racine, and
Molière respectively.

One of the first established ideas in Molière criticism that
Bénichou reviewed was the notion that the poet was the representative of bourgeois morality. Logically, because of Molière's
success at the court and in Paris, the opposite would seem to be
true. Bénichou argued that in the comedies, "le bourgeois est
presque toujours médiocre ou ridicule," and that Molière's ideal
of "bon sens" was not Chrysale's version ("prosaïque et risible"),
but the more elegant notions of a Clitandre. [64] But this is not the

---

[62] *Ibid.*, pp. 311-312.
[63] Cf. also, John Cairncross, *Molière bourgeois et libertin* (Nizet, 1963).
The author asserts that, "Molière est bien libertin et non-conformiste." His
thesis is that Dom Juan is conceived as an ideal and that whenever he is
made to look ridiculous or repugnant, it merely serves the mythological
convention and prepares for the inevitable end. The libertine innuendoes
of *Le Misanthrope* suggest strongly, dixit Cairncross, that Acts I and II
were really written around 1661, at the time Molière was working on the
Lucretius translation. These arguments are debatable.
[64] Paul Bénichou, *Morales du grand siècle* (Gallimard, 1948), p. 172.
F. Gaiffe in *Le Rire et la scène française* (Boivin, 1931) had the same
intuition. He suggested that Molière wrote to please the court crowd but
that for the playwright this was a practical expediency and not a firm philosophical conviction. Bénichou is more systematic. For him, Molière chose freely

only dimension of Molière's posture. Bénichou detects a paradox and struggle between "Molière galant," defender of the aristocratic ethic, and "Molière libre et naturel" who is really plebeian in spirit. What is important is that there is no intermediary, bourgeois attitude. According to Bénichou, the reconciled "ton moliéresque" is "le mélange de l'agrément noble avec la raillerie plébéienne et cet accord se fait en sautant par dessus les régions de l'honorabilité bourgeoise." [65] The paradox is resolved in the crucial years 1664-1666, when Molière firmly establishes himself as the defender and promoter of the aristocratic ethic. At this point, the author sketches a "Molière conformiste" who is the exact opposite of the traditional Molière conforming to bourgeois moderation. In the great plays, the poet reaffirmed the ethical standards of the galant court. What is unacceptable both in Molière and in the ethic of Louis' court, is any attempt at constraint other than what is innate in the *générosité* of the *honnête homme*. Hence, *Tartuffe* is not specifically directed against a religious group, but against "tout ce qui dans le christianisme pouvait permettre de censurer, persécuter, envahir." [66] But this ideal aristocratic liberalism can be threatened from a position other than that of the "dévots." For example, Alceste incarnates "l'idéalisme réformateur" and is no less a threat. It follows that Molière must treat him harshly and not allow him to triumph. So Alceste's "droiture" is portrayed as the result of shortcomings in his character and accordingly, it functions more as a sort of compensation than as a disinterested virtue. Therein lies his failure. Dramatically, Célimène "est la femme la mieux faite pour lui faire sentir son échec, et pour justifier la colère moralisante par laquelle il essaye de compenser cet échec." [67] In the end, the one character who could have threatened the "moeurs dociles et adroites ... l'ouvrage et le soutien du pouvoir absolu" is exiled, and the royal status quo is maintained. This is the best example of Molière's conformity and of his special morality. "Toute la morale de Molière consiste à savoir s'incliner

---

to ridicule the bourgeois and to align himself with the aristocratic *honnêtes hommes*.

[65] *Ibid.*, p. 195.
[66] *Ibid.*, p. 206.
[67] *Ibid.*, p. 213.

devant un certain nombre de faits. La force des usages défie autant chez lui la justice que la force des désirs défie la bienséance ... tout au moins a-t-il réduit la morale à n'être que l'accompagnement le plus discret possible de la vie." [68]

Obviously, Bénichou does not attach negative value to Molière's ethic. Corneille's heroism, Pascal's stringent morality and Molière's flexible ethic are all part of the "révalorisation de l'humain," which takes on special impetus in the seventeenth century and continues through the following Age of Enlightenment. These ideals "prennent naissance dans la nature qui lui doivent leur attrait, lui communiquent leur valeur." [69] Involved as they were in a common effort, the seventeenth and eighteenth centuries are complimentary, "par la valeur qu'ils attribuent, dans l'ensemble, à la qualité d'homme, à l'équilibre de la lucidité et de l'instinct, par la façon dont ils allient tous deux, le beau et le naturel, dont ils dessinent le caractère et les exigences de la véritable humanité." [70] Molière's works are part of this honorable effort.

Through the various opinions on this question, what trends emerge? In general, modern critics have not been prepared to discard the idea that Molière could have been influenced by the major philosophical preoccupations of his day and that his comedies might have a moralistic side. When the formalists, Moore and Bray, suggested that the dramatic construct and the internal functioning of the comedies are the most important considerations in Molière criticism, they were accused of hiding behind esthetics and willfully ignoring the obvious. But Jasinski's work, which represents the other extreme, has also been accepted with considerable caution. In the midst of these arguments and counter-arguments, Bénichou's book has been very significant. Highly controversial, but original and perspective, his *Morales du Grand siècle* provided many new perspectives on Molière and his times and influenced the entire generation of critics after 1950. The temper of recent time has clearly favored Bénichou's conception of Molière's *morale*, as well as his sociological method for studying the entire seventeenth century.

[68] *Ibid.*, p. 214.
[69] *Ibid.*, p. 222.
[70] *Ibid.*

The New Approach

Literary history contributed greatly to our knowledge and understanding of Molière and his time. Precisions on dates, circumstances, and sources establish a context in which the work itself can be more fully appreciated. The works of Despois and Mesnard, Michaut, Lancaster, and Adam attest to the quality and value of literary history in the study of Molière. The discipline has its limitations however, as Adam suggested when he observed that research on "la cabale" was erroneously interpreted as providing keys to understanding *Tartuffe*. In spite of the considerable historical research from previous generations, scholars had left many aspects of the comedies untouched and detailed studies of circumstances and sources had not answered a number of central questions. Literary science had done its work but now there was a need to proceed further.

The shift of interest began in the first years of the century. The first phase is represented by a renewed interest in the practical aspects of Molière's career. Paul Fischmann's long article, "Molière als Schauspiel Direktor" (1906), deals with the "recettes" of each play and their importance to the players. [71] Henri Bidou wrote that "les considérations de l'affiche" were the primary concern for Molière and his troupe. "Faire l'affiche et que le public vienne, voilà la préoccupation de tous les jours." [72] Karl Mantzius' book, translated from the Danish in 1908, traced the evolution of French theatre in the seventeenth century with Molière as the focal point. In this perspective, he too emphasizes Molière's role as director, actor, and "orateur," and the importance of the material conditions of theatres at the time. [73]

---

[71] Paul Fischmann, "Molière als Schauspiel Direktor," in *Zeitschrift für französischen Sprache und Literatur*, vol. 29 (1906), pp. 1-55.

[72] H. Bidou, "Molière directeur de théâtre," in *Journal des débats*, (28 August 1931), vol. 38, p. 356.

[73] Karl Mantzius, *Molière: Les Théâtres, le public et les comédiens de son temps*, traduit du danois par Maurice Pellisson (Armand Colin, 1908); see especially chapters VI and VII, pp. 97-146.

In 1935, Valdemar Vedel wrote that above all, "Molière est né dramaturgue et acteur." [74] In his opinion, moliéresque comedy functions primarily as a visual spectacle intended to entertain and not merely as literary parody or social satire. In fact, it is most successful when it operates as pure theatrical prestidigitation. [75] The play of masks, for example, provides Vedel with one of the keys to Molière's sepecial art. "La comédie est la sorte de ruse que Molière emploie de préférence. Jouer de la comédie dans la comédie, jouer un personnage qui à son tour joue un autre, voilà certes, de quoi satisfaire en Molière le démon de théâtre." [76]

Applied to Molière in Vedel's context, the felicitous phrase, "le démon du théâtre," indicates the new direction emerging in Molière criticism. It maintained that the object for study should no longer be the man or the milieu, but Molière's dramatic technique elaborated over thirty years in the profession. Among other things this implies seeing Alceste and Célimène, Tartuffe and Dom Juan, only in terms of what they were originally intended to be, fictitious characters in a comic drama. As Professor Guicharnaud put it, the new conception of Molière is not of a man but of a theatre. [77]

Implicitly, Gustave Lanson's important article, "Molière et la farce" (1901), had already suggested new insights into the crucial Italian element in Molière. Lanson distinguished between the coarse, exterior effects of farce (lazzi, bâtons, obscenities), and an underlying "principe d'esthétique" which in Molière's case was more important and more lasting. According to Lanson, a close study of the genre indicates strongly that farce was more than unwritten, spontaneous set-pieces played randomly by players of limited skills. On the contrary, farce as a genre had "son esthétique, sa méthode d'invention et une façon originale de

[74] Valdemar Vedel, *Deux Classiques français vus par un critique étranger: Corneille et son temps-Molière*, traduit du danois par Madame E. Cornet (H. Champion, 1935), p. 464.

[75] *Ibid.*, p. 476. Pierre Kohler also wrote about "l'impersonnalité dramatique" in Molière: "... le comique de Molière est de pur réalisme dramatique." See his *L'Esprit classique et la comédie* (Payot, 1925), p. 231.

[76] Vedel, *Ibid.*, p. 484; this passage and the previous one are quoted in W. G. Moore's *New Criticism*, p. 71 and p. 38 respectively.

[77] J. Guicharnaud, "Molière in the Light of New Criticism," in *The American Society of the Legion of Honor Magazine*, vol. 29 (1959), # 3.

traiter la matière de la vie." [78] It was this established Italian form which heavily influenced Molière's technique, even in the "high comedies" between 1664 and 1666. For example, action in farce operates in a special way because "l'action n'a pas pour objet de produire des modifications de sentiments, mais de faire jaillir inépuisablement en des actes divers et sous des jours variés le sentiment qui est le ressort unique du caractère." [79] It follows that the characters in this comic form tend to have fixed dispositions because "ils doivent être tels à la fin qu'au début, ils ne peuvent dire 'oui' après avoir dit 'non', un 'non' qui était dans la nécessité de leur essence." [80] Lanson's descriptions clearly indicate that Molière created his characters in the mold of Italian farce and that these characters can be best understood in terms of roles interacting with other roles in a purely dramatic, theatrical, world. Although Lanson himself did not develop this line of argument in detail, his article represented a good beginning and was often cited by later critics following the new approach.

The most radical break with traditional moliéresque criticism and the most substantial contributions in the new method came from Professors Will G. Moore and René Bray. Professor Moore's *Molière: A New Criticism* (1949) is generally considered to be the source of the renaissance in Molière studies, but Professor Bray's *Molière Homme de théâtre* is of equal importance. In any case, both books "ont fait date" in Molière criticism.

Mr. Moore's slim volume suggests that "in Molière we may find the comic art in its most vigorous and vital expression and that this is the matter for analysis rather than imputed assumptions and doctrines." [81] Moore's inquiry is simply "a dispassionate analysis of the comic art as practised in plays which are universally acknowledged as masterpieces of comedy." [82] Chapter headings

---

[78] G. Lanson, "Molière et la farce," in *Essais de méthode, de critique et d'histoire littéraire,* edited by Henri Peyre (Hachette, 1965), p. 200. See also M. Peyre's vigorous and somewhat polemical introduction to this volume.

[79] *Ibid.,* p. 206.

[80] *Ibid.,* p. 207. Gustave Rudler's classic edition of *Le Misanthrope* (Oxford: Blackwell, 1947) is an excellent *mise en œuvre* of much of Lanson. See particularly the fine discussion on "le comique externe" and "le comique interne," pp. xxvii-xxxv.

[81] Will G. Moore, *Molière: A New Criticism* (Oxford: The Clarendon Press, 1964), 5th impression, p. 6.

[82] *Ibid.*

indicate the "various strata of comic material," including "Mime," "Mask," "Speech," and "Scene," with a view to establish that the plays are constructed according to the necessities of the stage and the actor. At every level of analysis, the investigation revises old opinions and suggests new insights into the working of Molière's art.

"Mime" reviews Molière's experience as an actor. In Moore's argument, Molière's realism "is the outcome not of poetic or satiric intention, or of literary attitude, but of a type of acting which proved successful in practice." [83] The discussion on "Mime" leads to reflections on "Mask" which Moore elaborates in detail, believing that "consideration of the mask as symbol would lead us to the animating principle of comedy as Molière evolved it. [84] In "Speech," Moore shows how Molière successfully achieved comic effects in his use of language. "Language in Molière shows with almost infinite variety the clash of man and speech." [85] The language of the comic character invariably reveals his lack of understanding and his incoherence. But there is a more subtle and psychological use of language which operates like a verbal parallel to the mask. Moore calls it "language as disguise," and it is often manifested in the rogue's use of speech to mystify and mislead, without always lying. The outstanding examples are Diafoirus and specially Tartuffe. In confrontation with Orgon, the "faux dévot" pushes irony to its extreme with his revelation that "Tout le monde me prend pour un homme de bien / mais la vérité pure est que je ne vaux rien." In Le Malade imaginaire, the verbal mask falls. Argan gives himself away when he unconsciously admits, "Je ne suis pas bon, je suis méchant quand je veux." And Moore remarks that, "It is not what he would ever want to say. It is however a deeply true statement about him, and about all of us. Comic drama elicits the utterance of what in most of us is buried, suppressed, unutterable." [86]

In "Scene," Moore inquires into the structure of the comedies and consequently into some old notions in moliéresque criticism. For example, he suggests that plot in the comedies is built neither

---

[83] Ibid., p. 29.
[84] Ibid., p. 35.
[85] Ibid., p. 57.
[86] Ibid., p. 65.

on sequential succession of events, nor on linear evolution of characters. Instead, the dramatic principle underlying Molière's plots is a "struggle between deceiver and deceived, . . . between fraud and foolishness." In *Le Malade imaginaire,* tension builds between the rogue Diafoirus and the fool Argan. Around this central conflict, the action evokes "a suggestion, no more, of the gulf that separates the mind from reality, the products of thought from the nature of things . . . the mixture of what is probable and what is grotesque." [87] In *Le Misanthrope,* the basic structure is more complex, for it operates on a new idea. "This new principle of structure might be said to depend on suffusion rather than on deduction. The loosely linked scenes all stand in direct relation to the master concept; they build up a vision not of a person nor of a plot but of a choice of attitudes . . . . Each element may be said to be progressively revealed, but not on any register of a progression in time, from cause to effect: they appear as successive illuminations of facets, of aspects." [88] In this light, the critic reconsiders the role of the "raisonneur," traditionally thought to be the author's spokesman, standing aside from the action "in the manner of the ancient chorus." Not so, contends Mr. Moore: "These characters have a better reason for their presence, an esthetic reason. They ensure symmetry and roundness of comic presentation. Excess is more distinguishable if its opposite is exhibited at the same time. Sense shows up nonsense, sobriety offsets bad temper." [89] The resolution of the comedies also follows in this line of reasoning. "Fantasy is indeed highly appropriate to end a spectacle in which the distinction between the probable and the improbable is designedly vague, and which any realistic happy ending would mean an alteration or violation of character." [90] Moore's arguments here on structure were new and far-reaching, and the chapter is perhaps one of the most revolutionary in the entire book.

Among some of the established ideas which Professor Moore attempts to dismiss is the conception of the comic playwright as

---

[87] *Ibid.,* p. 78.
[88] *Ibid.,* pp. 78-79.
[89] *Ibid.,* p. 74.
[90] *Ibid.,* p. 83.

purveyor of bourgeois morality. Paradoxically however, one observation in the conclusions of this book seems to attribute a bourgeois attitude to Molière. "Molière exhibits the limits of human nature no less than its power. It apparently implies a sober sense of man's place in nature, of his function, of that order and sobriety to overstep which is to be unnatural." [91] While this statement could suggest that Molière always clearly delineated between what he considered morally acceptable and morally reprehensible, Mr. Moore indicates that this is not regularly the case. "In the contest of mask and face, of wit and nature, of mind against life, let us not ask who wins. The comedy does not determine the relative strength of the forces pitted against each other; it illustrates in bewildering variety, their juxtaposition and coexistence" [92] These are but a few of the many new insights in this elegantly simple book. Its importance for the new orientation in Molière studies is an uncontested fact.

René Bray's book, *Molière Homme de théâtre* (1953), is often believed to be à continuation of Moore's work. In fact, Bray's study was the "aboutissement" of many years of work and reflection on Molière, including two important editions of the playwright's complete works. The first of these editions already showed signs of Bray's originality. As early as 1935 he had begun to formulate ideas which later became part of the emerging new attitude in Molière criticism. To the question, "Quel est l'objet de la comédie?", Bray responds that it is not satire but amusement primarily, Molière's first preoccupation. "Il n'est pas poéte satirique, c'est un poète comique et cela implique une différence essentielle." [93] Later, Bray suggests that in works written in and for the theatre, the study of sources can be of limited value. For example he takes lightly the fact that no source has been found for *Le Sicilien*, and even if some persistent scholar finds one someday, "en quoi aura-t-on avancé l'étude de la pièce?" [94]

---

[91] *Ibid.*, pp. 120-121.

[92] *Ibid.*

[93] Molière, *Théâtre - de 1655 à 1660*, edited by René Bray (Société des Belles lettres, 1951), 2nd edition, p. 29.

[94] Bray, editor, *op. cit.*, *Théâtre - de 1666 à 1668*, p. 362. See also R. Rolland's excellent remarks of the effect of music in *Le Sicilien* in his *Les Origines du théâtre lyrique moderne* (E. Thorin, 1895), pp. 270-273.

Bray's idea about what is important in this obscure one-act play is revealing, for it indicates the tenor of his thinking even at this time (1946). "Ce qui en fait la valeur, c'est justement ce qui est propre à son créateur, la fantaisie d'une imagination qui se joue de toute vraisemblance, non pas de toute vérité, et s'amuse ici d'un décor, là d'un sentiment, ailleurs' d'un geste ou d'une situation; c'est la légèreté de la trame, c'est l'évocation d'une Sicile de convention (n'allons pas avec Mesnard nous demander doctement s'il y avait des esclaves à Messine en 1666!), c'est l'entrain et la galanterie, c'est pour mieux dire, la poésie." [95] In his "Notice" on Le Misanthrope, Bray displays impatience with ". . . les hypothèses auxquelles s'arrêtent des critiques qui veulent à toute force ignorer ce qu'est une comédie." [96] He himself always presents the plays exclusively as "pièces de théâtre," and shows little interest for other extraneous considerations. Bray's effort on his second edition of Molière's complete works was interrupted by his death in 1955. The edition was completed in the same spirit by J. Scherer, and it pushes the "optique théâtrale" even further, stressing the theatrical aspects of the comedies, such as technique, staging, décor, etc. [97]

Now let us consider Molière Homme de théâtre, which Bray called a "post-face" to the recently published edition of the playwright's complete works. To begin with, the simple title is to be taken literally. Bray's study focuses on Molière's long professional commitment to the theatre which he considers the primary influence in the comedies. "Il est d'abord et il reste jusqu'au bout un comédien. Il n'est poète qu'en tant que comédien. Non pas homme de lettres, mais homme de théâtre." [98] Having established this underlying assumption to his study, Bray surveys several traditional approaches to the comedies. In a series of ironic, rhetorical questions — "Est-il taciturne?" "Fut-il hereux?" "Molière, pense-t-il?" — he dismisses these matters for lack of information and because they are essentially irrelevant.

---

[95] Ibid.
[96] Ibid., p. 336.
[97] Molière, Œuvres complètes, ed. by R. Bray and J. Scherer (Club du Meilleur livre, 1954-1956), 3 vols.
[98] René Bray, Molière, Homme de théâtre (Mercure de France, 1953), 2nd impression, p. 8.

La vie privée a peu à faire avec un comédien lorsqu'il
écrit des comédies. L'existence du comédien a sur leur
composition des répercussions que ne saurait avoir sa
vie d'homme. Cette existence comporte en effet des exigences qui suscitent, précipitent, ralentissent la naissance
des œuvres, qui déterminent, conditionnent jusque dans
le détail leur forme et leur contenu ... Molière homme
privé n'intéresse guère le critique: Molière le comédien
est de son gibier; bien plus, c'est son gibier de choix. [99]

This is the *prise de position* from which the critic elaborates his
study, admitting from the beginning that this book is "notre
ouvrage de combat."

One of the most engaging parts here concerns Molière as director of his troupe. Within the company, he was "la grande vedette,"
for he had mastered the sterling qualities of an accomplished
actor, "drôlerie, ... agilité corporelle, ... virtuosité oratoire." [100]
And Bray is convinced that acting and directing were Molière's
primary concerns; the efforts at playwriting and publishing his
works were secondary occupations born out of necessity. Molière-
actor-director began writing in order to provide his troupe with
new material which would otherwise have been meager. Pierre
Corneille's contribution to Molière was rather thin and it came
late. The ambitious Racine was erratic and undependable, as
the *Alexandre* affair of late 1665 proved. Besides, tragedy was
not the *forte* of Molière's troupe. The comic authors at this time,
Donneau de Visé, Chappuzeau, Brécourt and Subligny, all made
small contributions but only over short periods of time. They were
hardly able to provide enough material for the major comic troupe
in Paris and Versailles during the brilliant decade of the 1660's.
Although Molière obviously attempted to secure a substantial and
lasting collaboration with several authors of his day, he was
unsuccessful. During his last four seasons, with few exceptions,
his troupe was sustained by Molière's own works. "Le Palais-Royal
avait perdu à peu près tout contact avec les auteurs," writes Bray.

---

[99] *Ibid.,* p. 17.
[100] *Ibid.,* p. 165; for good notes on Madeleine Béjart and other players,
cf. pp. 227 ff.

Having written several plays, Molière was forced to have them officially published as a safeguard against the flourishing commerce of pirated, unauthorized editions, a problem for all authors of the time. [101]

Once Bray has established the primacy of Molière as actor and director of his troupe, he proceeds to a detailed and penetrating analysis of moliéresque dramaturgy. Molière's adaptation of Italian farce techniques are discussed, including the uses of *sketches, lazzi* and *masque*. On the question of the *dénouements* in the comedies, Bray concurs with Moore — and both with Jouvet — that the resolutions are logical within the play's system of theatrical fantasy. [102] Bray then considers the importance of the number, quality and talent of the players Molière had at his disposal in terms of the conception and elaboration of each play. From the very start of his study, Bray had expressed the view that "... pour comprendre comment *Le Misanthrope* a été composé, il importe moins de savoir si son auteur était taciturne ou atrabilaire que de connaître le nombre et la qualité des actrices dont il disposait." [103]

The short chapter, "L'Imaginaire et le déraisonnable," is an interesting redefinition of Molière's art. According to the author, Molière's world is essentially theatrical and illusory. In spite of the illusion of realism it projects, it is based on "le chimérique ... l'invraisemblable ... l'imaginaire et le déraisonnable." [104] Artifice here is not arbitrary, but controlled and carefully manipulated, for "le théâtre a sa logique à lui.... L'imagination comique n'est ... pas absolument libre. Loin de là: elle obéit à des règles strictes, mais qui lui sont propres, et sont liberté à l'égard du réel. [105] Finally, there is this definition of the play which is germane to the thinking of actors such as Copeau and Jouvet. "Une pièce est une création de l'imagination, dominée dans sa structure

[101] For one aspect of this problem, see H. C. Lancaster, "Molière and Jean Ribou," in *Romantic Review*, vol. 28 (1937), pp. 32-35; for Bray's synopsis of Molière's difficulty with Ribou, pp. 36-37, in his *Homme de théâtre*.
[102] *Ibid.*, pp. 212-219.
[103] *Ibid.*, p. 18.
[104] *Ibid.*, pp. 267-268.
[105] *Ibid.*, p. 273.

par la bienséance interne, c'est-à-dire par la cohésion établie entre
les éléments entrant en jeu, et dans son efficacité par la bienséance
externe, c'est à dire par l'accord cherché entre le spectacle et
le spectateur . . . la pièce s'avance d'un seul élan dans une harmonie
que crée l'obéissance aux lois du monde enchanté de la scène . . .
L'univers merveilleux [des pièces de Molière] est un royaume
enchanté où règnent l'imaginaire et le déraisonnable." [106] In a final
part, Bray reaffirms that in all its forms, moliéresque comedy
is "outré" vis-à-vis reality, and is only justified by the poet's
attempt at providing pleasure. "Ce monde comique est le monde
du plaisir . . . . Le poète crée pour plaire." [107]

Bray's *Molière Homme de théâtre* is a considerable accomplish-
ment both in substance and import. Substantively, it follows in
the best tradition of literary history. Discreet and elegant in its
use of documentation, every important proposition of a historical
nature is nonetheless supported by impressive erudition. The book
teems with dates, figures, enumerations and comparisons, in the
best tradition of French literary history. But there is another
dimension perfectly blended into this one. Moore had said that
his book owed much to the criticism of men of the theatre. The
same is obviously true for Bray, who defers more than once to
such men as Copeau and Jouvet. The book's entire argument
as we have seen, remains steadfastly in the optic of the theatre.
It is difficult to imagine a non-theatre professional being more
concise, penetrating, and more convincing on theatre matters than
René Bray. But finally, what is impressive in Bray's approach
is not simply recalling that Molière was a player, director and
"pleinement homme de théâtre," but in pursuing this line of
argument further than any academic critic had before. *Molière
Homme de théâtre* is a basic book, and it will last.

---

[106] *Ibid.*, p. 274 and p. 278.
[107] *Ibid.*, p. 297.

Chapter IV

THEATRE PROFESSIONALS FROM COPEAU TO JOUVET

In the preceding pages, we saw how Bray and Moore articulated a new approach which viewed Molière not as a "littérateur," but as a highly skilled professional of the theatre. This attitude, which caused a veritable renaissance in academic studies, was not completely new for it had been elaborated, albeit in different fashion, by a number of well-known theatre professionals. These two approaches to understanding Molière, the academic and the theatrical, existed in mutually exclusive isolation during most of the first thirty-five years of this century, with only ocassional exceptions.

How do the *hommes de théâtre* view Molière? In essence, they view him first and foremost as an "homme de métier," a highly gifted actor, director, and troupe leader who, from these experiences primarily, evolved into a distinctively great technician of comedy. In this optic, the text itself, the play's inner working and possibilities as drama, becomes the singular focus of attention. Even the critical vocabulary is different. There is no more "penseur," "philosophe," "bourgeois" for the theatre professionals; their terminology evolves around "gestes," "positions," "destination." This reaffirms the play in its plenitude as theatre, and at once both the artistic work and criticism assume a new flexibility and freedom.

When dealing with the writings of theatre professionals, a number of problems arise. Although several French actors and directors have written well on Molière, the roles they have played

and the Molière productions they elaborated are their best statements on the matter. The following considerations are therefore
subject to qualification, for they rest primarily on their writings on
Molière, their lectures, notes, prefaces, etc., and only secondarily
on the limited material available on their acting and/or direction. [1]

It might be said from the outset that the *rencontres* between
Molière and modern theatre professionals have not always been
particularly original or revealing. For example, Jean Anouilh's
confrontation with the classical dramatist. Anouilh seems obsessed
with Molière and his time, believing that the French seventeenth
century was fraught with mystery and danger. In this atmosphere,
"Molière, dans un moule de comédie raisonnable, a écrit le
théâtre le plus noir de la littérature de tous les temps." [2] Anouilh
detects this paradox in all of Molière's life and works and often
refers to the classical dramatist's life as "inconsolable et gaie."
In fact, much of his writings on Molière seems to evolve around
similar kinds of antitheses: "rire énorme, rire heureux . . . petitesse,
laideur. . . . Nous sommes drôles . . . désespoir . . . l'horreur de
la condition humaine." [3] And this message is not mere rhetoric,
but the final thrust of all of Molière's works, "le grand message."
"Grâce à Molière le vrai théâtre français est le seul où on ne dise
pas la messe, mais où on rit, comme des hommes à la guerre — les
pieds dans la boue, la soupe chaude au ventre et l'arme à la
main — de notre misère et de notre horreur." [4]

This attitude, which tells more about Anouilh than about Molière, is best expressed in Anouilh's *La Petite Molière*. Orignally

---

[1] The following articles on stage productions of Molière are good.
Dussane's historical and technical account, "Molière et la scène," in *Molière,
Œuvres complètes*, edited by Bray-Scherer (Club du Meilleur livre, 1954),
vol. 1, pp. 55-95; Jean Duvignaud, "Répertoire des mises en scène," in
J. Audiberti, *Molière Dramaturge* (Arche, 1954), pp. 135-146; Hélène Henry,
"Toujours combattant, ou le grand Molière de Jacques Copeau à Roger
Planchon," in *Europe*, vols 441-442 (1966), pp. 136-150; Jacques Guichar-
naud, "Memorable Twentieth Century Performances of Molière's Play in
France," in *Molière, A Collection of Critical Essays* (New Jersey: Prentice
Hall, 1964), pp. 178-181.

[2] See "Textes critiques de Jean Anouilh," in Pol Vandromme, *Jean
Anouilh, Un Auteur et ses personnages* (La Table ronde, 1965), p. 141.

[3] *Ibid.*, pp. 141-143.

[4] *Ibid.*, p. 143; see J. Harvey's interesting comment in his *Anouilh, A
Study in Theatrics* (New Haven: Yale U. Press, 1964), p. 33.

a film scenario, it consists of a series of scenes from Molière's life, animated with dialogue from his comedies. In this skit, we are once again in search of the "Molière intime," the lover, husband, cuckold, a bitter man, old before his years, who resembles some of the protagonists of Anouilh's *pièces noires*. Instead of an exploration into some aspect of Molière *homme de métier*, we have a long series of petty domestic squabbles, tears, and false laughter, interspersed with scenes of questionable taste, including a rather grotesque one transposed from *L'Amour médecin*. [5] Many of the elements of the legend naturally find place here. Molière is really in love with the more-or-less faithful Madeleine, but he is obsessed with the deceitful and unsympathetic Armande, lusts after la de Brie and la du Parc, is watched over by the lovingly maternal La Forest, is deceived by the ingrate Baron, and jostled by contemptuous noblemen. *La Petite Molière* reads like a combination of subjectivist biography and *Le Roman comique*. The critic Guy Dumur aptly characterized this production when he wrote that, "Pour Anouilh, comme autrefois pour Pierre Brisson, la vie et l'œuvre de Molière se réduisent à l'image d'un petit bourgeois — 'moi qui ai été tapissier' — qui a eu bien tort d'abandonner sa chère Madeleine pour cette petite peste d'Armande, mais bon type au fond, pas méchant . . . . Une vie de Molière racontée aux lecteurs de *Match* ou de *Marie-Claire*." [6]

Jean-Louis Barrault's *Portrait de Molière* is more engaging. Here too are occasional references to the sad state of affairs in Molière's family. There is a long quote from Pierre Brisson which describes in imaginative detail Madeleine Béjart and her first meeting with Jean-Baptiste Poquelin. [7] Nonetheless, Barrault's portrait of Molière is a more interesting meeting of two theatre minds. From the start of this production, all the actors are on stage as in an *impromptu* and they perform as in a play within a play, with a narrator for the "enchaînements." Rapid movement, gestures, dance, and pantomime, all of the "commedia" features

---

[5] Jean Anouilh with Roland Laudenbach, "La Petite Molière," in *L'Avant Scène*, vol. 210 (1959), p. 34.

[6] Guy Dumur in *Théâtre populaire*, vol. 34 (1959), pp. 103-104.

[7] Jean-Louis Barrault, "Portrait de Molière," in *Cahiers Renaud-Barrault*, vol. 49 (1964), p. 12.

of which Barrault himself is a master, enliven the presentation. The scenes from Molière's works suggest Barrault's predilection for moliéresque farce, including excerpts from *Les Fourberies de Scapin, Le Bourgeois gentilhomme, Le Médecin malgré lui, Le Malade imaginaire, Le Sicilien, George Dandin,* among others. The long scenes from *Les Fourberies,* played zestfully and with a full measure of mime and movement, give a dimension which is authentically theatrical and appropriate to Molière. It is typical of Barrault to have searched in Molière for a synthesis of "ivresse dionysiaque" from the Italian tradition, and a very French and classical rhythm and poetry. This, at least, is more in the spirit of the "new Molière." [8]

Jacques Arnavon, an admirer of Antoine, proposed a number of methods for playing Molière in the naturalist style. His *Notes sur l'Interprétation de Molière* (1923) provides an interesting contrast to Jacques Copeau's notions of the "tréteau nu," a conception diametrically opposed to the naturalistic style. For Arnavon, the prime concern of the director in modern times is to establish "entre l'interprétation et la réalité un contact direct." [9] This can be best achieved by securing "un rapport permanent de vraisemblance entre le texte et le décor." [10] Arnavon argued that Copeau's technique, utilizing a minimum and highly stylized décor, demanded too much concentration and effort from the public and that these abstractions were accessible only to an elite. Moreover, without directly refuting Copeau's emphasis on the Italian style in moliéresque comedy, Arnavon denies that the "commedia" influence was important in the major comedies. Instead, he thinks the Italian farce tradition provided Molière only "artifices" and "ficelles" of the trade. For the great works, Molière composed carefully and slowly and was exclusively

---

[8] It should be recalled that these texts are not definitive statements on Molière by these two theatre professionals. Anouilh's direction of *Tartuffe* "en smoking," and in turn-of-the-century costumes, won considerable acclaim. Barrault's famous playing of Scapin (in Jouvet's production), and his playing of Mercure (in his own production of *Amphitryon*), are still considered memorable performances. This is the best medium for *rencontres* between Molière and contemporary men of the theatre.

[9] J. Arnavon, *Notes sur l'Interprétation de Molière* (Plon, 1923), p. 29.

[10] *Ibid.,* p. 49.

French in inspiration and execution: "... dans les grandes comédies, le souvenir du modèle italien, lorsqu'il y en eut un, est si vague, si intermittent, qu'il faut une sorte de recherche exégétique pour le découvrir." [11]

In his "éditions techniques," Arnavon expounded at length on his method. In *Le Misanthrope*, for example, "Si toute la pièce se joue dans un salon de la maison de Célimène, on se heurte aux invraisemblances les plus flagrantes." [12] Thus he imagines a scene on "la terrasse de Célimène" for Act I, "le salon de Célimène" for Acts II-IV, and "le parc de Célimène" for Act V. [13] The last act is typical of the entire method. For Alceste's final rejection and departure, the setting is dark and heavy with metaphoric meaning. The lines are taken literally, excluding any possible comic irony. In the final scenes Alceste speaks "... d'un air repentant, un peu humilié, mais en conservant la note pathétique et poétique." [14] There is clearly a direct relationship between "vraisemblance" and "sérieux" here, and the naturalistic approach leaves little room for comedy. The description of the closing scene is typical of the entire interpretation: "... le rideau tombe avec une extrême lenteur, de façon à grandir l'effet que produisent le départ d'Alceste, son sacrifice héroïque, solitaire, inconnu et probablement inutile. La lumière de la maison a baissé peu à peu. Alceste s'en va dans la nuit, où règne une vague clarté, un peu laiteuse." [15] It is perhaps not surprising that this production met with considerable succes in Scandinavia, for in pace and impulse it recalls the dramas of Ibsen and Strindberg. The underlying truth in Molière is sought in silences and innuendos, and the décor is always heavy. What these productions lack are the nervous dance-like movements which enhance and lighten the comedies and make them distinctively Molière's own.

Arnavon's reading of *Dom Juan* is even more debatable. As a "naturaliste," Arnavon could justify neither the ghost scene, nor the one depicting the don's supernatural damnation. The

---

[11] *Ibid.*, p. 401.

[12] *Ibid.*, p. 184.

[13] See the sketches in Arnavon's *Le Misanthrope de Molière* (Plon, 1930), hors texte, after pp. 16, 96, 240.

[14] *Ibid.*, p. 266.

[15] *Ibid.*, pp. 272-273.

critic-director is convinced that even for Molière, this hocus-pocus was but "un merveilleux qui l'encombrait." Judging that the modern sensibility could not accept such blatantly irrational events ("pratiquement impossible à supporter de nos jours"), he deleted the scene. To reconstruct the truncated last act, Arnavon imagines a more plausible and dramatic *dénouement*. By the fifth act, Done Elvire's brothers have come to wit's end in their attempt to coerce the capricious don into reassuming his marital responsibilities. Don Carlos, "homme de cœur ... entièrement sous l'empire de ses préjugés de caste," has argued and threatened but to no avail. Don Alonse however, is a man of fewer scruples and a more flexible sense of honor. He and a number of hired assassins wait in ambush for Dom Juan behind heavy mediterranean shrubbery and, at just the right moment, "Une salve de coups de feu claque ... Dom Juan reçoit les balles en pleine poitrine, et tombe, les bras étendus, l'épée lui échappant.... On entend les hommes remonter à cheval et le groupe s'éloigner." [16] Sganarelle appears briefly to cry "mes gages," and the curtain falls.

Arnavon's obsessions with coherent reality and his desire to fit Molière into a naturalistic mode tend to subvert all the elements of poetic fantasy which keep the comedies open to endless possibility. The result is a levelling of meaning, a diminished complexity, and a seriousness which many recent critics consider inappropriate to Molière. One can of course argue the merits of Arnavon's efforts and the assessment of his work has been mixed. [17] It is undeniable that he was attempting to rescue one of Molière's most ambiguous plays from some of the worst stage traditions of the nineteenth century. In so doing, he continued the efforts of his "maître à penser," Antoine, who had engaged well-known popular actors from the *cafés-concerts* to play Molière in a way more accessible to "le grand public." In spirit, these efforts at a form of *théâtre populaire* with Molière's works at the core of the comic repertory are laudable, and Arnavon's works should be seen in this context.

---

[16] J. Arnavon, *Le Dom Juan de Molière* (Copenhague: Gyldendal, 1947), pp. 433-434.

[17] In his *Molière: A New Criticism*, W. G. Moore expresses a generally favorable opinion on Arnavon's work; J. Guicharnaud, in his *Molière, Une Aventure théâtrale*, is more critical.

The most important and far-reaching *renouvellement* of Molière came from Jacques Copeau. Where Arnavon conceived of movement on stage only in practical terms, Copeau's conception is more poetic. For him, "mouvement" is a kind of body poetry (mime, gesture, acrobatics), which establishes its own dimension of metaphoric meaning when integrated into the action and ambience of the play. The inspiration for Molière is of course Italian farce, which Copeau believes Molière "a complètement assimilé et épuisé." [18] For maximum freedom of movement, Copeau designed an open stage, free of all unnecessary décor, one which was diametrically opposed in concept and function to the stage in the naturalist tradition. The idea was to utilize the entire open space exclusively for the action of the play, without any concern for local color or pedestrian realism. Copeau's new stage was called the "tréteau nu," and it consisted of a raised platform built in the form of connecting cubes; narrow stairs led from one level to another, with nothing to interfere with the direct visual contact between spectator and player. Raised and isolated, each actor assumed superhuman proportions and, in this dramatic framework, gestures became as important an idiom as language itself. The accent on gesture and action minimized the relationship between the play and literature and gave the play a new independence, the possibility of creating itself on stage according to its own laws. In this regard, Copeau's conception of *Les Fourberies de Scapin* is revealing: "Il n'y a ni forme dramatisée, ni psychologie possible, il y a du théâtre, il y a un mouvement." [19] This does not imply that moliéresque comedy can be reduced to a "charabia nerveux." Copeau staged his Molière productions, especially the farces, in such a way that every gesture is precisely executed within a highly stylized but dynamic décor. This kind of staging gave the effect of a rapid dance and demonstration, a synthesis more visual (theatrical) than literary. Fernandez referred to this special quality as "la profonde poésie du jeu" and described it aptly as, "des gestes bouffons se voulant tels et se moquant

---

[18] J. Copeau. *Le Théâtre populaire* (PUF, 1942), p. 60.
[19] Molière, *Les Fourberies de Scapin*, edited by J. Copeau (Le Seuil, 1951), p. 20.

quelque peu d'eux-mêmes [acquérant] tout à coup la dignité intellectuelle d'une analyse." [20]

The best example of Copeau's style was his 1917 production of *Les Fourberies de Scapin*. This production is largely responsible for the continued succes of the play since that time. In the director's own account of his *mise en scène*, he emphasizes that "Le tréteau, c'est déjà l'action, il matérialise la forme de l'action . . . ." [21] For *Les Fourberies* specifically, the bare juxtaposition of blocks connected by steep stairs represents a kind of physical obstacle course which will, of itself, differentiate the characters "selon leur aptitude physique." Copeau called his special stage a "piège à veillards . . . il doit donner la sensation de péril, on doit voir Argante suspendu au bord de l'incréé." [22] Thus the décor is integrated into the very substance of the comedy, underscoring the tension between youthfulness and dotage, vitality and senility, vigor and decrepitude. This tension, based as it is on physical aptitude, justifies Copeau's insistence on constant, rapid movement in the play. Thus, the *commedia* style is the impulse animating the action of the entire play. This production of *Les Fourberies de Scapin* is probably as close as Copeau ever came to his ideal of "une réalisation purement théâtrale et de pur mouvement."

Copeau always insisted upon the *destination* of Molière's works, the simple fact that they were written to be performed, that they were designed for actors and for the stage, and that this attitude implied a certain commitment to the public. But Copeau's outstanding contribution to understanding and renewing Molière remains his defense and illustration of the Italianate, *commedia dell'arte* style, the theatre-for-theatre aspect of moliéresque comedy. This is theatre of pure fancy, creating and recreating itself in a close interplay between the essence of human comedy and *le jeu scénique*. For Copeau, this latter element is the crux of Molière's theatre, for the works are not primarily comedies of ideas, but of technique. Only after the director has controlled the movement and action of the play, only after a complementary

---

[20] Ramon Fernandez, "Molière et Copeau," in *NRF*, vol. 33 (1929), p. 249.

[21] *Les Fourberies de Scapin, op. cit.,* p. 17.

[22] *Ibid.,* p. 21.

rhythm between language and the human body has been established in a dramatic composition, only then can ideas implicit in
the play spring forth. Copeau's commentaries on Molière's plays
in his edition of 1930 return to these concepts. Although his
notices on each play are often brief, they exude an intimacy
with the subject, at once professional and personal. The final
impression of Molière that emerges from Copeau's commentaries
is that of a man who lived primarily for the theatre, and who
managed to control and integrate technical proficiency and personal feeling into a unique comic form.

The ritualization of farce as an integral part of the ceremony
of moliéresque comedy, the stylization of gestures and décor,
and the rediscovery of the fun and value of elemental comic
forms profoundly reoriented staging and interpretation of Molière
in our time. Copeau's innovations have marked the most original
performances of all the lighter comedies, from Jouvet and Dullin,
to Vilar, Barrault, and Robert Hirsch.

Louis Jouvet's contribution to Molière was also quite substantial. While Copeau often passed as an over-analytical elitist,
Jouvet's public lectures on Molière in the late 1930's and after
the War thrust him into broad public view, and even the universit-
ies took note.

Jouvet's point of departure was his basic definition of Molière's comedies as *irréalité* or *surréalité*. "Une comédie de Molière
est un conte irréel, une chronique légendaire . . . . Les personnages
de Molière sont fous, non pas de cette folie qui occupe les
psychiatres, mais de cette sublime déraison, de cette extravagance,
de cet absolu qui différencient les humains et qui en isolent un
certain nombre au-dessus de la normale dans une zone où l'on
ne retrouve que les héros, les poètes et les saints. Car Molière,
qu'on a étiqueté l'homme de la raison, est l'homme qui a le mieux
senti et le mieux compris ce que c'était que le déraisonnable, et
son théâtre, qui paraît être le triomphe de la raison aux yeux de
ses commentateurs, est surtout, en vérité le royaume de cette
merveilleuse déraison qui s'appelle la poésie." [23] Reduced to the
fantasy of poetry, the source for the comedies could hardly be

---

[23] L. Jouvet, "Molière," in *Conférencia*, vol. 18 (1937), p. 291 and. p. 294.

literature, biography, philosophy, etc. As early as 1937, Jouvet
was certain that Molière could be explained and understood only
"par la tradition théâtrale, par le sens d'un métier éminemment
pratiqué par un homme marqué de la vocation." [24]

In truth, Jouvet is somewhat scornful of what he considers
the irrelevancy of academic and journalistic criticism. For him,
the actor and professional director alone can grasp the inner
meaning of Molière. In his writings, Jouvet suggests a mystical
union between the actor and the playwright once the former has
reached the peak of his role, once he has slipped imperceptibly
into the part and it in turn has consumed him. During this *réincar-
nation professionnelle*, Molière himself lives again in the actor
and the play takes on its original force. This idea of theatricality
runs through all of Jouvet's writings. "Une œuvre théâtrale ne
s'explique pas, elle se joue." [25] And, "La littérature dramatique
n'est pas préalable à l'art de jouer, elle est une conséquence
du jeu." [26] This "conséquence du jeu" is the only valid medium
for undestanding poetry and truth in moliéresque comedy. Jouvet
eschewed dubious traditions, exterior data (criticism), and pre-
conceived notions which might in any way have distorted his
understanding of a role. In other words, the actor alone is responsible for seizing upon the truth of his role in all of its theatrical
and poetic substance.

Paradoxically, it was his preoccupation with this noble ideal
which caused Jouvet so much anguish over his productions
of *Dom Juan* (1947) and *Tartuffe* (1950). In both cases, Jouvet
refused to compromise with traditional interpretation of the main
parts. His Dom Juan is not a "coureur de femmes," a mocking,
gay-blade libertine, but a reflective, self-conscious, and frightened
man on the verge of repentence. For Jouvet, Dom Juan's struggle
represented "l'angoisse de l'homme vis-à-vis de son destin: c'est
de salut et de damnation qu'il est question dans le *Dom Juan* de
Molière." [27]

---

[24] *Ibid.*, p. 297.
[25] *Ibid.*, p. 298.
[26] L. Jouvet, "Problèmes de la mise en scène des chefs d'œuvre classiques," in *Revue d'Histoire du théâtre*, vol. 4 (1951), p. 386.
[27] L. Jouvet, *Témoignages sur le théâtre* (Paris: Flammarion, 1952),
p. 32.

His Tartuffe is likewise troubled and ambiguous. Again Jouvet refused to cast the protagonist as the traditional hypocrite. In printed programs distributed at these performances, Jouvet quoted Georges Bernanos on "l'illusion de juger du menteur sur son mensonge." This key line is significant: "L'imposteur n'est peut-être sorti [de la verité] qu'une seule fois mais il n'a pu rentrer. C'est bien joli de dire qu'il le fait exprès. Qu'en sait-on?" [28] Jouvet accepts this idea for Tartuffe, believing that "il y a au fond de chaque être une énigme et un secret,... [une] ambiguïté, [une] dualité." [29] On stage, his Tartuffe was young, intelligent, rather melancholic, and gave the impression that he was not "totalement responsable de son mensonge." Actually he is often sincere, and Elmire shares the responsibility for his burst of passion. Jouvet's final statement on his reading is quite eloquent. "Au nom de qui juger? C'est au milieu de ces contradictions, de ces jugements partisans et singuliers, que s'élèvent et apparaissent l'impartialité, la générosité, l'universalité de l'œuvre classique et le génie même de Molière. Si Tartuffe ressemble à quelqu'un, il ne ressemble à personne en particulier, mais un peu à tout le monde en général." [30] As one critic put it, this effectively gives Tartuffe the benefit of the doubt. It is known that Jouvet suffered a crisis of the spirit in his last years and many believe that his *Dom Juan* and *Tartuffe* interpretations reflected his personal religious anxieties.

In his productions, Jouvet sought to renew Molière constantly and to surprise and engage the spectator, even the one seeing *Tartuffe* for the twentieth time. He denied tradition the right to predetermine the sense of any role or scene, and he played the text in all its complexities and ambiguities, letting it work out its solutions within its own framework. Only in this way can theatre redeem and sustain itself in total freedom. This is what Jouvet believed and what he thought Molière lived for. If Jouvet's interpretations occasionally went astray ("a superb mistake," said someone of his *Tartuffe*), no one could deny that his efforts had revitalized Molière's comedies for our time.

---

[28] *Ibid.*, p. 87.
[29] *Ibid.*, p. 88.
[30] *Ibid.*, p. 93.

The works of Arnavon, Copeau, and Jouvet represent the major
substantial contributions of professional men of the theatre to
Molière exegesis since 1900. But there were others. After her
sentimental biography, Mme Dussane also wrote an excellent
historical account of the technique of Molière productions from
the seventeenth century to Jean Vilar. Although she persists "à
rêver" on a number of issues, she does manage to contain her
reveries "toujours selon l'optique du métier." She believes that
Molière's great protagonists are essentially reflections of the
poet himself, that he drew them primarily from his own experiences, and that the evolution of his heroes follows the "trame" of
his own life. Occasionally this point of view leads to interesting
speculation. For example, Dussane maintains that Molière's "mous-
taches en parenthéses" were both a key and symbol for the
"masque" Molière adopted early in his career, particularly in
Sganarelle. For Alceste, however, and for that role only, Molière
opted to play without his usual moustache, and this immediately
changed the meaning and impact of the character. In Le Misanthrope, the "masque" has degenerated into nothingness revealing
the face of Molière, so that Alceste is a mirror image of his
creator. [31] In Le Malade imaginaire, she points out that Argan's
role is essentially an armchair role. Without having predicted
his death, as the old canard suggests, Dussane says simply that
Molière was ill and fatigued and so he designed the part with
"la possibilité de ne point porter les très lourds costumes d'alords,
et de jouer en robe de chambre et en pantoufles, en bonnet et
sans perruque, avec la ressource de longues scènes assises dans
un fauteuil." [32] Although many ideas remain speculative, Dussane's
keen sense for theatre and her admiration for Molière are unfailing.

Aside from Jouvet, at least two more of Copeau's students
established themselves in Molière interpretation. Charles Dullin's
playing of Harpagon is legendary, and his staging of L'Avare did
much to establish that play as one of the most popular of Molière's works for the general public. The idea of this production
was to broaden the perspective of the play beyond Harpagon's

[31] B. Dussane, "Molière à la scène," in Molière, Œuvres Complètes, edited
by Bray-Scherer (Club du Meilleur livre, 1954), vol. 1, p. 61.
[32] Ibid., p. 64.

massive presence and to develop the action as a complex inter-
working of the protagonist's obsessions and the plight of the
young lovers. This fuller presentation avoided the traditional,
narrow conception of the play as primarily a "portrait" of Harpagon. Technically, Dullin made sure the garden was partly visible
on the left of the stage, for it was considered "le lieu dramatique
par excellence." [33] The delightful, short ninth scene of Act III
"doit être réglée avec la précision d'un ballet." [34] Dullin suggested
further that on stage, Molière's prose should be delivered in a
special cadence which can be adapted to the rhythm of the action.

In his *Molière*, Léon Chancerel gave a brief and pertinent
account of the technical aspects and the operations of Molière's
troupe. Student of Copeau, player, director, president of the
"Société d'Histoire du théâtre," Chancerel was particularly know-
ledgeable about the practical side of theatre. He discusses Molière's directing, the architecture of the theatres in which he
played, the costumes and props, the *jeu*, and the uses of *masques*.
Chancerel also recalls how Molière kept active on two fronts
in order to keep his troupe at the center of attention: the grand
machine plays impressed the general public, and the more discreet
private showings *en visite*, in the residences of the nobility, kept
Molière in touch with the powerful courtisans. [35] The machine
plays were so succesful that in 1671, the King offered Molière
"la Grande Salle des machines des Tuileries." It was on this
stage, built and equipped by Vigarani, that Molière gave *Psyché*,
an unrivalled visual spectacle. The invitations for the *en visite*
performances began in 1661 when Molière and his troupe graced
Foucquet's guests at his Château de Vaux with an impressive
production of *Les Fâcheux*. Afterwards, Molière was often com-
manded to present plays in various *résidences royales*. In these
instances, the troupe played on a portable stage.

The importance of the material aspects of theatre in Molière's
works, which professional players and directors had always stress-
ed, was confirmed by a very academic volume in 1950. Jacques

[33] Molière, *L'Avare*, edited by C. Dullin (Le Seuil, 1946), p. 16.
[34] *Ibid.*, p. 121.
[35] Léon Chancerel, *Molière* (Presses littéraires de France, 1953), pp. 39
ff.; see also the long note (no. 17), pp. 44-45.

122   MOLIÈRE: TRADITIONS IN CRITICISM

Scherer's *La Dramaturgie classique en France* documented the importance of the material and technical sides of classical dramaturgy between 1600-1670, and the increasing need for adjusting esthetic requirements to the material reality of the theatre. The evolution he traces emphasizes the gradual shift from literary, rhetorical, and often non-dramatic forms in the early part of the century, to a fully elaborated, purely theatrical system of scene structure, machines, etc., around 1665. Scherer also stresses the technical aspects of Molière's art in his contribution to the Bray-Scherer edition of the *Œuvres complètes* which remains the outstanding edition for those interested in this aspect of the comedies.

Clearly, the contributions of professional men of the theatre in this domain have been special. By definition, Molière studies suggest academic, systematic inquiry, while the writings of the theatre professionals have been intuitive and imaginative. As it was for Molière, directing a troupe and playing the boards are often the main source of inspiration for their commentaries. The result is that their insights have been fruitful both in themselves, and for more systematic explotation by the academic critics. In any case, this dimension has added freshness and originality to Molière exegesis.

CHAPTER V

BOOKS AND BOARDS
EXEGESIS AND PERFORMANCE: 1960-1970

Documentation

In the area of scholarly documentation, there have been several major works of the highest interest and importance published during the last decade. Together they have added both quantity and precision to the sum of factual knowledge concerning Molière's private and professional life.

Mmes. M. Jurgens and E. Maxfield-Miller's *Cent Ans de recherches sur Molière, sur sa famille et sur les Comédiens de sa troupe* [1] is an excellent compendium which follows in the tradition of Beffara (1831) and especially Soulié (1863). The volume contains abstracts of all the major documentation research since Soulié's work and includes many contributions from the authors. By the most exacting standards, this volume is a model of its kind. To supplement and breathe life into the documents, the authors provide a sober and highly structured narrative of Molière's life. In the research section, over 700 items are either transcribed or synthesized in succinct résumés. Among the most interesting is the lease, dated 1644, for the "Jeu de Paume de la Croix-Noire." It was here that the *Illustre Théâtre* was first housed. After only six months it floundered, sending the young Poquelin first to debtor's prison and then into a thirteen-year exile from the Capital. Another item of interest is the detailed contract for the building and painting of the sets for the first *Dom Juan* production in 1665.

---

[1] M. Jurgens and E. Maxfield-Miller, *Cent ans de recherches sur Molière, sur sa famille, et sur les comédiens de sa troupe* (Imprimerie Nationale, 1963).

Here is first-hand information on the actual staging of this controversial play which is of particular interest since subsequent editions
indicate only that "la scène est en Sicile." Marie Hervé Béjart's
birth certificate is also reproduced here establishing her birth
date as 1593. This effectively proves that she was 48 years old
at the time of Armande's birth (and not 53 as was supposed), and
is another good reason to believe that Armande was Mme Béjart's
child and Madeleine's youngest sister. Mmes. Jurgens and Maxfield-Miller assume this as fact and inscribe Armande's name
in that place on the Béjart family genealogical table (p. 793). The
documents in this valuable volume are arranged chronologically
for easy consultation and are followed by a series of pertinent
historical "notices biographiques" on all important personages
in the dramatist-player's family and entourage. This imposing
"outil de travail" will serve well and for a long time to come.

Georges Mongrédien's edition of *Recueil des textes et des
documents du XVIIe siècle relatifs a Molière* [2] is a good companion
volume to the *Cent Ans*. The author extends his collections to
1705 and includes "tous les documents du XVIIè siècle, impri-
més et inédits, témoignages littéraires ou pièces d'archives relatifs à
Molière, à sa vie et à ses ouvrages" (p. 8). The *Receuil* is especially
complete in the area of "témoignages littéraires" which the *Cent
Ans* had not systematically recorded.

To add to this impressive list, there is A. J. Guibert's *Bibliographie des œuvres de Molière publiées au XVIIè siècle,* with
a *Supplément*. [3] Mlle Suzanne Dulait's *Inventaire raisonné des
autographes de Molière* [4] is a complete report on the subject,
with facsimile reproductions of the known signatures: there are
seventy-seven, and all but six are dated. There is also an excellent
mise au point on all related questions, including the problems of
authentication.

On the "ballet de cour," two important publications combine
for a good compendium on the subject: *L'Art du ballet de cour*

---

[2] Georges Mongrédien, *Recueil des textes et des documents du XVIIè
siècle relatifs à Molière* (C. N. R. S., 1964), 2 volumes.
[3] A. J. Guibert, *Bibliographie des œuvres de Molière publiées au XVIIè
siècle* (C. N. R. S., 1961); *Supplément* (C. N. R. S., 1965).
[4] Suzanne Dulait, *Inventaire raisonné des autographes de Molière* (Geneva: Droz, 1967).

en France, 1581-1643,[5] and its sequel, *Le Ballet de cour de Louis XIV, 1643-1672, mises en scènes.*[6]

Finally, two volumes by Maurice Descotes are of the highest interest to Molière studies. *Les Grands Rôles du théâtre de Molière* offer a good review of the evolution in stage interpretations of some fifteen-odd "grands rôles," including four from *Tartuffe* alone.[7] More recently, Descotes published a useful rapid account of Molière's "survie littéraire." His *Molière et sa fortune littéraire* parallels this study in its attempt at showing how succesive generations have understood and appreciated Molière's theatre.[8]

Biography

Contributions to Molière biography and related subjects have been exceptionally valuable during the 1960's. The most important publications range over two areas, research in literary history on the Armande problem, and straightforward biography.

One of the most vigorous pieces of literary history on Molière and his entourage in the last ten years is Georges Couton's long and substantive "L'Etat civil d'Armande Béjart, femme de Molière, ou Historique d'une légende."[9] This article is clearly intended to dispel the "brouillard" which has obscured this element in Molière's life, even since the poet's own time. No single argument will probably ever completely settle the matter, but Couton's

[5] M. McGowan, *L'Art du ballet de cour en France, 1581-1643* (C. N. R. S., 1963).

[6] M.-F. Christout, *Le Ballet de Cour de Louis XIV, 1643-1672, mises en scènes* (A. et J. Picard, 1967). On the theatres and troupes in seventeenth century France, see the excellent volumes by S. Wilma Deierkauf-Holsboer: *L'Histoire de la mise en scène dans le théâtre français à Paris de 1600 à 1673* (Nizet, 1960); *Le Théâtre de l'Hôtel de Bourgogne*, v. 1, 1548-1635 (Nizet, 1968); *Le Théâtre de l'Hôtel de Bourgogne*, v. 2, *Le Théâtre de la Troupe royale, 1635-1680* (Nizet, 1970).

[7] M. Descotes, *Les Grands Rôles du théâtre de Molière* (P. U. F., 1960). On *Tartuffe* exclusively, see H. P. Salomon, *Tartuffe devant l'opinion française* (P. U. F., 1962).

[8] M. Descotes, *Molière et sa fortune littéraire* (Bordeaux: Guy Ducros, 1970). A recent bibliography also lists, Brian Masters, *A Student's Guide to Molière* (London: Heinemann, 1970).

[9] Georges Couton, "L'Etat civil d'Armande Béjart, femme de Molière, ou Historique d'une légende," in *Revue des Sciences humaines*, 1964, pp. 311-351.

arguments should surely help to bring a measure of moderation. In method and style, this brief is in the best tradition of "la critique scientifique" which Michaut had mastered so well. Couton attempts to destroy the Armande legend and to establish that Armande was Madeleine Bejart's youngest sister and not her daughter. Having profited from the *Cent Ans de recherches*, Couton stands on the solid ground of the most recent findings, including Marie Hervé's birth certificate. But even that is not a clinching document, and the weight of this article is in its rational argumentation. Couton's summation is a good synthesis of how the calumnious legend was probably born, how it grew, and how it achieved credibility.

> A l'origine se situe une calomnie, que certains ont sans doute cru n'être qu'une bonne médisance, née dans le petit monde cancannier du théâtre et bien servie par les apparences. Elle a fait son chemin à la faveur des haines que suscitaient Molière et Armande, voire Madeleine. Certains de ses bons confrères comédiens ont fait de la sorte à Molière un mal plus durable et plus profond que les dévots les plus acharnés. Le prestige de l'imprimé aidant, le goût assez morbide, mais si largement répandu de l'information scandaleuse aussi, *La Fameuse comédienne* a été acceptée et même par Bayle, mieux inspiré d'ordinaire. L'entrée au *Dictionnaire* est une consécration.... Un dogme était établi contre lequel les actes les plus authentiques n'ont pu tout à fait prévaloir." [10]

Georges Couton's contribution appears to have attracted little attention. Thus far it has been rarely quoted and does not even appear in bibliographies where one might expect to find it. And yet no one dealing with the Armande question could avoid dealing with this excellent piece. More recently, Professor Jacques Scherer offered a gentlemanly general essay reaffirming Couton's findings. In a modest way it offers all the obvious, rational motives for believing that Armande was Madeleine's sister, and that Molière's marriage was less tumultuous and burdensome to the playwright than the legend suggests. [11] Perharps M. Scherer's quiet approach

---

[10] *Ibid.*, p. 351.
[11] Jacques Scherer, "Réflexions sur Armande Béjart," in *Revue d'Histoire littéraire*, 1969, 393-403. Before Couton and Scherer's contributions, Jacques

is an indication that interest in this marginal question is fading and that perhaps, as Michaut would have wished, it can finally be put to rest.

The contributions to interpretive biography have also been interesting. Jean Meyer's *Molière* [12] is the last biography to date by an actor and it follows in the tradition of Mme Dussane and Pierre Brisson. A number of old trinkets are resold: Molière's father is "le bonhomme Poquelin que l'on sait avare" (Michaut has some spirited pages against that canard); Madeleine is the mother of Armande; *L'Ecole des femmes* is the story of Molière's marriage, etc. Other interpretations are debatable, but less patent. In the chapter "La Politique du Roi," Meyer suggests that Molière was a willing and obedient servant to his king, and that it was Louis who pressed Molière into service for his political intrigues. Thus *Tartuffe* was written on commission and directed specifically against the "dévots." When the King left his hired poet-playwright in the lurch after the play was discontinued, Molière became disabused with his role and began concentrating on his art, leaving political issues to the professional courtiers. The rest of his career, from *Le Misanthrope* on, was spent in "Les plaisirs de la forme." But Molière had been "engagé" and had made commitments. Meyer then speculates on possible explanations for Molière's "sudden" deaht. The final lugubrious chapter is aptly entitled, "Au delà du rideau." His theory is that if Molière had lived and had had the leisure of a natural death, he might possibly have left behind a revealing and incriminating testament and many people could not allow this to happen. The biographer's conclusion suggests that Molière might have been poisoned, or at least was the victim of foul play.

Inconclusive speculation aside, there are other pertinent passages in Meyer's *Molière*, particularly a number of insights into character roles. For example, Meyer sees Orgon as frightened and spineless, a complex and very disturbing character. His avowal in the fifth act that he had prepared a "faux-fuyant" in the event

---

Chabannes had offered yet another installment in the long series of Armande novels: *Mademoiselle Molière* (Fayard, 1961). There is also a good dose of fiction in Léon Thoorens, *Le Dossier Molière* (Intercontinental du Livre, 1964).

[12] Jean Meyer, *Molière* (Librairie académique Perrin, 1963).

of an investigation is proof of his fear and hypocrisy. Tartuffe is no worse nor more illusive than he. But in Orgon this moral position is more cause for alarm for he had, in the recent past, been a responsible head of the family and loyal citizen. It is this sudden "envoûtement d'Orgon pour Tartuffe" which marks his painful downfall. This view and Meyer's insistence on the importance of the structure of Orgon's family within the total work are very much in line with recent major stage interpretations of the play.

Georges Bordonove's *Molière, génial et familier* is a more comprehensive and objective biography. The author apparently has no axes to grind, although he does object to some modern directors (Bourseiller, for one) who are only ideologues brandishing plays like *Dom Juan* "comme une oriflamme préalablement retouchée et peinte à leurs couleurs." [13] This "vie" profits from all the important recent documentation, making it the most up-to-date work available at this time. Its strength lies in the successful integration of all elements of Molière's life and career, without falling into domestic anecdote or excessive technicalities of the "métier." Documents are used efficiently and judiciously, and the synthesis on the complex Armande question is lucid and comprehensive. Inevitably, one can bicker with some of the biographer's interpretations, the short-sighted assessment of *Amphitryon* for example, Nonetheles, this is a solid, reliable biography, better than most in the last few years. Finally, for the general reader, Hallam Walker has provided a very readable and sound introduction to Molière's life and works in the well-known Twayne Series. [14]

Morality and Philosophy

Molière studies in the twentieth century have been especially preoccupied with the playwright's *morale,* with his moral, metaphysical and religious attitudes. This concern continued unabated in the 1960's and underlies much of the critical debate in the books and articles of the past decade. The Moore-Bray thesis did much to alter the framework of criticism in this area of exegesis,

---

13 Georges Bordonove, *Molière génial et familier* (Laffont, 1967), p. 264.
14 Hallam Walker, *Molière* (New York: Twayne Publishers, 1970).

attempting as it did to minimize the importance of "la morale
de Molière" in the comedies, preferring instead to view Molière
as a master technician in the craft of comedy. In this argument
for example, the *raisonneur* was no longer considered a character
of exemplary virtue, but an integral working part of the comic
construct. [15] Some still believed that Molière's *morale* was more
difficult to define than previous critics had believed and if
it could be explained, it would have to be deduced from the comic
fantasy of the total oeuvre. But this too is a tenuous procedure for
the "reason" of a comic text is often difficult to ascertain. Judd
Hubert alluded to this problem when he pointed out that "One
of the axioms in these comedies is that no amount of *raisonnement*
can ever persuade a person to change the impertinence of his con-
duct." And the would-be reasoners do not help a wit. They are often
"the most frustrated characters who, though rarely ridiculous in
themselves, provoke laughter by the inextricable situations in which
they find themselves — and by the inevitability of their failure." [16]
No single character tells all, no one role directs the consciousness of
the complex whole play. If there is a moral sense in the comedies,
it seems to take the form of "tâtonnements," gropings, which
do not seem to be directed toward some predetermined grand
scheme of universal truth. On the contrary, there was a growing
feeling in criticism that if in fact there was a spiritual voyage
in Molière's works, it was directed less toward society at large
than toward the poet's own inner consciousness. Robert Jouanny
wrote that *Le Misanthrope* projects "la trajectoire sauvage d'une
destinée que Molière dessine pour lui, parce qu'il a besoin d'y
voir clair." [17] In the great plays at least, Molière seems less concerned with moralisms of general edification, than with seeking
himself, with "seeing clear" in his on destiny.

---

[15] At least one well-known American critic dissented from this view.
Lionel Gossman argued that the reasoners are exemplary because they are
the only authentic personnages in Molière's works and that their genuineness
is the source of their equilibrated well-being. See Gossman's *Men and Masks:
A Study of Molière* (Baltimore: Johns Hopkins Press, 1963), especially
pp. 92-99.
[16] J. D. Hubert, *Molière and the Comedy of Intellect* (Berkeley: University of California Press, 1962), p. 118.
[17] *Molière: Œuvres complètes,* edited by Robert Jouanny (Classiques
Garnier, 1962), vol. 1, pp. 813-814.

Jacques Guicharnaud's conception of Molière's "aventure théâ-trale" is germane to this idea. In the three great plays at the apex of Molière's career, Guicharnaud plots a movement toward an impasse which is finally manifested in *Le Misanthrope*. This impasse is double: dramaturgical, in that it reaches the ultimate limits of comedy and veers towards the darker domain of "le drame," and profoundly moral, for it rests on an implicit concept-ion of the human condition. In the masterpiece of 1666, Guichar-naud suggests that Molière reached the zero degree of conflict, revealed in the irreducibility of human nature, and the total impossibility of beings to relate unselfishly to each other, to share intimately a common destiny. The root "défaut irréductible" is the cardinal sin all classical moralists warned against, "l'amour de soi." Accordingly, in terms of its resolution, the play opens not onto a harmonious world, but onto one ultimately defined by "la confrontation des exigences qui se solde . . . par l'affirmation d'une permanence du désaccord . . . la dispersion des êtres. Le monde n'est plus fait du conflit de la tyrannie et du consentement, mais du jeu sans solution des résistances mutuelles." [18] But there is no method or scheme on the poet's part, no intention of purpose. Guicharnaud deals deftly with what he thinks Poquelin's most intimate intuitions might have been, but only in terms of his art. From Brunetière to Guicharnaud, "la philosophie de Mo-lière" evolved from a conscious, systematic engagement to a subtle, poetic, more private impression.

In more recent years, debate has continued and diversity of opinion still prevails. In some cases, old questions resurfaced. For example, a recent critic on *Dom Juan* and *Tartuffe* has asked again, "Molière, fut-il impie?" The response of course, was markedly less peremptory than in the days of Jeannel, Veuillot, and Perrins. Nonetheles, the general opinion persists that to a degree, the playwright did express an attitude which was essentially irreligious. For Richard Coe, Molière might indeed have been impious, but he was "not an atheist." Dom Juan is struck down for his intellectual arrogance ("immense, almost transcendental self-confidence"); his sin is wanting "to argue

---

[18] J. Guicharnaud, *Molière, Une Aventure théâtrale* (Gallimard, 1963), p. 533.

with God on God's own level, God being the only form of mind that can make the argument worth while." [19] Raymond Picard nuanced the case by suggesting that the play was "impie" only to the extent that, "pour les docteurs et les prédicateurs," it represented "une satire diabolique de la vraie religion." [20] But for members of Louis' court, Molière's most important constituency, *Tartuffe* was almost certainly not considered offensive. In their view, "la religion [doit] de toute nécessité — il faut s'y résigner — être adaptée au monde." [21] Jacques Scherer argues that an unprejudiced reading of *Tartuffe* reveals that Molière was more or less indifferent to religion. And yet this indifference was sufficient to keep him in the mainstream of his contemporaries, as his attitude in *Dom Juan* suggests. Here Profesor Scherer sees Molière taking a clear stand against one of the more dangerous elements of the libertine creed: "la leçon manifeste de la pièce qui est si claire ... [et] aisée à formuler: l'athéisme, racine des vices et des crimes de Dom Juan, appelle une punition exemplaire et spectaculaire par le Ciel... La pièce est contre l'athéisme, ce qui est parfaitement admissible pour le public de Molière." [22] Philip Butler's reading of *Tartuffe* insists more on the author's intent. Like Michelet, he argues

---

[19] R. N. Coe, "The Ambiguity of Dom Juan," in *Australian Journal of French Studies*, v. 1 (1964), p. 34. These remarks seem to have been inspired by Jean Vilar's famous production of *Dom Juan* at the T. N. P. (1953). For an opposite view of the same Vilar production, see R. Barthes' "Le Silence de Dom Juan" in *Les Lettres nouvelles* (1954). Here the "silence" Vilar projected in the title role is a blatant epression of atheism, brandished at a bourgeois public for the first time in recent history. See also R. Grimsley, "The Dom Juan Theme in Molière and Kierkegaard," in *Comparative Literature*, v. 6 (1954), pp. 316-334.

[20] R. Picard, "*Tartuffe*, production impie?" in *Mélanges ... offerts à Raymond Lebègue* (Nizet, 1969), p. 239. In *Le Malade imaginaire*, C. François thinks Molière went much further in attacking religion: "Médecine et religion chez Molière, deux facettes d'une même absurdité," in *The French Review*, v. 42, pp. 665-672. See also Peter Nurse's good edition of *Le Malade imaginaire* (Oxford: The University Press, 1965) and his discussion of these problems.

[21] *Ibid.* George Couton brings some noteworthy clarifications of a historical nature on the connotations of "hypocrisie" and "imposteur," showing how "hypocrisie" could actually be used in service to dogma instead of being a sin against it. "*Tartuffe* et le péché d'hypocrisie, cas réservé," in *Revue d'Histoire littéraire*, 1969, pp. 404-413.

[22] Jacques Scherer, *Sur le Dom Juan de Molière* (Sedes, 1967), p. 79.

that Molière's play is directed especially against the insidious authority of the "directeur de conscience." To this end, the dramatist's resolve is deliberate: "la position prise par l'auteur et ses intentions polémiques sont parfaitement nettes: ce qui'il raille et discrédite, ce n'est pas simplement le mauvais directeur . . . c'est le principe de la direction telle que l'a conçue la Contre-Róforme." [23]

These bids at specifying a religious attitude in moliéresque comedy are perhaps a less recurring preoccupation in criticism than the desire to situate the comic poet in a philosophical or ethical tradition. Here again, practically all views have been restated since 1963. A recent study interprets *Dom Juan* in light of a determined libertine philosophy. In terms of critical opinion, its conclusions take us back many years when asking, "Molière, dont les malheurs de sa vie ont dû accentuer la gravité naturelle de son esprit, n'était-il pas Dom Juan? N'a-t-il pas éprouvé les mêmes craintes que lui, partagé les mêmes préoccupations?" [24] Another decided opinion views Alceste's drama as an internal conflict between stoicism and epicureanism. Originally a neo-stoic in matters of love, the hero is tempted and almost compromised by Célimène's forceful epicureanism. In the end however, Alceste recognizes the futility of such a pact and comes to the only possible solution: "il ira s'enfermer dans la retraite . . . il va devenir un stoïcien renforcé." [25]

These attitudes are not typical however. The more common efforts of the past decade on this question have avoided untenable theories associating the playwright with a single, well-defined

---

[23] Philip Butler, "*Tartuffe* et la direction spirituelle au 17è siècle," in *Modern Miscellany Presented to Eugene Vinaver* (Manchester: Manchester University Press, 1969), p. 61. See also Butler's companion piece to this article, "Orgon le dirigé," in *Gallica* (Cardiff: University of Wales Press, 1969), pp. 103-119. Michelet's vigorous contribution to the subject is in his *Du Prêtre, de la Femme, de la Famille* (Comptoir des imprimeurs. 1845), especially Part I, Chapter 6.

[24] Jean-Marie Teyssier, *Réflexions sur Dom Juan de Molière* (Nizet, 1970), p. 185. For another uninspired contribution which insists on perceiving "la foi religieuse" in all of Molière's works, see A. Garreau, *Inquisitions* (Editions du Cèdre, 1970).

[25] L. Hippeau, *Essai sur la morale de La Rochefoucauld* (Nizet, 1967), p. 180.

dogma. There remains nonetheles, a strong feeling that the total œuvre does reflect "an attitude of mind" on certain moral issues of the poet's time. "Après tout, dixit Raymond Picard, il n'est pas interdit à un homme de théâtre d'avoir des idées." The real problem as it now exists for the objective commentator was summed up recently by an English academic: "The difficulty is not to find social, ethical and religious statements in Molière's plays, but to establish which one of them, if any, he stood by." [26]

In line with this opinion, the same critic, R. Fargher, opines that Molière was in fact a moralist, that his reasoners are spokesmen who express a kind of proto-Voltairian rationalism. "It seems to me abundantly clear that the Molière who mocked Holy Scripture, who created the sceptic Béralde, who poured scorn on the obscurantist opponents of modern science, was something less than 'bien pensant' and that his plays do manifest an attitude of mind which in the following century informed another comic genius, Voltaire." [27] For Peter Nurse, Molière's characteristic "voice" is his scepticism. "The final impression that emerges from Molière's work . . . is one which was formulated by the Sceptic Montaigne." Thus Molière's attitude is "the traditional Sceptic-Epicurean view of the 'human comedy'; one if its earliest formulations is in Lucretius' De Natura rerum, while it is also found in La Mothe le Vayer." [28] The humanistic impulse in Molière's work is all the more remarkable in that it flourished under duress, at the center of Louis XIV's court. But even in this alien environment, "jamais Molière . . . ne s'est trahi comme dramaturge humaniste, héritier

---

[26] R. Fargher, "Molière and his Reasoners," in *Studies in French Literature Presented to H. W. Lawton* (Manchester: Manchester University Press, 1968), p. 114. See also, Jacques Morel, "Molière ou la dramaturgie de l'honnêteté,) in *L'Information littéraire*, v. 15 (1963), p. 189.

[27] *Ibid.*, p. 116. For an opposing view, see the excellent essay by F. L. Lawrence, *Molière and the Comedy of Unreason* (New Orleans: Tulane Studies in Romance Languages and Literatures, 1968); also his "The Raisonneur in Molière," in *L'Esprit créateur*, v. 6 (Fall 1966), pp. 156-166.

[28] Peter Nurse, *Classical Voices* (London: Harrop, 1971), p. 178 and p. 184. From the same author, see also: "Le Rire et la morale dans lœuvre de Molière," in *XVIIè Siècle*, v. 52 (1951); "Essai de définition du comique moliéresque," in *Revue des Sciences humaines* (1964), pp. 9-24; "Molière and Satire," in *The University of Toronto Quarterly* (1967), pp. 113-128. A similar and interesting view is in G. S. Burgess, "Molière and the Pursuit of Criteria," in *Symposium* (Spring 1969), pp. 5-15.

de la tradition d'Erasme et de Montaigne." [29] This idea has become, particularly since Antoine Adam's influential *Histoire ...*, an accepted view in most academic criticism today. It should be repeated that this view considers the humanistic thrust in Molière's work as an inherent, instinctive impulse, as opposed to polemical proselytizing. It is one thing to place Molière within the tradition of Erasmus and Montaigne, and quite another to see him as a disciple of Gassendi or La Mothe Le Vayer.

But questions persist and responses remain provisional for moliéresque criticism continues apace. Although no definitive conclusions are possible, there are a few discernable tendencies. In terms of definable dogma, no specific religious or philosophical credo emerges clearly from Molière's work. Even the attempt at organizing ideas and determining the nature of their meaning seems a most perilous task. In truth, efforts to particularize anything concerning ideas, philosophy or religion in the thirty-odd comedies seem destined to remain on the level of transient hypothesis. This accounts for the reorientation in criticism recently from specificity to generality. The fact of the matter is that Molière's comic structures function too efficiently within the multi-levels of fantasy, irony, and those qualities of the imagination which are the most ethereal, the most illusive. As someone pointed out years ago, the sum total of Molière's work represents "une œuvre de dislocation" wherein necessarily, "la pensée hésite sur les conséquences à tirer." [30] In the arguments and counter-arguments on Molière's *morale,* at least one idea seems to have been permanently dashed, the conception of Molière as revolutionary thinker. "La belle plaisanterie pourtant: Molière ne s'est pas dit un beau matin, comme pourrait le faire quelque personnage humouristique d'un film de René Clair: 'Je m'en vais déblayer le chemin pour l'Encyclopédie, souffler des apostrophes célèbres à Beaumarchais et préparer la Révolution Française!'" [31]

---

[29] Marc Fumaroli, "Microcosme comique et macrocosme solaire," in *Revue des Sciences humaines*, v. 145 (1972), p. 114.

[30] A. Villiers, "Dom Juan ou le libertin de l'esprit," in *La Revue théâtrale*, v. 4 (1947), p. 33.

[31] *Ibid.*

It seems finally, that the Moore-Bray "estheticism" steered opinion away from the excesses of the "Molière penseur" attitude. Bénichou's work also rendered virtually untenable, for most critics, the view of Molière propagandist of the prudent, "bon bourgeois" ethic. Finally, without addressing itself directly to these questions, Professor Guicharnaud's magistral study clearly avoids systems and suggests that Molière's real "aventure" was deeply personal, quasi-existential. The sum of these shifts of focus toward more suppleness is reflected in this recent statement on "la philosophie de Molière": "Elle ne se réduit pas aux théories simplistes professées par Ariste, Cléante, Philinte et autres adeptes de la raison: accepter la vie comme elle est, agir avec prudence, fuir toute extrémité. Elle est dans l'atmosphère de son théâtre, plus facile à sentir qu'à formuler. Elle s'exprime sous forme de suggestions discrètes et non de conseils impérieux." [32]

But all is not yet said. For surely Alfred Simon's dictum was prophetic: "On risque de disputer encore longtemps sur la leçon qui émane des comédies de Molière." [33]

Structure Studies

Although not "structuralist," several studies of recent date have dealt with various types of structure in the comedies. In *Structures de Tartuffe*, [34] Jacques Scherer defined four "structures": "historique, idéologique, dramaturgique, gestuelle." His analyses of the acts, scenes, action, and resolution of the play follow the lines of inquiry already established in his *Dramaturgie classique*, and in his part of the "Club du Meilleur Livre" edition of Molière's works. Perhaps the most original pages of this study of *Tartuffe* are devoted to the "structure gestuelle. A few

---

[32] P. Salomón, *Précis d'Histoire de la littérature française* (Masson, 1964), p. 158.

[33] A. Simon, "La Puissance de l'illusion comique," in *Cahiers Renaud-Barrault*, v. 26 (May 1959), p. 13.

[34] Jacques Scherer, *Structures de Tartuffe* (S. E. E. S., 1966); see also his *Le Dom Juan de Molière* (S. E. E. S., 1967). For an interesting account of Louis Jouvet's notes and statistics on *Tartuffe*, see J. Jomaron, "A Propos d'un document de mise en scène," in *Revue d'Histoire du théâtre*, v. 18 (1966), pp. 210-215.

exaggerations aside (i. e., the function of the door), there are some excellent pages on the "gestuelle" of surprise, warning, desire, dance, etc. Many of these remarks coincide with some of the current interpretations of Molière on stage. Marcel Gutwirth's *Molière ou l'Invention comique* traces the evolution of prototypes in the early comedies to the protagonists of the great comedies.[35] The development here moves from traditional types in older French sources ("la matière gauloise"), and from Italian farce ("la matière d'Italie"), toward a new form of social comedy.

By far the most ambitious — and debatable — structure study of the 1960's was Charles Mauron's *La Psychocritique du genre comique.* Here, of course, the structures are "psychiques." Attempting to establish the comic poet's personal and psychological "mythe personnel" as he had for Mallarmé and Racine, Mauron found that the recurrent image in moliéresque comedy, "le blondin fourbant un barbon," could hardly be construed as Molière's personal and psychological obsession. They were quite obviously traditional types of the comic genre and so, using Molière as a departure and constant point of reference, Mauron set out to apply his psycho-critical method to the entire genre. Essentially Mauron sees the traditional types ("canevas comiques") functioning in a complex series of "renversements triomphaux de situations achétypiques angoissantes." In this context, comedy is understood as being a "fantaisie du triomphe" in favor of "le fils" ("jeune blondin"), over "le mauvais père" ("le barbon"). This basic construct is derived from the Oedipus conflict and although comedy constantly suggests, it never really confronts the violence and parricide of this elemental conflict.

Mauron distinguishes between indirect expressions of violence in farce ("l'esprit tendancieux"), with aggressiveness, obscenity, scatology, etc., and the more sublimated expression of a potential "fond oedipien" in precious, overly galant and un-comic comedies ("l'esprit inoffensif"). Molière's art consists in combining these two tendencies in viable comedy, with *L'Ecole des femmes* as an example of the first synthesis: "Le rapport Arnolphe-Agnès

---

[35] Marcel Gutwirth, *Molière ou l'invention comique* (Minard, 1966).

sert de thème à l'esprit tendancieux; le rapport Arnolphe-Hora-
ce sert de thème à l'esprit inoffensif." [36]
What Mauron finds most interesting in Molière's comedies
is the almost total absence of the mother and the fact that the
"ridicule" is always directed to the father or to a father-image
type. This attitude has a particular significance: "la fantaisie
de triomphe sur le père, dans l'œuvre de Plaute devient, dans
celle de Molière, une fantaisie de cocuage." [37] Mauron refrains
from a detailed interpretation of these signs, but devotees of Freud
and other contemporary psychoanalysts would have sufficient
theoretical data here to make a prognosis of Molière's "personna-
lité inconsciente." The reader of Mauron occasionally regrets
that analyses of individual plays are often brief and elliptical,
and that many of the insights are very abstract. But this remains
a very laudable contribution to modern Molière studies.

Baroque

It would be extraordinary if the considerable vogue of the
Baroque in literary history and criticism on seventeenth century
French Literature had not touched Molière exegesis. It did of
course, especially with regard to *Tartuffe, Dom Juan*, and, to a
lesser degree, *Le Bourgeois gentilhomme*. It began, discreetly,
as early as 1948 with W. G. Moore's article on *Tartuffe*. [38] Without
using baroque terminology, Moore's explication of *Tartuffe* in
terms of masks and role-playing clearly suggested characteristics
which later critics of the baroque would use extensively. A decade
later, Alfred Simon contended that all of Molière's theatre could
be described in baroque features: "ce grand jeu des métamorpho-
ses ... ce jeu de la comédie dans la comédie par quoi le théâtre
réfléchit sur lui-même, et engloutit la réalité de l'homme dans
la puissance de l'illusion comique." [39] More recently, Jacques

---

[36] Charles Mauron, *La Psychocritique du genre comique* (José Corti,
1964), p. 48. The inquiry on Molière began in Mauron's *Des Métaphores
obsédantes aux mythes personnels* (José Corti, 1964), pp. 270-298.
[37] Charles Mauron, *La Psychocritique du genre comique, op. cit.*, p. 133.
[38] W. G. Moore, "*Tartuffe* and the Comic Principle in Molière," in
Modern Language Review (1948), pp. 47-53.
[39] Alfred Simon, "La Puissance de l'illusion comique," in *Cahiers
Renaud-Barrault*, v. 26 (May 1959), p. 14 and p. 16.

138 MOLIÈRE: TRADITIONS IN CRITICISM

Guicharnaud also referred to baroque elements in *Tartuffe,* especially in the "vocabulaire baroque" of the protagonist's seduction
attempt, the role of the *Exempt,* and in the play's resolution. [40]

It is Jean Rousset's work however, which specifies most clearly
the points of contact between Molière's comedies and the baroque
temperament of the seventeenth century. For Rousset, one of the
basic elements of the baroque imagination — especially as manifested in the theatre — is the emphasis on sumptuous décor, movement, inconstancy, masks, all the primary ingredients for creating
illusion. And according to Rousset, in all of seventeenth century
French theatre there is an effort at maximizing illusion. This
effort attempts to convince the spectator that he is involved in
reality, and the actor that he is not playing a fictive role. From
this point of view the critic contends that Molière's comedies
offer good examples of baroque style. Arguing against Guicharnaud's contention that the structure of *Tartuffe* is basically classical, Rousset sees the protagonist as "un personnage de souche
baroque... un personnage en mutation, ou un personnage en
état de déguisement, se donnant pour autre qu'il n'est." [41] But it is
Dom Juan who best exemplifies the baroques sensibility in Molière.
He belongs to the class of baroque heroes who are the "deliberate
comedians, the masked men who remain masters of their masks
and of their power of illusion." [42] This "unequalled virtuoso of
inconstancy and disguise" is Molière's most talented mask-player:
"The son and heir who sows wild oats has been transformed into an
outlaw impatient of any dependency, whether it be social or religious. At the same time, he has become a reasoning philosopher
for whom 'the heavens' and their manifestations represent an
absurd joke, a scandal in the eyes of reason that also wants
to be autonomous and sovereign." [43] *Le Bourgeois gentilhomme*
reflects another tendency in the later baroque, a movement toward
death, and in theatrical terms, a sumptuous décor which crashes

---

[40] J. Guicharnaud, *Molière, Une Aventure théâtrale* (Gallimard, 1963),
pp. 93 and 166-169; on the non-baroque structure of *Dom Juan,* cf. p. 337.
     [41] J. Rousset, *La Littérature de l'Age baroque en France* (Corti, 1961),
p. 248.
     [42] J. Rousset, "Dom Juan and the Baroque," in *Diogenes,* vol. 14
(Summer 1956), p. 13.
     [43] *Ibid.,* p. 15.

in on itself. "M. Jourdain, se persuadant de son identité imaginaire par le spectacle vestimentaire qu'il déploie pour lui-même [est] victime heureuse de l'illusion, entrant en bonne foi dans une féerie qu'il se crée, circulant émerveillé dans le palais enchanté que devient à ses yeux son salon bourgeois — mais uniquement à ses yeux seuls, tous les autres refusant d'y croire. C'est ce dernier trait, ce refus exprès ou sournois de se laisser prendre au merveilleux du spectacle qui fait de la fête et du théâtre un dévoilement de l'univers de l'enchantement par le démontage des mécanismes de cette identification naïve au personnage fictif, fondement de l'illusion théâtrale." [44]

To date, baroque criticism has been but a small part of Molière studies. In the main, however, it has dealt with important problems in moliéresque comedy and has therefore been at the center of critical attention. At this stage, the groundwork has been done but the definitive work on "Molière baroque" is yet to be written.

Marxist-oriented Criticism

The literature of the seventeenth century has been an area of predilection for Marxist or Marxist-inspired critics of the past twenty years. Lucien Goldmann's *Le Dieu caché* is the outstanding work in the genre, but it deals only in a cursory way with Molière. In fact at this time, there is no substantial work from a Marxist critic on Molière's total œuvre, although there has been some activity on a more modest scale. Between 1959 and 1971, the Marxist-oriented series of texts, *Les Classiques du peuple* (from "Les Editions sociales"), published five critical editions of individual comedies: *Tartuffe* (1959), *Le Misanthrope* (1963), *L'Ecole des femmes* (1964), *Dom Juan* (1968) and *Les Femmes savantes* (1971). Each volume contains a substantial introduction and ample notes on the texts, usually inspired by a Marxist viewpoint. While not excessively doctrinaire in their critical method, the editors of these editions do accept the

---

[44] J. Rousset, *L'Intérieur et l'Extérieur* (Corti, 1968), pp. 179-180. See also, Rousset's "L'Ile enchantée. Fête et théâtre au 17ème siècle," in *Mélanges ... offerts à M. Brahmer* (Warsaw, Poland, 1967), pp. 435-441; and, in a related way, Regula Billeter, *Les valeurs spectaculaires dans l'œuvre de Molière* (Boulogne: Imprimerie Maleva, 1962).

basic Marxist principle that "l'existence sociale détermine la conscience." Hence, each Molière comedy is seen as deeply embedded in the historical and social matrix which constituted Louis XIV's "monde." Predictably, these critics reject the formalist approach to Molière and insist instead on the realism in the comedies. For them, René Bray's view of Molière as a man of the theatre is considered "excessif," "arbitraire," and tainted with "esthéticisme." Specifically, these critics oppose the tendency "qui consiste à vider l'ensemble de l'œuvre de Molière de tout contenu idéologique et à réduire l'auteur au rôle de faiseur génial de comédies, de metteur en scène et d'acteur." [45] Bray's formalism is not appropriate because, "pareille méthode convient particulièrement mal à Molière, dont les œuvres portaient sur la scène des questions étroitement liées à l'évolution et aux conflicts de la société sous le règne de Louis XIV." [46] An example, extreme perhaps, of the degree to which one can perceive Molière's work as embedded in a specific social context is this characterization of *Dom Juan:* "La pièce peint toute une époque, toutes les classes de la société française: la Cour, les bourgeois de Paris (M. Dimanche), le peuple et les 'culs-terreux' (Pierrot). Sganarelle n'est plus un valet italien, un fripon, comme Scapin ou Mascarille, toujours prêt, sans discussion ni remords, à servir les vices de son maître, mais un homme du peuple, sensé, naïf, craintif. Pierrot, le paysan, que l'on met souvent entre parenthèses, ce personnage épisodique, arbitraire, fait pour recevoir des coups, prend une conscience; ce pauvre bougre n'est-il pas, au bout du compte, une sorte d'anti-Dom Juan, d'anti-seigneur, victime et symbole des injustices de l'époque?" [47]

---

[45] Molière, *Le Misanthrope*, edited by E. Lop and A. Sauvage (Editions sociales, 1963), p. 91, n. 1. L. Goldmann's most pertinent remarks on Molière are in his *Sciences humaines et philosophie* (Editions Gonthier, 1966), pp. 114-115. Also, there is a substantial study by a Russian scholar which one assumes is Marxist-inspired, but it has not yet been translated: G. Bojadziev, *Molière* (Moscow: Iskusstvo Editions, 1967).

[46] Molière, *Le Tartuffe*, edited by Suzanne Rossat-Mignot (Editions sociales, 1959), p. 11.

[47] Molière, *Dom Juan*, edited by Guy Leclerc (Editions sociales, 1968), p. 19. Out of fairness, let it be restated that these editions are not "hardline" Marxist interpretations. They are heavily oriented toward History and present Molière and his art as consciously reflecting the conflicts and ideolog-

In the view of these Marxist-oriented critics, Molière was without doubt an "auteur progressiste." In *L'Ecole des femmes*, he
is a feminist: "il attaque les survivances de la morale féodale,
c'est-à-dire une oppression séculaire qui pesait encore sur les
jeunes filles, et dans une moindre mesure, sur les jeunes gens
dans la deuxième moitié du XVIIè siècle." [48] The same liberalism
is at work in *Les Femmes savantes*, contrary to the opinions of
many other critics. "L'auteur de *L'Ecole des femmes* n'est pas,
dix ans après, devenu antiféministe parce que dans *Les Femmes
savantes* il fustige Armande, qui récuse, par principe et par gloriole,
toute féminéité, ou Philaminte, dont le féminisme ne tend qu'à
singer les hommes, et pas les meilleurs. Et si, maintenant, il
semble être à la fois avocat et détracteur de la cause féminine,
c'est que toujours partisan convaincu de l'accès des femmes à
l'instruction, il condamne les extravagances d'un certain monde.
Ce qu'il dénonce, une fois encore, c'est l'excès, le pédantisme, la
fausse science qui conduisent à la sottise." [49]

Following the same lines of argument, it was Molière's "conscience" which gave his own version of *Dom Juan* a special value.
In contrast to earlier interpretations of the same theme, Molière
minimizes the supernatural and exotic elements in his play, as
well as the anecdotal and romanesque marginal adventures. In
place of these insignificant ingredients, he adds a sharp satire
of hypocrisy in a realistic framework which contemporary spectators immediately recognized as reflecting their situation, their
country, their time. "Et puis il y a toutes ces allusions à des
questions d'intérêt contemporain: les railleries contre les méde-
cins, ... l'allusion à la question du tabac, l'évocation des grands
problèmes philosophiques (acte III)." [50] *Tartuffe*, "un chef d'œuvre
réaliste," has similar value, for it reflects all the problems of the
time: conflict over Port-Royal, polemics concerning the Jesuits

---

ical struggles in Louis XIV's France. In that sense it would seem more
accurate to call this criticism "marxistic;" in French, the term is simply
"marxisant."

[48] Molière, *L'Ecole des femmes*, edited by Suzanne Rossat-Mignot (Editions sociales, 1964), p. 47.

[49] Molière, *Les Femmes savants*, edited by J. Cazalbou and D. Sévely
(Editions sociales, 1971), p. 37.

[50] *Dom Juan, op. cit.*, p. 19.

and their casuistry, animosity toward "la cabale des dévots" and "les directeurs de conscience." Moreover, it is particularly enlightening for its "valeur historique profonde, saisissant le développement de la société de classes." [51]

Although P. Bénichou's *Morales du grande siècle* is anything but patently Marxist, its orientation is sufficiently sociological and historical to interest all "marxistes" and "marxisants" and, along with L. Goldmann's work, it is often cited in these *Classiques du peuple* editions. Surprisingly however, all of these critics disagree sharply with Bénichou on whether or not Molière was a bourgeois author. Bénichou's dictum (which Goldmann apparently accepted) was that Molière was "antibourgeois" and "conformiste," at least in relation to the status quo of "la noblesse de cour" at Louis' court. Since the classic Marxist view of the bourgeoisie in the *ancien régime* insists on its progressive character, Molière "progressiste" could not have been anti-bourgeois. The editor of the *Tartuffe* volume, Suzanne Rossat-Mignot, argues that Molière was not at all contemptuous of the bourgeoisie. On the contrary, by his criticisms he put that social class on guard against the danger to its potential power within the Court and to its future progressive development. In terms of "l'idéologie progressiste," this fore-warning was invaluable because "la première condition de l'humanisme véritable est de voir clair et de se débarasser des illusions." [52]

For these critics, *Le Misanthrope* presents the most critical view of society at the peak of Louis XIV's reign. Here the marxist critics refuse all recourse to universal values and to "psychologisme" to explain the comportment of the protagonists, like for example, Jasinski's idea of Célimène exemplifying "l'éternel féminin." The coherence of these characters can be explained only in view of their station and function in the society of the 1660's, a society which was overwhelmingly male-dominated, relegating women to ignorance and servitude without even minimal rights

---

[51] Molière, *Le Tartuffe, of. cit.,* p. 47.
[52] Ibid. For another vigorous reconsideration of Bénichou and Goldmann, cf. Guy Leclerc's introduction to the *Dom Juan* edition in this series, pp. 36-37, note 2.

or privileges; for every intelligent, ambitious woman, Paris was a jungle where "sauve qui peut" was the rule. Thus Célimène's *coquetterie* is anything but "frivole" (Jasinski); it is a calculated "politique... un procédé d'économie, qui permet de donner peu à beaucoup et de s'attacher le maximum d'amis aux moindres frais. Dans cette société, une femme qui ne veut pas se confiner dans son domestique et qui prétend avoir une vie sociale et agir personellement... est nécessairement conduite à s'attacher par un marchandage subtil et calculé les hommes dont l'influence lui est utile, et cela tout à fait indépendamment des sentiments ou des désirs qu'ils peuvent lui inspirer."[53] Arsinoé's prudery serves the same function. By her "zèle," she is able to win favor amongst influential "dévots" discreetly placed at the Court and in high places in Paris. *Coquetterie* and prudery, contrary tactics, are thus both in service to disadvantaged women trying to survive "les vices du temps."

The men also express an ethic which is comprehensible in terms of their social class. Philinte is the exemplary "honnête homme de cour." A rich, bourgeois member of the rising class which has not yet seized the dominant position in society, he has had to learn that "la complaisance est... avec la modération, l'une des règles essentielles de cet art de vivre en société."[54] The critics interpret this attitude as being inherently generous and practical and, inevitably, as a compromised political and ideological position. At a corrupted court, dominated by a decadent, fading aristocracy, the civilized bourgeoisie can only hold its own and wait its day. Philinte understands and accepts. Alceste, on the other hand, is the "anti-honnête homme," a "féodal" living in the past. "Chez le féodal toute résistance à sa puissance, tout affront subi provoquent un courroux dont la dissimulation est inutile et contraire à son honneur."[55] Alceste's "feudal" and energetic temperament make him an old-style aristocrat, regardless of his birthright. Ironically then, "un gentilhomme rebelle aux accommodements courtisans et doté de vertus chevaleresques devient d'une certaine manière le représentant de

[53] *Le Misanthrope, op. cit.*, pp. 27-28.
[54] *Ibid.*, p. 50.
[55] *Ibid.*, p. 72.

valeurs progressistes." [56] In spite of his excesses, Alceste is clearly a model, for his passion and intransigency show up the moral bankruptcy of compromise and insincerity in the "société courtisane." But he is not an ideal and he cannot survive; his retreat is foreordained. Nonetheless, Louis' world is on the wane. Philinte and the "idéologie bourgeoise" were gradually assuming the prestige and power that would bring them into the dominant position in the following century.

It has been said that the constant recourse to history gives Marxist criticism a determinism which limits its insights and mitigates its critical value. Perhaps. And yet in their relative flexibility, sound scholarship, and pertinency, these modest commentaries merit close consideration.

A Special Few

On the myriad books and articles of the last decade, two books and one set of articles merit special attention for they are among the most original recent contributions to Molière studies.

Molière and the Comedy of Intellect [57] is an ambiguous and ironic title. The author, Judd Hubert, sees comedy as a conscious choice on Molière's part, an intellectual vantage point from which the value of the intellect could be measured. The book investigates primarily stylistic devices, conventions, metaphors, themes, word and image patterns, etc. The result is a modern book which says surprisingly little about dramaturgy *per se*, its primary concern being moliéresque comedy as a literary form. At the same time, Hubert suggests how the comedies project a view of the human condition. After farce and parody in the first few works, *Dom Garcie de Navarre* marks a turn toward a more complex vision

---

[56] *Ibid.*, p. 86. For an elegant view of Molière's theatre with regard to its essence and purport, see Octave Nadal, "Molière et le sens de la vie," in *A Mesure haute* (Mercure de France, 1964), pp. 91-108. In dealing with Corneille and Racine, Nadal has always been close to Bénichou; in this piece on Molière, however, he is resolutely in the Moore-Bray formalist camp.

[57] Judd Hubert, *Molière and the Comedy of Intellect* (Berkeley: University of California Press, 1962). H. Gaston Hall's fine article recently took a similar view, insisting on the importance of "assimilated literary traditions" in Molière's works: "The Literary Context of *Le Misanthrope*," in *Studi Francesi*, v. 40 (1970), pp. 20-38.

of human nature. More and more, the comic insight reveals at the center of conflict a deep-rooted *"décalage"* "between man's dreams and the reality with which he must contend. In line with this vision, the two *Ecole* plays represent the futility of illusions. The confrontation between wish and fullfillment is never resolved, but *Le Misanthrope* and *Amphitryon* represent the most mature attitude: here at least, the protagonists have a clearer idea of what they must do to survive. After 1668, the plays reflect the confusion of those who cannot adapt. The conclusion is that, as a "militant entertainer," Molière's choice of comedy led the poet to an extreme form of poetic comedy which was similar to and equally as efficacious as tragedy in expressing human emotion. Nonetheless, for Hubert, the traditional conception of the comic genre remains intact. The genre remains essentially optimistic, exposing to ridicule any social or personal aberration which deviates from an accepted standard of social or moral behavior.

Jacques Guicharnaud does not accept the idea of a Molière who continues to work within the limits of optimistic, reality-illusion conflict. It is especially on this theoretical point — the limits of moliéresque comedy — that his *Molière, Une Aventure théâtrale* [58] takes a new turn. The author has described his work as "showing how Molière's use of the comic mask, in greater and greater depth, leads to an awareness of the irreducibility of human nature and a dramaturgical impasse." The conditions leading to the impasse are analyzed in great detail in *Tartuffe, Dom Juan* and *Le Misanthrope.* (Earlier, Guicharnaud had defined Anglo-American "new criticism" as a derivative form of the French "explication de texte" and his study follows in this tradition.) Although the book's critical perspective is very broad (dramaturgy, history, social ideology, etc.), the "aventure" is essentially an intellectual and moral one. The "irreducibility of human nature" implies that human beings find it impossible to relate to one another, to share a common destiny. According to Professor Guicharnaud, *Tartuffe* still centered around "le problème de la nature profonde de l'anti-masque... (in which)...

---

[58] Jacques Guicharnaud, *Molière, Une Aventure théâtrale* (Gallimard, 1963).

le vrai drame humain reposait sur l'antithèse tyrannie-liberté, sur l'antinomie de l'illusion inconsciente des vérités." [59] But this optimistic and analytical vision gradually gives way to a synthesized view of human nature, essentialistic, quasi-jansenistic, devoid of freedom, of which the basic essence is "Nature-Corruption." "Chacun étant doué d'une nature fermée sur elle-même et différente de celle de tout autre, les harmonies, quand il s'en produit, ne sont que des illusions ou des faits de hasard. Il n'y a pas d'ordre, de bonheur vrai, d'équilibre social authentique par rapport auquel la Comédie puisse dénoncer et du coup ridiculiser les 'défauts' des hommes. L'être lui-même est un défaut irréductible, contre lequel la comédie vien s'achopper." [60] The "défaut irreductible" which isolates each individual from another has its roots in a profound "amour de soi." This is the dominant trait of each of the main protagonists in *Le Misanthrope* and the source of the despair which leads to the impasse. "Ce qui éclate à la fin du *Misanthrope,* c'est que Célimène se préfère à Alceste, c'est qu'Alceste se préfère à Célimène. Et ce qui est évident d'un bout à l'autre, c'est que chaque personnage se préfère à tous les autres." [61] At that point the limits of comedy break down, the genre has gone beyond itself and at the end of *Le Misanthrope,* "la Comédie... apparaît comme un genre illusoire, qui s'évapore dans un néant." [62] The essential elements of comedy, wisdom and laughter, are found to be illusory and the genre has evolved into "un drame très particulier."

Professor Guicharnaud's study has been widely read and discussed and some have taken issue with it. Most of the criticism concerned the book's intricate, detailed explications, its debatable conception of comedy, and its interpretation of the impasse and breakdown of the comic genre in Molière's masterpiece of 1666. And yet the overwhelming consensus of opinion was that the coherent and sophisticated analyses of this difficult book marked

---

[59] *Ibid.,* p. 529.
[60] *Ibid.,* p. 532.
[61] *Ibid.,* p. 510.
[62] *Ibid.,* p. 532. Professor Guicharnaud also published a useful anthology: *Molière: A Collection of Critical Essays* (Englewood Cliffs, N. J.: Prentice Hall, 1964.)

it as one of the single most impressive contributions to Molière exegesis during the past twenty-five years.

In the large harvest of articles devoted to Molière in the last decade, two pieces by Professor Jules Brody deserve special mention. In their breadth and scope, they reflect almost all of the major works on Molière since Bénichou and Moore. In the process of his argumentation, Professor Brody is constantly scrutinizing and testing the ideas of the past, either to corroborate or to differ, and his fine critique often takes certain points further than his predecessors had. In his "Esthétique et Société chez Molière," the author begins with Bénichou's well-known contention that Molière's works promoted an aristocratic ethic; Brody suggests instead that Molière actually supported an aristocratic esthetic. Since, in the dramatist's eyes, society seemed so insensitive to the most basic values and so vulnerable to the excesses of tyrants and maniacs, one's best defense was in esthetic beauty. Thus, if the bourgeois characters in Molière always seem to come out second best, it is because they are incapable of attaining "cette vraie noblesse," the absolute esthetic of elegance and natural grace. And regardless of their material wealth, they are incapable of buying these qualities. The main conflict in the comedies then is not between morality or immorality, but between grace and *gaucherie*. [63] In this view, M. Jourdain's fault is "une insuffisance esthétique plutôt qu'une tare morale" and, although morally right, George Dandin is "esthétiquement dans son tort." [64] Brody's conclusions to this first part have implications for all of Molière's work: "Le rôle comique est toujours réservé à ceux qui ne savent trouver, malgré la justice de leur cause, ni motif impérieux ni stratégie harmonieuse qui leur permettent d'ajuster leur contenance selon les pressions et les vicissitudes de l'existence sociale." [65]

In a second essay in English, "*Dom Juan* and *Le Misanthrope*, or the Esthetics of Individualism in Molière," Professor Brody

[63] Jules Brody, "Esthétique et Société chez Molière," in *Dramaturgie et Société au 16è et au 17è siècles* (C. R. N. S., 1968), pp. 316-317.

[64] *Ibid.*, p. 318 and p. 322.

[65] *Ibid.*, p. 323. The extended conclusion, insisting on the permanence of "corruption" and "mal" in Molière's works, seems to parallel Guicharnaud's thinking at the end of his book.

148   MOLIÈRE: TRADITIONS IN CRITICISM

focuses on Dom Juan's "deft histrionics" and Célimène's "imperturable grace," both outstanding examples of the "esthetics of individualism." Departing from Moore's view of a Dom Juan dashed by the limits of his humanity, and essentially comic because of his blindness to those limits, Brody thinks that the don's imposing individuality keeps him immune to the leveling effects of comedy, as though he were "exempt from the laws governing the common destiny of mankind." [66] Dom Juan's incomparable, sublime egocentricity remains beyond human check, allowing him "to exercise indeterminate freedom." That this is possible is proof that the protagonist inhabits "a rotten world falling apart at the seams, ruled by vanity, self-interest, hypocrisy and indifference; a world in decline..." [67]

The don's counterpart is Célimène. More insightful than Alceste, she has realized that in their tarnished world there are no absolutes, no perfection. For her, happiness is "the result of the same conscious, energetic enterprise on which the viability of social life itself depends: the harmonization of a multitude of warring elements, the disarming of hostility, the reconciliation of rivalries, the persistent imposition of decorum, the constant assertion of form." [68] Taking issue this time with Guicharnaud and others, Brody contends that, in the resolution of the play, Molière did not intend Célimène to suffer defeat; Alceste's ultimatum merely provokes a "déconvenue ... a momentary reversal, a pause in her progress toward elegant felicity." [69] In the final analysis, the individuality of Dom Juan and Célimène is projected beyond mere crass and valueless egomania. It is part of a "noble esthetic" designed to assure "a modicum of levity, style and beauty in a world that would otherwise be devoured by folly, ugliness and mediocrity." [70]

One could say that Professor Brody's two pieces represent just one more viewpoint on Molière, one more grain of sand on

---

[66] Jules Brody, "*Dom Juan* and *Le Misanthrope*, or The Esthetics of Individualism in Molière," in *P. M. L. A.*, v. 84 (May 1969), p. 559.
[67] *Ibid.*, p. 568.
[68] *Ibid.*, p. 573.
[69] *Ibid.*, p. 575. M. Guicharnaud (and Moore) had a different idea: see his *Aventure*, pp. 488 ff.
[70] *Ibid.*, p. 576.

a large and ever-growing dune. And yet, as this judgment tried to show, the special value of his contributions lies in their ability to incorporate and extend some of the best criticism on Molière in the past decade.

Molière on Stage

Molière belongs primarily to the theatre and some effort must be made to assess how the theatre of our time has produced his work. For if Molière had not been rediscovered and recreated on stage during the twentieth century, all the myriad books and articles on him would be but artifacts for historians and specialists. For those, like René Bray, who minimize the importance of Molière "littérateur," it is the work on stage of the "hommes de théâtre" that represents the ultimate contribution to the patrimony of letters. We have seen, however, that the work of theatre professionals has almost always been somewhat marginal to the total effort of assessing Molière's work, and that there has been rather little contact between the theatre and the university. With the exception of Copeau and Jouvet, little attention had been given to the original and innovative dramatic productions by professional directors and board players. One obvious reason for this state of affairs lies in the ethereal nature of the theatrical performance. Somewhat akin to a fireworks display, there is a flash of light, a swell of sound, and then nothing. And regardless of how impressive it was, for history it will quite likely be reduced to a column or two of thin prose by a critic who perhaps never fully understood all of what he saw. Such, alas, is the destiny of every theatrical performance. [71] Nevertheless, a number of vigorous theatre professionals have left their mark on the posterity of Molière's work, and they more than anyone else deserve credit for revitalizing the spirit of Molière for "le grand public"

---

[71] There are films which preserve, as it were, the essence of some memorable stage productions: the BBC films of Shakespeare plays, the RTF films of Comédie Française performances, etc. But the live theatrical performance is a unique, non-transferable medium, and a film of a play is a film, not a play.

and for making Molière a contemporary for successive generations. Without them, there would be fewer books on Molière.

The consideration of selected innovative productions of Molière's comedies during 1960-1969, and of the statistics of Comédie française performances in the same period, suggests a few hypotheses and raises a number of only partially answerable questions. During the 1960's, *Dom Juan* established itself as the Molière play most germane to the temper of our time. At the Comédie française alone, there were 60 performances during this period, as opposed to 37 in the preceeding ten years, and only 135 during the entire period 1680-1959. [72] *L'Avare* persists in popularity, second only to *Tartuffe* in total performances since 1680 (2232); during the time in question, *L'Avare* was the most oft played work with 234 performances. *Tartuffe* however has always been the overwhelming choice, with 2851 showings since 1680, and 184 during the 1960's. [73] *Le Malade imaginaire, Le Misanthrope* and *Le Bourgeois gentilhomme* all played more than 150 times during the last decade. For *Le Bourgeois gentilhomme* however, this represented a reduction by more than 50 % from its inordinate number of runs during the preceding decade (325).

One might ask why certain plays are able to sustain a long impetus of success while others have not been so susceptible to renewal? Established tradition surely plays a role here. Dullin's *L'Avare*, Jouvet's *Dom Juan* and *Tartuffe*, Louis Seigner's Monsieur Jourdain, all of these well-known directors and players gave their productions new impetus since 1948 and helped to maintain general public acceptance. But stage tradition is a two-sided coin, at once an invitation to persist in the established direction, and a challenge to resist and to seek new possibilities. It is clear that several innovative Molière productions of recent years repre-

---

[72] The statistics used in the text and reproduced in rearranged form at the chapter's end are taken from *Molière*, edited by Sylvie Chevalley et al. (La Comédie Française, 1969.) Many other troupes are playing Molière, but accurate statistics are difficult to obtain. Since La Comédie Française remains the national center in France for classical theatre, the choice of Molière comedies played there and the number of performances represent somewhat accurately prevailing trends and attitudes to the comic playwright's works.

[73] For a detailed account of critical appreciation through the ages, see H. P. Salomon, *Tartuffe devant l'opinion française* (Paris: P. U. F., 1962).

sented a conscious attempt at breaking with popular tradition: Antoine Bourseiller and Patrice Chéreau's productions of *Dom Juan*, Roger Planchon's *Tartuffe*, and Bernard Ballet's *Le Bourgeois gentilhomme* are the most obvious examples. Aside from tradition, the changing moods of the times have favored some plays over others. *Tartuffe*, of course, fascinated almost every generation, but the recent emergence of *Dom Juan* seems linked with a prevailing preocupation with ideology, liberty, hubris, and with what one director called the "univers concentrationnaire." This work exemplifies well the intellectual and emotional kinship that can exist between a play and a public separated by over 300 years. On the other hand, some once popular plays seem to be on the wane: unless recent attempts at renewal are successful, *Le Bourgeois gentilhomme* seems to be losing ground. Over-exposure (film and stage) may be one of the factors, or perhaps Louis Seigner's highly stylized production which has dominated the stage for the past twenty years has lost touch with the new, more combative styles in the recent theatre. The same might be said for *Les Fourberies de Scapin*. Launched into the twentieth century by a brilliant production by Jacques Copeau (in 1917), it was often considered the first Molière play to be completely modernized for our time. Subsequently, serious actors such as Louis Jouvet, Jean-Louis Barrault, and Robert Hirsch revived interest in it. More recently, however, it has not been played with great success and it does not rank among the ten most played works during the last decade. Might one hypothesize that the *Commedia dell'arte* style (the tradition for this play since Copeau) is fading in competition with our own modern *commedia* idiom, which tends to be darker, more absurd?

Aside from changes in taste which influence the theatre and questions of repertory, other questions arise from the work itself: why have some plays, by their very nature, been more resistant to change and new interpretations? Here *Le Misanthrope* is the most striking example. [74] More than any other play by Molière, this one seems most entrenched in the seventeenth century. *Tartuffe*

---

[74] Antoine Bourseiller's "new" *Misanthrope* of 1972 has apparently had much less success and acclaim than his brilliant *Dom Juan*, and it does not appear to have established an innovative new style.

and *Dom Juan* are surely very much a part of their age and of
Molière's career, and yet between myth and myth-making, the
spirit of these plays easily transcends their epoch. But what about
Alceste's self-righteousness, Célimène's presciosity, Philinte's moral pusillanimity? Is it not really the vast game of charade being
conducted, and particularly the passion and deftness with which
it was played within a certain privileged society around 1660
which fascinate us today? In this view, the play could be seen
less in terms of ideas and more as a brilliant set-piece, a delicate
item for exhibition in the "musée imaginaire" we have built
to our vision of seventeenth century French society. Our imaginative modern theatre has renewed *Tartuffe, Dom Juan* and
several other Molière works, while Célimène's salon and the
relationships she maintains with her suitors have resisted major
changes in interpretation. Of all Molière's major comedies, *Le
Misanthrope* "reste à réinventer." [75]

It is clear, nonetheless, that several theatre professionals since
1950 have forcefully established their right to re-invent Molière. Certain dicta which seemed arrogant at first, are virtually
axiomatic today, especially those which insist on the necessity of
renewing Molière and the classics in general: Antoine Bourseiller's
claim that "tradition" should mean playing the classics according
to the prevailing temper of the time, and Roger Planchon's suggestion that a classical play is one that was written yesterday.
Not surprisingly, some critics considered this new-found flexibility
excessive, and there has been considerable hostility toward the
work of Planchon, Bourseiller, Patrice Chéreau, Marcel Maréchal,
and others. It is true that their contributions have been uneven and
it is unlikely that all of their interpretations will leave the same
mark in the history of Molière performances. But to reduce their
energetic efforts to "dégats" and "pseudo-messages de contem-
porains à la mode" is to deny at once the unique plasticity of

---

[75] Some aspects of the play have, of course, been renewed, but mostly
surface elements: costumes, settings, Alceste's choleric temperament. But
these have been variations on a similar theme and have not resulted in
a new, coherent interpretation of the whole work. For the variations, see
M. Descotes, *Les Grands Rôles dans le théâtre de Molière* (Paris: P. U. F.,
1960).

Molière's comedies and our right to reinterpret them in a new light.

Finally, it is worth noting that the majority of new and innovative interpretations of Molière were offered by relatively new troupes, made up of young directors and players, many from outside Paris. For several directors and/or actors, a notable effort in a renewed Molière production was one of the highlights of their career: Roger Planchon's productions of *George Dandin* and *Tartuffe* did much to reaffirm his talents as an original director; J.-P. Roussillon's productions of *L'Avare* and *George Dandin* showed that he was as fine a director as he was an actor; Antoine Bourseiller proved himself a forceful and original talent with his new *Dom Juan;* and Marcel Maréchal emerged as a Molière-like "bête de théâtre" with his powerful portrayals of Monsieur Jourdain and Sganarelle. The energies of these and other theatre professionals in service to Molière have won for them the esteem and support of a large French public, and it is in large part due to their efforts that Molière has been renewed for our time and is being appreciated by more spectators than ever before. It is also why one critic during the 1971 theatre season could proclaim that "Molière est l'auteur le plus actuel." In sum, the 1960's were memorable years for Molière, for French theatre, and for a new generation of theatre professionals.

SOME NOTEWORTHY PERFORMANCES OF MOLIÈRE COMEDIES IN FRANCE DURING THE 1960'S

L'Avare

Directed by Jean-Paul Roussillon. (Paris: La Comédie Française, 1969.)

This staging did not break decisively with the Dullin or Jean Vilar interpretations of 1941 and 1952 respectively. Nonetheless, Roussillon's production embraced the entire Harpagon household in such a way as to make the intrigues and frustrations of the young lovers stand out more clearly, and the entire décor reproduced in more detail the interior of a not overly austere bourgeois house. Michel Aumont as the miser avoided the excesses of caricature and yet managed to create a Harpagon more unattractive and more menacing than for example, Jean Vilar's protagonist. At least one new element appeared in the set: a staircase which was functional but more modest than M. Jourdain's baroque ornamentation and which allowed for more vertical movement to break the routine of entrances and exits limited to "cour" and "jardin."

Le Bourgeois gentilhomme

Directed by Bernard Ballet. (Sartrouville: La Compagnie du Cothurne, 1970.)

A provocative interpretation intended to break the Comédie Française-Louis Seigner tradition of Jourdain as an unwitting dupe who deserves the scorn and abuse he brings upon himself. Insisting on Molière's idea of a spectacle, Marcel Maréchal plays an energetic Jourdain, so rich that he can buy any pleasure he desires from any of the crass, pusillanimous parasites who gravitate around him. Thus, the entire play unfolds like "un immense rêve baroque," willed and controlled by M. Jourdain, culminating logically in the Mamamouchi ceremony, an apotheosis of sound and color. To enliven the spectacle, Lully's delicate "musique pour divertissement" is discared in favor of the more modern and lively sounds of "Les Pink Floyd."

Dom Juan

1.   Directed by Antoine Bourseiller. (Marseille: Centre dramatique du Sud-Est, 1967.)

Along with Roger Planchon's Tartuffe, this is the most striking Molière production of the decade. Bourseiller's Dom Juan (played by Georges Descrières) wanders unattached and arrogant through a décor of stylized forms in copper and leather ("un univers concentrationnaire"). A romantic figure in many ways, the don is clearly in revolt, but perhaps only in order to reaffirm his "moi." Or, is his libertinage a form of political consciousness ... ? Jacques Charon's substantial portrayal of Sganarelle forged that role to form a couple "à égalité" with the role of Dom Juan. This turned out to one of the most disputed elements of the production.

2. Directed by Patrice Chéreau. (Sartrouville: Théâtre du Co-thurne, 1969.)

This production was the Molière scandal of the 1969-1970 season. Considering it "ignoble" and a "niaiserie," the then director of La Comédie Française, Maurice Escande, refused to allow this production in the national theatre. Here, Dom Juan and Sganarelle, in snug leather pants, seem bent on defiling everything. The hero, "un intellectuel de gauche du 17ème siècle," lives the contradiction of betrayer and hypocrite: a willful traitor to his noble class, his feudal society is nevertheless the only world in which he can continue to enjoy his privileged existence. No fixed couple here, Sganarelle is as cynical as his master and, with the clear vision of the peasant class, he becomes more and more alienated from his master. Thus his "Mes gages, mes ga-ges!" is simply a demand to know who will pay him for his work now that his irresponsible master has absconded. The women in Chéreau's production hardly speak. Instead, they con-vulse, scream, faint, and have wild, erotic fantasies. Apparently the director's idea was to seek, within a pre-verbal condition, an intellectual and emotional coherence not immediately apparent in the illusive construct of Molière's text. This production was debatable from almost every point of view.

George Dandin

1. Directed by Roger Planchon (Villeurbanne: Théâtre de la Cité, 1958.)

This was Roger Planchon's first major production of a Molière play. There was no music or dance interludes, none of the "divert-issement" elements of the original, thereby projecting into promin-ence the "côté drame" of Dandin's dilemma. Here is an essentially sympathetic George Dandin who is nonetheless reprehensible for betraying his peasant origins by attempting to merge into the "gentilhommerie" through an ill-conceived marriage. Verbal delivery was considerably slowed and occasionally lines are reinforced by mute scenes in which appear large reproductions of paintings by Louis LeNain and Bourdon, realistic scenes of abject peasant life during Molière's time. The entire production was oriented toward depicting realistically and with great sympathy the profound tedium of a nearly enslaved peasant class. There was a detailed mock-up of Dandin's barn occupying a good portion of the total décor, many extras in peasant-costumes milled around the stage, and Colin's presence was emphasized by having Jean Bouise play this normally muted part with unusual ubiquity. One critic called Planchon's production "a brilliant synthesis," an admixture of the styles of Antoine, Brecht and Visconti.

2. Directed by Jean-Paul Roussillon. (Paris: La Comédie Française, 1970.)

More intense than one might have expected from a Comédie Française production, the sustained tension came mostly from Robert Hirsch's interpretation of Dandin. Potentially violent, always angry, seething with frustration, he is constantly on the verge a nervous breakdown. Thus, his threat at the end of the play has the chilling effect of a real possibility, bringing the play close to a *drame*. Curiously, because of the suppressed tensions, there is more of a feeling of class struggle here than in Roger Planchon's would-be "brechtian" interpretation in which the hero seemed more like a passive victim. A good comic addition was having the Sotenvilles appear stiff, overdressed, always walking one behind the other in lock-step, tapping in cadence with extra-long walking canes. They alone are a comic, highly stylized marionette show.

Tartuffe

Directed by Roger Planchon. (Villeurbanne: Théâtre de la Cité, 1962.)

Perhaps the single most original and contested reinterpretation of a Molière comedy during the last decade. After opening at Villeurbanne, this production played at the Odéon in Paris in March 1964, and in New York in July 1968. Planchon emphasized the aristotelian aspect of his *mise en scène,* as opposed to the brechtian. The idea was to play the text exactly as it is, insist on the "fable" (action), let only this element bring out the meaning of the text. In other words, show what Tartuffe and Orgon do instead of speculating on who they are, insist on "faire," not "être." In contrast with established tradition (especially of Jouvet and Ledoux), Orgon emerges here as the central figure of the drama. He is a strange and complex man, forceful and potentially dangerous, as opposed to a puerile *martinet*. He is motivated through the first four acts by a strange obsession with Tartuffe, which might have homosexual connotations. Refusing to speculate on Tartuffe's religious sentiments, Planchon's protagonist is a "fourbe," a villainous knave who profits from Orgon's credulity. The production created an overall feeling of extreme cruelty and projected a cynical vision of a world fraught with arbitrariness and unrelieved chicanery. Some critics accused Planchon of projecting a modern leftist's view of life in Louis XIV's *ancien régime*. The action unfolded in a sumptuous décor of rich, polished wood interiors and, on the walls, large photo-reproductions of realistic paintings from the seventeenth century depicting erotico-religious scenes of Christ in anguished suffering and convulsing mystics. Thus, instead of being mere ornamentation, the décor complements the meaning of the action. Some other modern touches were added: Marianne is much like a spoiled, middle-class adolescent, and the guards who accompany the *Exempt* at the end of the play are dressed and act like agents of the C. R. S. (French security police). This last detail, which provoked negative criticism, has been much misunderstood. Many critics considered it a gratuitous touch of modernity, unrelated to the sense of the drama. Within the coherent logic of Planchon's production however, the opposite is true. Orgon does live in Louis' world, the epitome of the police state, and in fact he has been involved in political intrigues against the King's authority. Tartuffe himself, it is suggested, belongs to a secret *cabale* of fanatics, which could pose a potential threat to the authority of the throne. Hence, the end is doubly political, in that Tartuffe's arrest solves the problem of his criminality and strikes a blow against the *cabale,* and Orgon's pardon by the King's grace absolves the bourgeois protagonist from his past crimes of *lèse-majesté*. In Louis' regime, both of these cases are matters for the police, and yet contemporary audiences, particularly viewing a stilized production, tend not to recognize the police in the presence of the *Exempt* and the guards who accompany him. Planchon's high-booted, authoritarian, suspicious "flic" types bring us back to the reality of *Tartuffe*. [76]

STATICS OF MOLIÈRE PERBORMANCES IN FRANCE *

		NUMBER OF PERFORMANCES: NOVEMBER 1658- AUGUST 1680	COMEDIE FRAN- ÇAISE PERFORMANCES FROM 1961-1969	TOTALS 1658- 1969
1.	Tartuffe	128	184	2.979
2.	L'Avare	88	234	2.320
3.	Le Médecin malgré lui ...	60	70	2.175
4.	Le Misanthrope	99	177	1.994
5.	Le Malade imaginaire ...	95	179	1.826
6.	Les Femmes savantes ...	50	109	1.784
7.	L'Ecole des maris	142	31	1.710
8.	L'Ecole des femmes	112	77	1.547
9.	Le Dépit amoureux	88	35	1.334
10.	Les Précieuses ridicules ...	60	17	1.300
11.	Les Fourberies de Scapin	37	44	1.297
12.	Le Mariage forcé	62	73	1.243
13.	Le Bourgeois gentilhomme	89	150	1.204
14.	George Dandin	73	18	1.148
15.	Amphitryon	101	66	1.121
16.	Sganarelle	159	25	920
17.	Monsieur de Pourceaugnac	76	13	858
18.	L'Etourdi	77	33	650
19.	La Comtesse d'Escarbagnas	45	——	624
20.	L'Amour médecin	85	——	468
21.	Les Fâcheux	142	——	435
22.	Psyché	82	8	371
23.	La Critique de l'Ecole ...	41	76	293
24.	Le Sicilien	32	——	271
25.	Dom Juan (from 1841) ...	15	60	210
26.	Les Amants magnifiques	——	——	182
27.	L'Impromptu de Versailles	20	2	164
28.	La Princesse d'Elide	25	——	114
29.	Le Médecin volant	14	——	61
30.	Mélicerte	——	——	22
31.	La Jalousie du Barbouillé	7	——	11
32.	Dom Garcie de Navarre ...	7	——	11

[76] Other views and reviews of Molière on stage can be found in the following: Wallace Fowlie, "Molière Today," in *Dionysus in Paris* (New York, 1960); Sylvie Chevalley, *Molière* (La Comédie Française, 1970); Gilles Sandier, *Théâtre et Combat* (Stock. 1970).

* These statistics were taken from *Molière*, ed. by. S. Chevalley et al (La Comédie Française, 1970). The plays are listed according to their ranking in total number of performances since 1658.

CONCLUSION

This book has attempted to outline some of the contours of Molière criticism in the twentieth century, and as we approach the tercentenary of the dramatist's passing, the number of critical studies on his works increases. It is clear that the comedies have had different meanings for people in different times, and that there can be no final word on Molière. In these last pages however, we might ask to what degree modern criticism has enlarged our understanding and appreciation of Molière and his works, what is the state of affairs since 1970, and what are some of the trends for the future.

One literary historian recently expressed the opinion that up to 1960, the twentieth century had not been a golden age of Molière criticism. In our view, that is an underestimation. It is undeniable that our age has broadened considerably the perspectives on the comedies and applied fruitfully many new methods in textual exegesis as well as in staging. Fernandez' brilliant *Vie de Molière* was both new and suggestive, in terms of biography and as an original reassessment of the comic principle in Molière. Pellison's re-evalation of the *comédies-ballets*, his insistence on Molière's originality in the genre, and the distinctive writing style in these works, did much to re-establish credit for this part of the total *œuvre*. In literary history, the works of Lanson, Michaut, Lancaster, Adam, to cite only the most obvious names, all contributed greatly to our knowledge of Molière and his time. On stage, the productions of Copeau, Jouvet, Vilar, Barrault, and even some of the more controversial young directors of the last two decades have imparted to us a Molière who is as contemporaneous as any modern playwright. An important part of this renewal on stage has been the rediscovery of comedies which had fallen into obscurity: *George Dandin, Les Fourberies de Scapin, Monsieur de Pourceaugnac, Les Amants magnifiques,* to mention only a few. But *Dom Juan* is really the most dramatic discovery of the twentieth century. Since its inception, for both moralistic and technical reasons, the play either intimidated or puzzled everyone, even in the benign rimed version of Thomas Corneille. During the hundred years between 1841 and 1941 when Molière's original text replaced the adaptation, it was still considered unplayable and was shown less than two hundred times, while *Tartuffe* enjoyed 2500 performances. It was Louis Jouvet's debatable interpretation in 1947 which proved decisively that the play could be produced in a coherent, exciting way, and that the play's audacity and ambiguities made it all the more appealing to contemporary audiences. The subsequent success of the play is well-known; it has become a Molière "classic."

Inevitably, Molière criticism has reflected some of the preoccupations of the times, including our predilection for mixing politics and history with literature. In its suggestion that the comedies consciously supported the established *louisquatorzième* aristocratic ethic, P. Bénichou's *Morales du grand siècle* had implications for Molière's work far beyond what earlier critics had proposed. On a related issue, Alfred Simon's provocative monograph on Molière and the recent Marxist-oriented editions of the comedies have enlarged our view on Molière's politics, although innuendoes have persisted on the subject since Chamfort's *Eloge* of 1796. Over two decades ago, Professors Moore and Bray reoriented criticism toward formalistic considerations of technique, while Judd Hubert's sensitive study insisted on the more purely literary aspects of Molière's style and temper. The "ideal spectator" who views Molière's three masterpieces in Jacques Guicharnaud's book has absorbed many of the various points of view in modern criticism. He proposes a synthesis which suggets that with *Le Misanthrope,* Molière's comedy went beyond itself and destroyed its own form. All of these original works have added valid new perspectives to Molière interpretation, in line with the modern temperament.

Even a cursory consideration of the current situation in Molière studies, 1971-1972, indicates that its characteristic diversity has not diminished. A new biography by the Academician Pierre Gaxotte, *Molière fameux comédien*,[1] is an excellent, concise presentation of Molière as actor, director of his troupe, and comic dramatist. The author cites as often as possible the works of professional men of the theatre, such as Jacques Copeau, who have always insisted on the value of Molière's *métier* for understanding the works. Coming from a prestigious Academician, this biography may indicate that the formalist views are finally being accepted by Establishment writers and critics.

In literary history, there is an engaging piece by Professor R. J. Nelson on "Classicism: The Crisis of the Baroque in French Literature."[2] He argues, as others had, in favor of broadening the view of classicism and allowing for a more flexible critical methodology in dealing with seventeenth century French literature. Specifically, Professor Nelson suggest that if critics could go beyond the "Classico-Racinian ideology" — reducing practically all classical dramatic literature to "an echo of the vision of Racine" — then it might be freer to concentrate on the baroque elements in Molière. This would be particularly helpful in dealing with "problem plays" between 1664 and 1666, and with the *comédies-ballets*. Professor Nelson writes that, ". . . in the twin motifs of theatrical self-consciousness and self-conscious theatricality, Molière, perhaps more than any of the great classics, satisfies that criterion which is for many theoreticians of the Baroque its principal hallmark: the transcendence of phenomenal reality — if not through the rediscovery of a divinely created world, then through the mental transformation of it in artistic creation."[3] Finally, the double perspective of theatricality reappears forcefully, according to Professor Nelson, in the *comédie-ballets* toward the end of Molière's career. ". . . the solution through art at which he [Molière] arrives in his final operatic, Baroque *comédies-ballets* is the artistic rendition of a dream, the formalized nostalgia for a poetic order tentatively and hesitatingly expressed in the earlier plays in

---

[1] Pierre Gaxotte, *Molière fameux comédien* (Hachette, 1971).
[2] R. J. Nelson, "Classicism: The Crisis of the Baroque in French Literature," in *L'Esprit Créateur* (volume also entitled *Paths to Freedom*), vol. 11 (Summer 1971), pp. 169-186.
[3] *Ibid.*, p. 175.

their more self-conscious preoccupation with theatricality." [4] In another piece concerned with "théâtre dans le théâtre," Marc Fumaroli also discusses levels of theatricality in Molière. He suggests that in *L'Impromptu de Versailles*, a mutation at once esthetic and political functions toward a double end. In the "microcosme comique" the play sketches in a comic mode the situation of the playwright at Court, while in the "macrocosme solaire," the play is a discreet celebration of Louis XIV's reign. [5] In the more traditional sphere of literary history, a number of recent articles trace the spirit of Molière in such diverse authors as Kleist, [6] Sartre, [7] and Anouilh, [8] while another study traces the Italian source of *L'Etourdi*. [9]

Surely the most striking contributions on Molière in the past two years have been two structuralist analyses which could be harbingers of things to come in Molière studies. The first, a massive piece by François Rastier, is the first rigorously scientific effort at a structuralist critique of one of Molière's works, in this case *Don Juan*. In *Niveaux d'ambiguïtes des structures narratives*, the critical method consists of "la mise en corrélation des deux systèmes sémiologiques [qui] équivaut à la construction d'un modèle d'interprétation totalisante." [10] In conception and elaboration, this methodology is derived from "la technique de descrip-

---

[4] *Ibid.*, p. 179. At least two other contributions in this volume of *L'Esprit Créateur* concern Molière: Hallam Walker's "*Les Fâcheux* and Molière's Use of Games," and some reflections on *Tartuffe* by E. B. O. Borgerhoff, to whom the volume is posthumously dedicated. The Fall 1966 volume of *L'Esprit Créateur* is devoted exclusively to Molière.

[5] Marc Fumaroli, "Microcosme comique et macrocosme solaire: Molière, Louis XIV et *L'Impromptu de Versailles*," in *Revue des Sciences humaines*, vol. 145 (January-March 1972), pp. 95-114.

[6] W. Wittkowski, "The New Prometheus: Molière's and Kleit's *Amphitryon*," in *Comparative Literature Studies*, 1971, pp. 109-124.

[7] Suzanne Larnaudie, "Molière et J.-P. Sartre: visages du Dom Juanisme," in *Annales publiées ... par l'Université de Toulouse* (also entitled, *Littératures*), vol. 18, pp. 67-85.

[8] P. W. Wood, *A Comparative Study of Jean Anouilh and Molière* (unpublished doctoral dissertation), listed in *Dissertation Abstracts*, vol. 31 (1970-71), p. 4801A.

[9] Phillip A. Wadsworth, "The Italian Source of Molière's *L'Etourdi*," in *Kentucky Romance Quarterly*, vol. 18 (1971), pp. 319-331.

[10] François Rastier, "Niveaux d'ambiguïtés des structures narratives," in *Semiotica*, vol. 3 (1971), p. 340.

tion des récits elaborée par les folkloristes," especially the Russian
V. Propp and other Slavic formalists, and in France, A. J. Greimas.
Rastier's conclusions on *Dom Juan* are not unlike the propositions
of other critics: the don is guilty of blatant hypocrisy, except that
here, hypocrisy is "le seul crime de Dom Juan." Earlier critics
are scored for having established elaborate interpretations of
Dom Juan's character which are tenous at best for they fail to
distinguish between unfounded allegations whose value is "indé-
terminé," and the one crime which is "reconnu" in the coherent,
assertive arguments of opposing roles within the play. [11] Although
hypocrisy is Dom Juan's only crime, its implications are broad.
"Précisons le statut de l'hypocrisie: c'est le seul contenu des deux
systèmes [sémiologiques] qui soit reconnu par deux locuteurs
actants opposés (Dom Juan et Sganarelle, V. 2); de plus il est
à deux reprises attribué à Dom Juan par des indications scéni-
ques (V, 1; V, 3): c'est donc le seul contenu des deux systèmes
sémiologiques qui appartienne, indéniablement d'ailleurs, à la
vérité-de-récit. D'après l'interprétation totalisante, son assomption
est alors le seul crime de Dom Juan; mais c'est un crime absolu,
car l'hypocrisie appartient aux deixis négatives des deux systèmes." [12]

The other article in question is Bernard Magné's fine contribution which attempts to show how the progressive stages in
Agnès' liberation from Arnolphe's tyranny are marked by her
"conquête de la parole," or, how the tyrant's gradual demise
and loss of power (essentially, a verbal monopoly over his victim)
is inversely proportionate to the heroine's increasing command
of lucid and meaningful language. Although Magné's structuralist
method is less exactingly scientific than Rastier's, it is nevertheless
coherent and rigorous. But, being less committed to the science of
literature, Magné allows his argument to move in the direction
of at least two propositions which imply historical and moralistic value judgments, normally disallowed by the structuralist
method. [13] While the subject of Magné's article is not entirely

---

[11] *Ibid.*, pp. 291-292.
[12] *Ibid.*, p. 341.
[13] B. Magné, *"L'Ecole des femmes* ou la conquête de la parole," in *Revue
des Sciences humaines*, vol. 145 (January-March 1972), p. 131 (footnote 15),

new, [14] his treatment is more thorough, and his perspective is larger and more penetrating than previous studies on the subject. Moreover, in its supple balance of scientific rigor and sensitive intuition, the method of this article may become a model for further lingusitic-oriented soundings of Molière's comedies. In any case, these two original pieces have introduced criticism to the linguistic method of analysing Molière's works, and a new approach to the comedies may follow.

For the future, what remains to be done? From the bulk of moliéresque criticism, one might think that all substantive areas of interpretation and documentation had been explored. To a point this is true, and yet as one critic remarked, "On n'aura jamais tout dit sur Molière." On the historical side, a comprehensive *Carrière de Molière,* modelled on Raymond Picard's study of Racine, would be very useful. Speculation aside, what was Mo- liére's actual relationship to Louis XIV and the powerful nobles at Court? To what degree did these ties influence his works, if in fact they did? The answers to such questions would demand minute research into all areas of court life and politics during the period 1658-1673, as well as a very close reading of the comedies. The so-called "sociological method" might be applied here, and the late Lucien Goldmann stated privately a few years ago that the facilities of the Centre de Recherches de Sociologie de la Littérature at the Institut de Sociologie in Brussels would be open to anyone willing to undertake this ambitious research. The obvious problem is finding pertinent documents on Molière's life and activities at Louis' court. Georges Mongrédien alluded to a veritable "conspiration du silence" in regard to Molière during his lifetime, and, aside from slanderous and irresponsible polemical texts, we have seen how little reliable information has come to us from the seventeenth century. Unless there is a major

---

and p. 138 (footnote 31); contrary to this attitude, see Rastier's definition of "la valeur de vérité" and his refusal to consider moral implications of Dom Juan's crime in "Niveaux . . . ," *op. cit.,* pp. 291-292, and p. 341, respectively.

[14] At least two articles in recent years discussed Arnolphe's tyranny and Agnès' liberation along somewhat similar lines: Serge Doubrovsky, "Arnolphe ou la chute du héros," in *Mercure de France,* vol. 348 (1961), pp. 111-118; and Jacques Ehrmann, "Notes sur *L'Ecole des femmes,*" in *Revue des Scien- ces humaines,* 109 (1963), pp. 5-10.

new find in this area of research, the existing approximations on Molière's *carrière* may have to suffice for the time being.

With regard to possible future structuralist analyses of Molière's comedies, at least one methodological problem will have to be solved. In the article discussed above, F. Rastier outlines briefly the special point which arises when attempting to establish models for linguistic analysis of "textes du genre dialogiques," in other words, for analysing the special language of dramatic literature. For his examination of *Dom Juan*, Rastier adapts models designed for inquiring into the structures of the "récit narratif." Now these common forms usually function in relation to a narrator, absent or present in the narration. In the language of theatre ("textes dialogiques"), there is either no narrator or else there are as many narrators as there are actors who speak in the play. Thus the narrator, usually a constant, invariable element in the total structure of the narration, is either non-existant or so variable as to be no longer functional in terms of a descriptive model for linguistic scrutiny. This situation raises several questions. Is there a particular "discours théâtral" structurally distinct from the "récit narratif?" Is there a unique "discours théâtral comique" whose constituent parts might be formulated into models for studying Molière's works? Aside from the categories already provided by traditional literary history, is there a specific "structure du langage comique moliéresque?" This type of inquiry could provide data for establishing certain myth patterns in the comedies, quite different from the recurring "psychic" obsessions already defined by Charles Mauron for the comic genre.

Another area worth sounding in Molière's works is madness. Ramon Fernandez' Freudian *Vie de Molière* made much of the obsessive nervousness in many of Molière's major characters and the author occasionally suggested possible links between this condition and a more profound derangement. More recently, Michel Foucault's impressive *Histoire de la folie à l'âge classique* defined a number of categories associated with madness in the seventeenth century. Is there any relationship between the hyper-nervousness of Molière's *persona* and some of the conceptions of madness at Molière's time? In the language of the time, *imaginaire* (like *visionnaire*) connoted a dimension of *déraison*. And, as Gaston Hall pointed out, there are in Molière's comedies a "cocu imaginaire," a "dévot imaginaire," a "gentilhomme imaginaire." But can one affirm with conviction that Sganarelle, Orgon, and M. Jourdain are really demented, or at least suffer from some form of "folie?" How does one distinguish in these works from the seventeenth centry between eccentricity and mild forms of madness? Foucault, for example, writes that madness in the classical age was considered one of the roots of family disorganization, social disorder, and a possible danger to the state. To what extent might the audiences of 1669 have considered Orgon a "fou?" There is also a dream-like quality associated with some forms of lunacy in the period in question, a recurring motif in baroque poetry of the time. Here the comic character Bélise, in *Les Femmes savantes* comes to mind, for she is surely the most obvious example of a "folle baroque" in all of Molière. Hypochondria too was considered a form of mental disorder, so does it follow that Molière intended Argan to be taken for a madman? These are but a few questions on this fascinating subject and they are primarily designed to suggest that a nuanced study on forms and functions of moliéresque madness would be welcomed. [15]

These unsystematic indications of possible directions in Molière research are intended only as tentative proposals. This book has shown that there is in Molière studies an infinite variety of approaches to the comedies and so critical exegesis during the coming years can go in any number of directions. Thibaudet wrote that "le moliérisme n'est pas une vocation de tout repos," and the twentieth century has been tireless in its attempts at making Molière meaningful for our times.

A decade ago Antoine Adam expressed the wish that "notre siècle renoue avec la tradition des moliéristes du XIXè siècle et que des recherches d'archives, des études patientes et précises, tirent les études sur notre grand écrivain de l'ornière où elles s'attardent depuis plus d'un demi-siècle." Undeniably there is more research to be done on Molière and hopefully literary historians will continue to contribute to our factual knowledge of

---

[15] In his *Toward Dramatic Illusion* (Yale, 1971), T. J. Reiss adopts Foucault's categories for analysing some early seventeenth century plays; see especially pp. 62-72. See also O. Mannoni, *Clefs pour l'imaginaire, ou l'Autre Scène* (Le Seuil, 1969).

the comic poet and of his age. But research of this nature should not be the only ambition of Molière studies. Contrary to Professor Adam's suggestion of a "rut" in contemporary exegesis, one could argue that never before have so many viable, substantive appreciations of Molière and his works been available to a large reading public. What we should wish for is a continuous, parallel progression in Molière studies, both in literary history and in textual exegesis, and that the quality and diversity of the latter will continue in the tradition already established. For if each successive generation does not reinvent its own Molière, then the great comedies will cease to speak directly to us and be relegated to some museum of culture, artifacts of only historical interest. But there is no indication that this will happen in the present century. Molière, his comedies, and moliéresque criticism are all as vigorously alive today as ever.

SELECTED BIBLIOGRAPHY

(The place of publication for all entries is Paris unless stated otherwise.)

A. BIBLIOGRAPHIES AND DOCUMENTS

Cioranescu, A., *Bibliographie de la Littérature Française du dix-septième siècle*. Volume 2. C. N. R. S., 1966.

Currier, T. F., and Gay, F. L., eds., *Catalogue of the Molière Collection in the Harvard College Library*. Cambridge: Harvard University Press, 1906.

Deierkauf-Holsboer, S. W., *L'Histoire de la mise en scène dans le théâtre français à Paris de 1600 à 1673*. Nizet, 1960.

————, *Le Théâtre de l'Hôtel de Bourgogne*, v. 1, 1548-1635. Nizet, 1968.

————, *Le Théâtre de l'Hôtel de Bourgogne*, v. 2, *Le Théâtre de la Troupe royale, 1635-1680*. Nizet, 1970.

Dulait, S., *Inventaire raisonné des autographes de Molière*. Genève: Droz, 1967.

Edelman, Nathan, ed., *The Seventeenth Century* ("Molière," pp. 226-243). Vol. III of *A Critical Bibliography of French Literature*. D. Cabeen and J. Brody, eds. Syracuse: Syracuse University Press, 1961.

Guilbert, A.-J., *Bibliographie des œuvres de Molière publiées au XVIIè siècle*. C. N. R. S., 1961.

Jurgens, M. and Maxfield-Miller, E., *Cent Ans de recherches sur Molière, sur sa famille et sur les Comédiens de sa troupe*. Archives Nationales, 1963.

Klapp, Otto, *Bibliographie der französichen Literaturwissenschaft*. Frankfort am Main: Klostermann, 1954—.

Mongrédien, Georges, *Recueil des textes et des documents du XVIIè siècle relatifs à Molière*. C. N. R. S., 1964. 2 volumes.

Rancoeur, René, *Bibliographie de la littérature française moderne, 16è-20è siècles*. Armand Colin, 1953.

Saintonge, P., and Christ., R. W., *Fifty Years of Molière Studies, A Bibliography, 1892-1941*. Baltimore: The Johns Hopkins Press, 1942.

————, "Omissions and Additions to *Fifty Years of Molière Studies*." *Modern Language Notes*, LIX (1944), pp. 282-285.

Young, B. E. and G. P., *Le Registre de La Grange (1659-1685)*. Geneva: Droz, 1947. 2 volumes.

B. Editions

Molière, Œuvres complètes, ed. E. Despois and P. Mesnard. ("Les Grands Ecrivains de la France"), 13 volumes. Hachette, 1873-1900.
Molière, Œuvres, ed. Jacques Copeau. 10 volumes. Cité des Livres, 1926-1929.
Molière, Œuvres complètes, ed. René Bray. 8 volumes. Les Belles Lettres, 1935-1952.
Molière, Œuvres complètes, ed. Gustave Michaut. 11 volumes. Imprimerie Nationale, 1949.
Molière, Œuvres complètes, ed. Bray and J. Scherer. 3 volumes. Club du Meilleur Livre, 1954-1956.
Molière, Œuvres complètes, ed. Robert Jouanny. 2 volumes. Classiques Garnier, 1960.

C. Molière Criticism

Audiberti, J., *Molière dramaturge*. L'Arche, 1954; cf. J. Duvignaud, "Molière et la critique," pp. 120-134.
Descotes, M., *Molière et sa fortune littéraire*. Bordeaux: Guy Ducros, 1970.
Guicharnaud, Jacques, "Molière in the Light of Modern Criticism," *The American Society of the Legion of Honor Magazine*, XXIX, III (1958), pp. 161-175.
Masters, B., *A Student's Guide to Molière*. London: Heinemann, 1970.
Mélèse, Pierre, "Activités moliéresques," *La Revue d'Histoire du théâtre*, I-II (1948), pp. 25-32.
Moore, W. G., "Molière Studies — The Present Position," *French Studies*, I (1947), pp. 291-301.
Morel, Jacques, "Quelques publications récentes relatives à Molière," *Journal des Savants*, 1967, pp. 250-252.
Nicolet, A., "Histoire des études sur Molière," *Edda*, XXXIX (1939), pp. 406-451.
Picard, Raymond, "Etat présent des études moliéresques," *Information Littéraire*, X (1958), pp. 53-56.
Rat, Maurice, ed. *Molière, Œuvres complètes*. Gallimard, "La Pléiade," 1962; cf. "Molière devant la critique," v. 1, pp. XL-LX.
Tenant, Jean, "La Critique de Molière," *Amitiés foréziennes*, I (1921-1922), pp. 121-126.
Thibaudet, Albert, "Molière et la critique," *Revue de Paris*, II (1930), pp. 365-394.

D. General

Adam, A., *Histoire de la littérature française au XVIIè siècle*, v. 3. Del Duca, 1952.
D'Almeras, H., *Le Tartuffe de Molière*. Amiens: E. Malpère, 1928.
Anouilh, Jean, "La Petite Molière," *L'Avant Scène*, CCX (15 décembre 1955).
Arnavon, Jacques, *Le Dom Juan de Molière*, Copenhague: Gyldendel, 1947.
————, *Le Misanthrope de Molière*. Plon, 1930.
————, *Morale de Molière*. Editions Universelles, 1945.
————, *Notes sur l'interprétation de Molière*. Plon, 1932.

Attinger, G., *L'Esprit de la Commedia dell'Arte dans le théâtre français.* Neuchâtel: La Baconnière, 1950.

Audiberti, J., *Molière dramaturge.* L'Arche, 1954.

Auerbach, Erich, *Memesis.* Princeton: Princeton University Press, 1953.

————, *Scenes from the Drama of European Literature.* N. Y.: Meridan Books, 1959.

Barrault, J.-L., "Portrait de Molière." *Cahiers Renaud-Barrault,* v. 49 (December-January 1964).

Baumal, F., *Molière et les dévots.* Bougault, 1919.

————, *Tartuffe et ses avatars.* Nourry, 1925.

Bénichou, P., *Morales du grand siècle.* Gallimard, 1948.

Billeter, R., *Les valeurs spectaculaires dans l'œuvre de Molière.* Boulogne: Imprimerie Maleva, 1962.

Bordonove, Georges, *Molière génial et familier.* Robert Lafont, 1967.

Bray, René, *Molière Homme de théâtre.* Mercure de France, 1954.

Brisson, P., *Molière, Sa vie dans ses œuvres.* N. R. F., 1942.

Brody, Jules, "*Dom Juan* and *Le Misanthrope,* or The Esthetics of Individualism in Molière." *P. M. L. A.,* v. 84 (May 1969), p. 559-576.

————, "Esthétique et Société chez Molière". *Dramaturgie et Société au 16è et au 17è siècles.* C. R. N. S., 1968, pp. 307-326.

Busson, H., *La Religion des classiques.* P. U. F., 1948.

Butler, Philip, "Orgon le dirigé." *Gallica.* Cardiff: University of Wales Press, 1969, pp. 103-119.

————, "Tartuffe et la direction spirituelle au 17è siècle." *Modern Miscellany Presented to Eugene Vinaver.* Manchester: Manchester University Press, 1969.

Cairncross, J., *New Light on Molière.* Droz, 1956.

————, *Molière Bourgeois et libertin.* Nizet, 1963.

Calvet, Jean, *Molière, est-il chrétien?* Fernand Lanore, 1954.

Chancerel, Léon, *Molière* ("Collection les Metteurs en scène"). P. L. F. 1953.

Chevalley, S. ed. *Molière.* La Comédie Française, 1970.

Christout, M.-F., *Le Ballet de Cour de Louis XIV, 1643-1672, mises en scène.* A. et J. Picard, 1967.

Copeau, Jacques, ed., *Molière, Les Fourberies de Scapin.* Le Seuil, 1951.

Couton, G., "L'Etat civil d'Armande Béjart ou Historique d'une légende," *Revue des Sciences humaines,* 1964, pp. 311-351.

Descotes, M., *Les Grands Rôles du théâtre de Molière.* P. U. F., 1960.

Doubrovsky, Serge, "Arnolphe ou la chute du héros," *Mercure de France,* CCCXLIII (September-December 1961), pp. 111-118.

Dullin, Charles, ed., *Molière: L'Avare.* Le Seuil, 1946.

Dussane, B., "Molière à la scène," *Molière, Œuvres complètes,* ed. Bray and Scherer. Club du Meilleur Livre, v. 1, 1954, pp. 55-95.

————, *Un Comédien nommé Molière.* Plon, 1936.

Ehing, Maria, *Hauptphasen der Molière-Kritik bis 1850.* Köln: Universität Köln, 1942.

Ehrmann, Jacques, "Notes sur *L'Ecole des femmes,*" *Revue des Sciences humaines,* CIX (January-March 1963), pp. 5-10.

Emard, P., *Tartuffe, sa vie et son milieu.* Droz, 1932.

Faguet, Emile, *En lisant Molière.* Hachette, 1914.

Fellows, Otis, *French Opinion of Molière, 1800-1850.* Providence: Brown University Press, 1937.

Fernandez, Ramon, "Molière." *Tableau de la littérature française*, ed. A. Gide. N. R. F., 1939, v. 2.

———, *Vie de Molière*. N. R. F., 1929.

Fowlie, W., "Molière Today." *Dionysus in Paris*. New York, 1960.

Garreau, A., *Inquisitions*. Editions du Cèdre, 1970.

Gaxotte, P., *Molière fameux comédien*. Hachette, 1971.

Gendarme de Bévotte, G., *Le Festin de Pierre avant Molière*. Cornély, 1907.

———, *La Légende de Don Juan*. Hachette, 1906.

Gossman, Lionel, *Men and Masks: A Study of Molière*. Baltimore: Johns Hopkins Press, 1963.

Guicharnaud, Jacques, *Molière, Une Aventure théâtrale*. Gallimard, 1963.

———, ed. *Molière, A Collection of Critical Essays*. Englewoods Cliffs: Prentice Hall, 1964.

Gutwirth, Marcel, *Molière ou l'invention comique*. Minard, 1966.

Hall, H. G., "The Literary Context of *Le Misanthrope*." *Studi Francesi*, v. 40, 1970, pp. 20-38.

Hubert, Judd, *Molière and the Comedy of Intellect*. Berkeley: University of California Press, 1962.

Huzár, G., *Molière et l'Espagne*. Champion, 1907.

Jasinski, René, *Molière et Le Misanthrope*. Armand Colin, 1951.

Jomaron, J., "A Propos d'un document de mise en scène." *Revue d'Histoire du théâtre*, v. 18, 1966, pp. 210-215.

Jouvet, Louis, "Molière." *Annales de Conferencia*, XVII (September, 1937).

———, "Problèmes de la mise en scène des chefs d'œuvre classiques." *Revue d'Histoire du théâtre*, IV (1951).

———, *Témoignages sur le théâtre*. Flammarion, 1952.

Lafenestre, G., *Molière*. Hachette, 1909.

Lancaster, H. C., *A History of French Dramatic Literature in the Seventeenth Century*. Part 3. Baltimore: Johns Hopkins Press, 1936.

Landolt, R. B., "Molière and Louis XIV." *History Today*, XVI (1966), pp. 756-764.

Lanson, Gustave, "Molière et la farce." *Essais de Méthode, de critique et d'histoire littéraire*, ed H. Peyre. Hachette, 1965.

Larroumet, G., *La Comédie de Molière*. Hachette, 1903.

Lawrence, F. L., *Molière and the Comedy of Unreason*. New Orleans: Tulane Studies in Romance Languages and Literatures, 1968.

LeFranc, Abel, "La Vie et les ouvrages de Molière." *Revue des cours et conférences*, IV, ii, 1906.

Magné, B., "*L'Ecole des femmes* ou la conquête de la parole." *Revue des Sciences humaines*, v. 145 (January-March 1972).

Magne, E., *Une Amie inconnue de Molière*. Emile-Paul Frères, 1922.

Mauron, Ch., *Des Métaphores obsédantes aux mythes personnels*. Corti, 1964.

———, *La Psychocritique du genre comique*. José Corti, 1964.

Mantzius, K., *Molière: Les théâtres, le public et les comédiens de son temps*. Armand Colin, 1908.

Martineche, E., *Molière et le théâtre Espagnol*. Hachette, 1906.

McGowan, M., *L'Art du ballet de cour en France, 1581-1643*. C. N. R. S., 1963.

Melèse, Pierre, *Le Théâtre et le public sous Louis XIV — 1659-1715*. Droz, 1934.

Meyer, Jean, *Molière*. Librairie académique Perrin, 1963.

Michaut, Gustave, *La Jeunesse de Molière*. Hachette, 1922.
————, *Les Débuts de Molière à Paris*. Hachette, 1924.
————, *Les Luttes de Molière*. Hachette, 1925.
————, *Pascal, Molière, Musset*. Editions Alsatia, 1942.
————, *Molière raconté par ceux qui l'ont vu*. Stock, 1932.
Mongrédien, Georges, "Les Biographies de Molière au 18è siècle." *Revue d'Histoire littéraire de la France*, XVI (1956), pp. 342-354.
————, *La Vie privée de Molière*. Hachette, 1950.
Moore, Will G., *Molière, A New Criticism*. Oxford: Clarendon Press, 1949.
————, "Molière's theories of Comedy." *Esprit Créateur*, VI (Fall 1966), pp. 137-144.
————, "The French Notion of the Comic." *Yale French Studies*, XXIII (1959).
Mornet, Daniel, *Molière*. Boivin, 1943.
Nadal, O., "Molière et le sens de la vie." *A Mesure haute*. Mercure de France, 1964.
Nelson, R. J., "Classicism: The Crisis of the Baroque in French Literature." *L'Esprit Créateur*, v. 11 (volume also entitled *Paths to Freedom*), (Summer 1971), pp. 169-186.
Pellisson, M., *Les Comédies-ballets de Molière*. Hachette, 1914.
Pintard, René, *Le Libertinage érudit dans la première moitié du 17è siècle*. 2 volumes. Boivin, 1943.
Poulaille, H., *Corneille sous le masque de Molière*. Grasset, 1957.
————, *Tartuffe ou la comédie de l'hypocrisie*. Amiot-Dumont, 1951.
Rastier, F., "Niveaux d'ambiguïtés des structures narratives." *Semiotica*, v. 3 (1971), pp. 289-342.
Rigal, E., *Molière*. 2 volumes. Hachette, 1908.
Robert, René, "Les Commentaires de première main sur les chefs d'œuvre de Molière." *Revue des Sciences humaines*, 1956.
Romano, D., *Essai sur le comique de Molière*. Berne: A. Francke, 1950.
Rousset, J., "*Dom Juan* and the Baroque." *Diogenes*, v. 14 (Summer 1956).
————, *La Littérature de l'Age baroque en France*. Corti, 1961.
————, *L'Intérieur et l'Extérieur*. Corti, 1968.
Rudler, Gustave, ed., *Molière, Le Misanthrope*. Oxford: Blackwell, 1947.
Salomon, H. P., *Tartuffe devant l'opinion publique*. P. U. F., 1962.
Sandier, G., *Théâtre et Combat*. Stock, 1970.
Scherer, Jacques, "Réflexions sur Armande Béjart." *Revue d'Histoire littéraire*, 1969, pp. 393-403.
————, *Structures de Tartuffe*. S. E. E. S., 1966.
————, *Sur le Dom Juan de Molière*. S. E. E. S., 1967.
Sauvage, Micheline, *Le Cas Dom Juan*. Le Seuil, 1953.
Sells, A. L., "Molière and La Mothe Le Vayer." *Modern Language Review*, XXVIII (1933).
Simon, Alfred, *Molière par lui-même*. Le Seuil, 1957.
Spink, J. S., *French Free Thought from Gassendi to Voltaire*. London: Athlone Press, 1960.
Teyssier, Jean-Marie, *Réflexions sur le Dom Juan de Molière*. Nizet, 1970.
Vedel, Valdemar, *Deux Classiques français vus par un critique étranger*. Champion, 1935.
Villiers, André, *Le Dom Juan de Molière*. "Masques," 1947.
Walker, H., *Molière*. New York: Twayne Publishers, 1970.

INDEX OF PROPER NAMES

174   INDEX OF PROPER NAMES

Jouvet, L.   107, 108, 112n, 117-
120, 135n, 149, 150, 151, 157,
159, 160.
Jurgens, M.   123-124.

Kleist, H. v.   162.
Kohler, P.   100n.

LaBruyère   35.
Lafenestre, G.   53, 54.
Laforêt   111.
LaFontaine   21, 28, 33, 92.
La Grange   26, 27, 28, 45, 53, 57,
59, 82.
Lamoignon   26, 42.
LaMothe le Vayer   90-91, 96, 133,
134.
Lancaster, H. C.   82, 83-84, 99,
159.
Landholt, R. B.   20n.
Lanson, G.   16, 29, 74-75, 88n,
100-101.
Larnaudie, S.   162n.
Larroumet, G.   47, 49.
LaSerre   32.
Lauzun, duc de   72.
Lawall, S.   89n.
Lawrence, F. L.   133n.
Lea, K. M.   79n.
LeBoulanger de Chalussay   31, 56,
59.
Leclerc, G.   140.
Ledoux, F.   157.
LeFranc, A.   52, 53, 55, 56, 71,
89, 92.
LeNain   155.
Lop, E.   140, 142-143.
Loquin, A.   63n.
Louis XIV   19, 20, 21, 38, 40, 41,
42, 44, 45, 68, 70, 97, 121, 127,
133, 140, 142, 144, 157, 162,
164.
Lowenstein, R.   32n.
Loüys, P.   62.
Lucretius   27, 49, 133.

Magné, B.   163-164.
Malherbe   20.
Mannoni, O.   166n.
Mantzius, K.   99.
Maréchal, M.   152, 154.
Marion, J.   88n.

Marmontel   35.
Martineche, E.   78.
Masters, B.   125n.
Matthew, B.   54.
Maurevert, G.   79n.
Mauron, C.   136-137, 165.
Maxfield-Miller, E.   123-124.
McGowan, M.   125n.
Ménage   70.
Mesnard, P.   48, 49, 99.
Meyer, J.   127-128.
Michaut, G.   16, 17, 31, 44, 54-60,
63, 64, 71, 82-83, 92n, 99, 127,
159.
Michelet, J.   41, 42, 86, 131, 132n.
Modène, baron de   45, 56.
Molé, F. R.   35.
Mongrédien, G.   22n, 31, 32n, 60,
61, 85n, 89, 124, 164.
Montaigne   88n, 133, 134.
Montfleury   22, 68.
Monval, G.   46.
Moore, W. G.   23, 25, 60, 76, 98,
101-104, 108, 109, 114n, 128,
135, 137, 160.
Morel, J.   133n.
Mornet, D.   60.
Musset, A. de   40.

Nadal, O.   144n.
Naves, R.   34.
Nelson, R. J.   161-162.
Nurse, P.   86n, 131n, 133.

Palissot   38.
Palmer, J.   54.
Pascal, B.   98.
Pellisson, M.   80.
Perrault, C.   58.
Perrins, F.-T.   92, 130.
Picard, R.   131, 133, 164.
Pintard, R.   92n.
Planchon, R.   151, 152, 153, 155-
158.
Plautus   21.
Poulet, G.   89.
Poulaille, H.   62-63.
Propp, V.   163.

Rabelais   50, 88n.
Racine   20, 22, 28, 33, 51, 70.
Rapin, N.   26.

176   INDEX OF PROPER NAMES

Rastier, F.   162-163, 164, 165.
Rébilliau, A.   80.
Riccoboni, L.   36.
Rigal, E.   53, 54.
Rohault, J.   31.
Rossat-Mignot, S.   140, 141-142.
Rouillé, P.   23, 86.
Rousseau   35.
Rousset, J.   138-139.
Roussillon, J.-P.   153-154.
Rudler, G.   101n.

Saint-Evremond   92.
Sainte-Beuve   39, 42, 43, 80.
Saintonge, P.   63n.
Salomon, H. P.   125n, 150n.
Sandier, G.   158n.
Sartre, J.-P.   162.
Sauvage, A.   140, 142-143.
Scramouche, T. Fiorelli, *dit*   79.
Scherer, J.   105, 121-122, 126, 127, 131, 135.
Schwartz, I. A.   79n.
Seigner, L.   150, 151.
Sells, A. L.   90.
Sévely, D.   141.
Simon, A.   72-74, 135, 137, 160.
Somaize   59.
Soulié, E.   46, 86, 123.
Spink, J. S.   91-92.
Staël, Mme de   40.
Stendhal   40, 41.

Subligny   106.

Taine, H.   46.
Tallement des Réaux   20.
Taschereau, J.   44.
Terence   21.
Thibaudet, A.   41n, 54, 64n, 166.
Teyssier, J.-M.   132n.
Tilley, A.   54.
Toldo, P.   79.
Tzoneff, S.   88n.

Vandromme, P.   110n.
Vauvenargues   35.
Vedel, V.   100.
Veuillot, L.   87, 130.
Vigarani, C.   121.
Vilar, J.   17, 117, 131n, 153, 154, 159.
Villiers, A.   134.
Voltaire   32, 33, 36, 38, 48, 50, 95, 133.

Wadsworth, P. A.   162n.
Walker, H.   128, 162n.
Wellek, R.   15, 89n.
Wittkowski, W.   162n.
Wood, P. W.   162n.

Young, B. E. & G. P.   82n.

Zanetta, C.   36n.

NORTH CAROLINA STUDIES IN THE ROMANCE LANGUAGES AND LITERATURES

I.S.B.N. Prefix 0-88438

Recent Titles

THE OLD PORTUGUESE "VIDA DE SAM BERNARDO," EDITED FROM ALCOBAÇA MANU-SCRIPT ccxci/200, WITH INTRODUCTION, LINGUISTIC STUDY, NOTES, TABLE OF PROPER NAMES, AND GLOSSARY, by Lawrence A. Sharpe. 1971. (No. 103). *-903-0.*

A CRITICAL AND ANNOTATED EDITION OF LOPE DE VEGA'S "LAS ALMENAS DE TORO," by Thomas E. Case. 1971. (No. 104). *-904-9.*

LOPE DE VEGA'S "LO QUE PASA EN UNA TARDE," A CRITICAL, ANNOTATED EDITION OF THE AUTOGRAPH MANUSCRIPT, by Richard Angelo Picerno. 1971. (No. 105). *-905-7.*

OBJECTIVE METHODS FOR TESTING AUTHENTICITY AND THE STUDY OF TEN DOUBT-FUL "COMEDIAS" ATTRIBUTED TO LOPE DE VEGA, by Fred M. Clark. 1971. (No. 106). *-906-5.*

THE ITALIAN VERB. A MORPHOLOGICAL STUDY, by Frede Jensen. 1971. (No. 107). *-907-3.*

A CRITICAL EDITION OF THE OLD PROVENÇAL EPIC "DAUREL ET BETON," WITH NOTES AND PROLEGOMENA, by Arthur S. Kimmel. 1971. (No. 108). *-908-1.*

FRANCISCO RODRIGUES LOBO: DIALOGUE AND COURTLY LORE IN RENAISSANCE PORTUGAL, by Richard A. Preto-Rodas. 1971. (No. 109). *-909-X.*

RAIMOND VIDAL: POETRY AND PROSE, edited by W. H. W. Field. 1971. (No. 110). *-910-3.*

RELIGIOUS ELEMENTS IN THE SECULAR LYRICS OF THE TROUBADOURS, by Ray-mond Gay-Crosier. 1971. (No. 111). *-911-1.*

THE SIGNIFICANCE OF DIDEROT'S "ESSAI SUR LE MERITE ET LA VERTU," by Gor-don B. Walters. 1971. (No. 112). *-912-X.*

PROPER NAMES IN THE LYRICS OF THE TROUBADOURS, by Frank M. Chambers. 1971. (No. 113). *-913-8.*

STUDIES IN HONOR OF MARIO A. PEI, edited by John Fisher and Paul A. Gaeng. 1971. (No. 114). *-914-6.*

DON MANUEL CAÑETE, CRONISTA LITERARIO DEL ROMANTICISMO Y DEL POS-ROMANTICISMO EN ESPAÑA, por Donald Allen Randolph. 1972. (No. 115). *-915-4.*

THE TEACHINGS OF SAINT LOUIS. A CRITICAL TEXT, by David O'Connell. 1972. (No. 116). *-916-2.*

HIGHER, HIDDEN ORDER: DESIGN AND MEANING IN THE ODES OF MALHERBE, by David Lee Rubin. 1972. (No. 117). *-917-0.*

JEAN DE LE MOTE "LE PARFAIT DU PAON," édition critique par Richard J. Carey. 1972. (No. 118). *-918-9.*

CAMUS' HELLENIC SOURCES, by Paul Archambault. 1972. (No. 119). *-919-7.*

FROM VULGAR LATIN TO OLD PROVENÇAL, by Frede Jensen. 1972. (No. 120). *-920-0.*

GOLDEN AGE DRAMA IN SPAIN: GENERAL CONSIDERATION AND UNUSUAL FEA-TURES, by Sturgis E. Leavitt. 1972. (No. 121). *-921-9.*

THE LEGEND OF THE "SIETE INFANTES DE LARA" (*Refundición toledana de la crónica de 1344* versión), study and edition by Thomas A. Lathrop. 1972. (No. 122). *-922-7.*

STRUCTURE AND IDEOLOGY IN BOIARDO'S "ORLANDO INNAMORATO," by Andrea di Tommaso. 1972. (No. 123). *-923-5.*

STUDIES IN HONOR OF ALFRED G. ENGSTROM, edited by Robert T. Cargo and Emanuel J. Mickel, Jr. 1972. (No. 124). *-924-3.*

A CRITICAL EDITION WITH INTRODUCTION AND NOTES OF GIL VICENTE'S "FLO-RESTA DE ENGANOS," by Constantine Christopher Stathatos. 1972. (No. 125). *-925-1.*

Recent Titles

LI ROMANS DE WITASSE LE MOINE. *Roman du treizième siècle*. Édité d'après le manuscrit, fonds français 1553, de la Bibliothèque Nationale, Paris, par Denis Joseph Conlon. 1972. (No. 126). *-926-X.*

EL CRONISTA PEDRO DE ESCAVIAS. *Una vida del Siglo XV*, por Juan Bautista Avalle-Arce. 1972. (No. 127). *-927-8.*

AN EDITION OF THE FIRST ITALIAN TRANSLATION OF THE "CELESTINA," by Kathleen V. Kish. 1973. (No. 128). *-928-6.*

MOLIÈRE MOCKED. THREE CONTEMPORARY HOSTILE COMEDIES: *Zélinde, Le portrait du peintre, Élomire Hypocondre*, by Frederick Wright Vogler. 1973. (No. 129). *-929-4.*

C.-A. SAINTE-BEUVE. *Chateaubriand et son groupe littéraire sous l'empire.* Index alphabétique et analytique établi par Lorin A. Uffenbeck. 1973. (No. 130). *-930-8.*

THE ORIGINS OF THE BAROQUE CONCEPT OF "PEREGRINATIO," by Juergen Hahn. 1973. (No. 131). *-931-6.*

THE "AUTO SACRAMENTAL" AND THE PARABLE IN SPANISH GOLDEN AGE LITERATURE, by Donald Thaddeus Dietz. 1973. (No. 132). *-932-4.*

FRANCISCO DE OSUNA AND THE SPIRIT OF THE LETTER, by Laura Calvert. 1973. (No. 133). *-933-2.*

ITINERARIO DI AMORE: DIALETTICA DI AMORE E MORTE NELLA "VITA NUOVA," by Margherita de Bonfils Templer. 1974. (No. 134). *-934-0.*

L'IMAGINATION POETIQUE CHEZ DU BARTAS; ELEMENTS DE SENSIBILITE BAROQUE DANS LA "CREATION DU MONDE," by Bruno Braunrot. 1974. (No. 135). *-935-9.*

ARTUS DESIRE, PRIEST AND PAMPHLETEER OF THE SIXTEENTH CENTURY, by Frank Giese. 1974. (No. 136). *-936-7.*

"JARDIN DE NOBLES DONZELLAS" BY FRAY MARTIN DE CORDOBA, by Harriet Goldberg. 1974. (No. 137). *-937-5.*

VISUAL VARIETY AND SPATIAL GRANDEUR: A STUDY OF THE TRANSITION FROM THE SIXTEENTH TO THE SEVENTEENTH FRENCH CENTURY, by John F. Winter. 1974. (No. 140). *-940-5.*

Essays

STUDIES IN TIRSO, I, by Ruth Lee Kennedy. 1974. (No. 3). *-003-3.*

Texts, Textual Studies and Translations

LAS MEMORIAS DE GONZALO FERNANDEZ DE OVIEDO, by Juan Bautista Avalle-Arce. 1974. (Nos. 1 and 2). *-401-2* and *-402-0.*

Symposia

LOS NARRADORES HISPANOAMERICANOS DE HOY, edited by Juan Bautista Avalle-Arce. 1973. (No. 1). *-951-0.*

ESTUDIOS HISPANOAMERICANOS EN HONOR A JOSE JUAN ARROM, edited by Andrew Debicki and Enrique Pupo-Walker. 1974. (No. 2). *-952-9.*

FRANCIS PETRARCH SIX CENTURIES LATER, edited by Aldo Scaglione. 1974. (No. 3). *-953-7.*

When ordering please cite the *ISBN Prefix* plus the last four digits for each title.
Send orders to:

> International Scholarly Book Service, Inc.
> P.O. Box 4347
> Portland, Oregon 97208
> U.S.A.